T0380262

THE BRANCH OFFICE

*Who says you can't have fun working
for an insurance company?*

Michael DeForest

BALBOA.PRESS
A DIVISION OF HAY HOUSE

Balboa Press books may be ordered through booksellers or by contacting:

Balboa Press
A Division of Hay House
1663 Liberty Drive
Bloomington, IN 47403
www.balboapress.com
844-682-1282

Cover Image Credit: Rachel Hurbrough

Print information available on the last page.

ISBN: 978-1-9822-6398-0 (sc)
ISBN: 978-1-9822-6400-0 (hc)
ISBN: 978-1-9822-6399-7 (e)

Library of Congress Control Number: 2021903285

Balboa Press rev. date: 02/12/2021

This book is dedicated to the memory of my wife, my son, and my mother.

Contents

Contents

The Waning Crescent Moon

*I*t was the night of August 12, 1985, on Highway 59, near downtown Houston, Texas. The moon was a waning crescent, which was not a good sign for most drunks on the road, since the moon showed only a small bit of light. However, Davis Bryant didn't care much about the moon or any other driver on the road, because he had just landed his dream job: a promotion to Houston branch manager at the Cleveland Insurance Companies.

He was celebrating in style. He had flown in a few days before and was getting his feet wet by holding meetings with his staff to size up who was a team player and who was not.

Davis was a large man at five foot ten and 330 pounds. He'd been a defensive lineman in college until a broken leg sidelined his college football career. He'd earned a football scholarship, but as one of the few players with a higher-than-average GPA at Auburn, he hadn't taken the standard basket-weaving classes most athletes got to choose from. Instead, he'd challenged himself with more demanding courses. Davis's father had advised him to get ahead in life through education and not be like him, an uneducated steelworker in a small northern town. Davis had graduated from Auburn with honors but had felt he needed a master's degree to get somewhere in the business world, so he'd applied at the Wharton School of Business, which quickly had accepted him. In the future, Davis would utilize everything he learned at the Wharton School to get ahead in the business world, which would also affect his personal life.

After graduating with a master's degree in business a few years later, Davis had been quickly scouted and hired by the Cleveland Insurance Companies and started his ascension in the company's ranks. Davis's first job had been in the sales department, working with independent insurance agents, whom companies like the Cleveland Insurance Companies—or CIC, as it was known—wrote their business through. A sales job was perfect for Davis because he was not an underwriting type. He was not built to sit at a desk for eight hours a day, endlessly crunching numbers; he had way too much personality for that type of work. It was too boring and mundane for his character and not where he pictured himself after graduating from college. Besides, most promotions to management came from the sales department at that time at CIC.

During his first year, Davis had learned about the independent insurance agency system while making agency calls with his sales manager. He'd noticed his sales manager always stopped by to visit with the customer service reps who worked for each agency to see how things were going, find out if they had any complaints or compliments about CIC, and, of course, ask for more business. Davis immediately had picked up the practice and instituted it on all his agency calls. Some of the customer service reps were gorgeous and friendly, but some were not. Davis had been instructed by his sales manager to discuss any problem he encountered on agency calls with either himself or the branch manager until he figured out the system and how to overcome objections and fix issues. His first and only question on the ride back to the branch office had been "Is it wrong to date these customer service reps?"

His sales manager had laughed and said, "I wouldn't recommend it. Try not to piss them off, because it could affect business writing! On the other end of things, dating a customer service rep might help you to write business. Just don't get too friendly unless there is an interest."

On agency calls, Davis would discuss everything from production results to current sports gossip. It depended on the relationship he had with the agent or customer service rep. But mostly, he would talk about how to increase production. There were two types of insurance a sales rep discussed with an agent: personal lines, such as homeowner's and auto, and insurance for a business entity. Davis had figured out quickly that commercial lines were more interesting, and the premiums were always higher than those of personal lines. Hence, he ignored personal lines most of the time because he thought they were a pain in the ass and a waste of time.

Independent insurance agents could place business with any company they felt could be advantageous for the agency, but they also could focus on companies they felt comfortable with and might earn a higher commission rate with. A good sales rep could increase production in many different ways, such as overcoming objections, becoming friends with the agency principal and the customer service reps, or figuring out how to increase business for the company in some other way. As with all independent agents, independent insurance agents represented many different companies. It was the sales reps' job to coax, bribe, become friends with, or use any other means necessary to get prospective consumers to write business with the company they worked for.

The relationship was like a triangle, with the top section being an insurance company, the bottom left portion being an independent agent, and the bottom right part being a consumer, whether a business or a personal consumer. This triangle defined the best relationship of the independent agency system with customers and the companies they represented. Since Davis concentrated on commercial lines, this area represented accounts he wrote or wanted to write and submitted to the company, which would hopefully be quoted by any of the underwriting departments he represented. For underwriting to quote anything always proved to be a monumental task, especially if it didn't fit the underwriting guidelines or had had negative results in the past. Getting underwriting to budge on anything was a difficult task and part of a sales rep's job.

Davis had picked up on the selling portion of the job quickly and knew how to skirt the system to increase business, but what he was truly after were the skirts.

Davis wasn't as interested in working with agents as he was with the customer service reps who worked for his agency force or the agents contracted with CIC. The agency force Davis utilized were agents assigned to his territory, and the total number of agents ranged anywhere from fifteen to forty at any given time. Since his sales manager had told him not to be overly friendly with the customer service reps, he attempted to ignore his interest in this target-rich environment; however, his hormones ruled the day. He talked with agency principals about business writings for short periods, but he spent most of his time becoming better acquainted with the customer service reps by using his expense account to pay for lunch, dinner, drinks, or whatever it took to succeed. This helped him become more successful at his job one customer service rep at a time.

With an extensive territory located in Missouri, there was a large agent and customer service rep base to choose from, and as luck had it, he was out on the road a lot and in hotels on overnight trips. Davis knew there were competitor reps who were better than he was and had less education; it was sheer luck that he had this job and everything it paid for. He would joke that the other reps got the business, but he always got the women.

Although he did get the women, he also managed to write a lot of business along the way. Within a few years, he'd been promoted in the Kansas office to sales manager, one step below branch manager. Davis had been on the fast track to becoming a branch manager—his dream job. A branch manager's position afforded more power, more prestige, better pay, a better company car, and a better choice of women.

After becoming a sales manager, he'd doubled his efforts to manage his reps to increase premium and show the higher-ups he was the man to choose for the next open branch manager position. Davis also had started looking for a nicer house to live in that would show his new job's status if he decided to entertain staff, clients, or new prospects. His only problem was that he was married with small kids by then, but that situation was only a temporary setback, as he had his sights and ambitions set on more significant things.

When Davis had received the Houston branch manager promotion, he'd left his wife and kids behind in Kansas and agreed to send for them when school was out; however, it never happened. His kids wanted to stay in Kansas, and he did not get along with his wife, so it was a wide-open atmosphere in Houston. Davis couldn't have been happier with the new prospects ahead of him and had no one to hinder his exploits.

The night was hot and sticky, like most summer nights in Houston, with a low of around 85 degrees. Usually, that would have been difficult for most Yankees to tolerate, but Davis didn't care about the weather or the moon. He was celebrating his recent promotion to branch manager with a few Houston branch employees he had just met. He drank his usual amount of beer to celebrate—his usual amount for the day was about thirty to forty beers. Davis did not drink one beer at a time either; he always ordered two at a time so he would not have to wait for a server to return.

He would extend his help to the Houston staff in any way he could, but secretly, his management style was to let people either sink or swim, which weeded out the undesirables and let the cream rise to the top—an approach learned from the Wharton School of Business. If one conducted him- or herself well under the Davis way of doing things, that person was well thought of by Davis, but if one sank, he or she was unceremoniously let go or transferred elsewhere. Davis's management style was unique. He referred to people who were undesirable as maniacs or numbies—short for *numb nuts*. Davis had a nickname for everyone and never called people by their real names, because he thought it was amusing, and most people thought it was a compliment. It wasn't a compliment in Davis's mind, just a reflection of his inner thoughts about a person and whether or not he liked someone. Davis referred to most people working in the home office or the regional home office as either numbies or maniacs, except for the higher-ups. He had respect for those folks because he knew their jobs were difficult at best, and he also knew they could fire him at any time for any reason, so he treated them with respect. His boss was the regional vice president, Tom Staben; however, the regional home office didn't get too involved with the Houston branch daily operations, because Davis was so politically motivated. Davis was a master in any political situation in business because of his education at Wharton. Hence, the regional home office was just a minor annoyance. Since Davis was new to town, he checked into a long-term hotel near the branch office, near Highway 59 in Houston, where he began to plan for future growth and who was to stay or go.

During that time frame, many hotels in the Houston area offered long-term hotel residents a Lincoln Continental to drive to and from work as a courtesy. Since Davis had flown in from Kansas recently, he had turned in his old company car and planned to look around for a new vehicle while in Houston. Branch managers were afforded a certain amount of money to buy a car as a company car, basically another perk. Davis hadn't decided what to buy, and he didn't care at that point, because he could use the hotel's courtesy vehicle to go to and from work. The hotel's courtesy vehicle allowed him to locate a new car and save some money on buying a new one. So the night of August 15, he was in a brand-new Lincoln, very drunk, and out on the town.

At the time, there was a lot of freeway construction on 59, or the Southwest Freeway, as it was known to most Houstonians. The road repair and construction on 59 seemed endless. Davis left the party after a few hours at a happy-hour haunt everyone knew called the Cellar Door, off Stella Link, and began his trek back to the hotel.

He exited the freeway but wasn't aware of the construction barrels or anything else in his drunken haze. He plowed right into some unfinished road concrete with only the rebar and plastic tips sticking up to stop his progress. The high-speed impact threw the car sideways, leaving the mangled vehicle to settle near some unfinished concrete with four blown-out tires. During the process, the car also hit a concrete barrier before it came to a stop. The crash was violent, and steel rebar stuck to the bottom of the undercarriage.

Davis didn't realize what was happening because of the twenty or thirty beers he had just consumed, but after the first impact, the jolt sobered him up fast. The courtesy car, as he later would find out, was a total loss due to all the undercarriage damage from the unfinished concrete and the rebar sticking out of the bottom of the vehicle. The rebar also had struck the engine, which made the car unrepairable.

Considering he was close to the hotel, Davis staggered his way back and called the company sales tech because he knew he could trust the sales department to keep things quiet. Davis remembered the name of marketing tech Susan Taggert, whom he thought was pretty hot looking, though he could tell she was trouble even after only meeting her once. Susan's name and number were written in his daily planner in case of emergencies. He called from a pay phone near his hotel and asked Susan to pick him up. Of course, there would be more emergencies in the future, but this was the first one.

Susan was ready for just about anything, as she was always the contact person for any emergencies; plus, she had done this type of thing many times in the past, as most of her previous managers had been drunks.

"Susan, I need your help. This is Davis, and I need your aid quickly."

Susan was always pretty quick on any response or request and arrived shortly to provide her much-needed assistance. Two heads were better than one, and in that situation, Davis needed all the help he could get. The plan was to develop an excuse for the hotel and call a local tow truck phone number that Susan had handy. They agreed to tell the hotel manager that the tires had been underinflated, which would explain the reason for his totaling the car. The vehicle needed a front-end alignment too, even though it was a fairly new vehicle type.

The hotel night manager was in shock and couldn't believe the story but was glad no one was hurt. The tow truck arrived, and no police arrived at the scene, so everything was going well. Davis would worry about the courtesy vehicle tomorrow, and he invited Susan to have one more drink at the hotel. Susan indicated she was married and said it wouldn't be a good idea. Davis was used to rejection, and it didn't bother him, but as he always said, "Hard dick has no conscience."

Davis continued to utilize the courtesy-vehicle program, changing hotels frequently because he always wrecked the courtesy vehicle and needed another car to get to and from work. Courtesy vehicles soon disappeared in the Houston area because Davis totaled three more vehicles during his first six months in Houston, usually after a night out on the town. The courtesy-car program was discontinued because the hotels could not afford that type of activity, even with insurance paying for the losses.

Still, Davis didn't care much about anything but writing business. It also seemed the hotel owners talked a lot to one another and passed on the information about the main perpetrator being one Davis Bryant. Hence, as Davis explained at many different happy hours, he got away with murder regarding the courtesy vehicles and was damn proud of it. He finally broke down and bought a new vehicle, but the car spent most of its time in the shop, under repair from the many different wrecks and body damage sustained after happy hour. Davis was endlessly trying to find a ride to one place or another.

As everyone joked in the office, giving Davis a ride should have been in the human-resources expectations and annual reviews, because everyone in the office was always giving him a ride everywhere. Davis usually picked the best-looking ladies in the office to get rides with, but he knew better than to hit on anyone in the office, because of past experiences. His hormones got the best of him, so it was business as usual. He'd learned in the Kansas branch that being too forward could get one fired quickly.

While in the Kansas branch office as the branch sales manager for a little more than a year, Davis had been on the lookout for a branch manager position, but a scandal had broken out with the previous branch manager, who had been unceremoniously fired due to his sexual escapades and heavy drinking, something Davis had taken to heart and learned from quickly. *Have fun, but don't get caught, and if you do get caught, lie your way out of it with every excuse in the book.*

Davis had been well behaved in the Kansas office because it had been too soon to act the fool. The Kansas office was a smaller branch than Houston but a good training ground to inherit a bigger branch office, which had been Davis's plan. His plan was always the same: make a small branch a big one, and enjoy the prizes that followed, which was another lesson he'd learned at Wharton. Accolades included bigger expense budgets, awards, new employees, mostly female employees, and, lastly, a bigger bonus. His first agenda item was always to hire female employees because having more female employees added up to a bigger target market to choose from, a new girlfriend, or at least a new mountain to climb and conquer. In those years before sexual harassment made so much news on television, it was open season. The doors were wide open now with his promotion, so Davis took full advantage of his good fortune. Even though he was married with two kids, that did not deter his ambitions. His idea was to leave his wife and kids in the Kansas area as long as possible to have a friendly hunting atmosphere. Especially in a big city like Houston, he could enjoy the fruits of his labor.

The Houston branch was ripe for growth, and Davis knew that. The Houston branch office just needed the right person at the helm and needed market conditions to change.

During that time, Houston enjoyed an oil boom again since the economy was oil-based, and most tax revenues came from the oil business. No one ever thought of expanding or diversifying the economy, because of the amount of money made in an oil-based economy and the considerable tax revenue in the oil business. Oil was king in Houston; however, after the bust of 1986, city leaders decided to change things a bit to attract different firms, with the hope of a more diverse economy that was not as oil-related.

With the oil boom in full bloom, business writings were up due to increased payrolls, which was what commercial insurance was based upon, so everything was clicking along gracefully for Davis and CIC. An oil boom was much like a steel boom where Davis had grown up, so he was used to that type of atmosphere. Additionally, many competitor insurance companies were having financial problems due to market conditions. A few would go out of business or be sold in the future because of poor market conditions, so things were beginning to heat up in the Texas market.

The branch office in Houston was a $40 million branch circa 1985. It should have been much larger with a growth-oriented person running the unit; however, market conditions were soft. It was a buyer's market at the time, and previous branch managers had been not the right fit or not aggressive enough to grow the branch. Within a few years, the atmosphere would change drastically, largely because the workers' compensation market and market conditions surrounding that coverage line would change drastically.

In most cases, workers' compensation was the largest premium in any commercial account, so it was the most critical expense to any business. Most insurance companies stopped writing workers' compensation in Texas, and it created a challenging market overnight. These types of market conditions would also help in the conquest department for the new branch manager because every independent agent would, sooner rather than later, want CIC as his or her leading company. CIC loved to write workers' compensation and never stopped writing this coverage line throughout the entire debacle, which lasted about six years, circa 1988–1994. Davis and his staff were in the right place at the right time to enjoy this growth and the accolades that followed.

Sales Managers

A description of a sales manager's role at an insurance company could have filled an entire book, and the job was a pivotal role. The position included everything from managing sales reps to successfully working with the regional home office and increasing business writings to enable the branch office to run like a well-oiled machine. Many different jobs were rolled into one, and it was a political career because the sales manager played devil's advocate most of the time, attempting to come out on top of most arguments and solve problems in the office. More tasks included running the sales department; working with underwriting; working with the home office; working with the services department; making the branch manager happy, which was an unusually difficult task; exceeding production targets; and, lastly, managing a tremendous amount of paperwork daily. It was almost a forest-killing amount of paper and probably a massive waste of time. These situations required answers in a short period or due dates that needed attention yesterday. If the branch manager were considered Captain Kirk of *Star Trek*, the sales manager was a mix between Spock and Scotty, always having the right answer for any question posed and being a miracle worker in the branch regarding production quotas—in other words, a miracle worker with some science behind it all. Most sales managers were as funny as the day was long, but they also had to be earnest at critical moments, which wasn't always the case, but they knew when and where to use humor as an antidote.

Usually, the underwriting manager and the sales manager would go toe to toe over an agent or, even more so, an account who was declined by an underwriter due to the exposure of the risk or some other incoherent, unheralded reason. The branch manager would intervene and become the referee during these shouting matches and always sided with the sales department. Under most circumstances, most branch managers had a sales background and disliked the underwriting department's short-mindedness; plus, there were production targets to meet or exceed. It was a check-and-balance system that most insurance companies utilized to conduct business, and it worked well in the Houston branch. Still, most underwriting managers who worked for Davis disliked him because he never heard their perspective and never once sided with them on any given dilemma.

Hal Marshall was the first in a long history of sales managers in Houston to make a great first impression but be a disappointment after a few drinks. While attending any given happy hour or lunch, he never stopped drinking, and he became a sloppy drunk after three to seven drinks.

The sales tech Susan had many jobs, but one of the most important jobs was taking care of the sales manager and, more often than not, the branch manager too—not babysitting but close to it. She kept everyone out of trouble because of her street smarts. A good sales tech could make or break a sales department but also could be a double-edged sword because the sales tech knew everyone's secrets, and Susan Taggert knew many of them. Much like Davis, she even made shit up occasionally to further her career. Of course, Susan had secrets too, and she was unhappily married and made sure everyone knew about it regularly. She also had financial problems because her husband could never keep a job, and she could be bought off for the right price or, more so, the right reason to keep things quiet.

Susan had been with CIC for a good number of years before Davis showed up, so she knew the ropes well and was an expert on how to get everything done quickly and quietly. Her knowing the ropes and her job helped out the sales department as a whole, but since Susan knew all the branch's secrets, no one tried to test her resolve on anything personal or business. Every sales rep who worked for the CIC wound up giving Susan some form of shit throughout the years, but she took it well because she gave shit out as well as she took it, and every rep or manager had to be careful on her bad days. She could be your best friend but could also be tough, so everyone did the Teddy Roosevelt around her: they walked softly but carried a big stick. In the past, she eloquently had set up a previous sales manager to get fired because she knew the system and how to exploit the system in her favor.

Hal knew these facts because one of the sales reps warned him at a bar one night, so he walked softly around Susan and treated her well. Hal was usually at a bar every night with Davis to discuss business or brag about a new female conquest, but the main focus was on women and where the next one could be found. Business concerns happily fit into the conversation somewhere, but the topic returned to women when the conversation became flat. Happy hour started at lunchtime and sometimes continued throughout the day, but Davis and Hal soon returned to the office and made a showing to sober up a bit. Since the office was on the third floor, Davis stopped on the first floor to go to the men's room to hide that they had been drinking heavily at lunch. The idea was to show they did not need to go to the bathroom immediately. It was a complete waste of time, but Davis was all about hiding his drinking at lunchtime.

As bad managers went, Hal also had a cocaine problem and usually ended up wandering the parking lot in a daze because of the drug's effects. Hal was a poster boy for drug and alcohol abuse. Susan always knew where to find him if a problem arose or a conference call was scheduled to happen at a specific time. The first place to look was the branch parking lot.

A big drinker, the sales manager was always the branch manager's drinking buddy. Hal could also be found in his company car with a new female conquest regularly, because the sales-manager types were always on the lookout for new gals. It didn't matter what time of day it was; whether morning, noon, or night, some form of action happened during the workday or night. Susan always complained about finding Hal in his company car, which seemed like his second office, usually illegally parked somewhere on the branch premises. Hal also invented new and improved uses for his company-provided vehicle. Even though it was his second office and a short-stay hotel for his sexual habits, it was too confining to be comfortable, so occasionally, he would leave the branch for an affair in a real hotel. The car's other use was for sex, drugs, and rock and roll. Susan would tell anyone who rode in Hal's vehicle never to touch anything in his car. No one knew who or what had been there, what had happened in the car, or the nature of any stain found on the seats.

When Hal needed to install a new basketball net at his house, he spent hours on the roof of his company car to install the goal instead of using a ladder, because it made sense to do so and was more stable than a ladder. The dents in the roof didn't bother him much, as Hal never had cared much for those types of cars, as they were always substandard vehicles anyway. As Hal put it, "They are a piece of shit anyway, so let's treat them like one."

Just as Davis had totaled many courtesy cars while staying at hotels, Hal totaled his company car while on a drinking binge with Davis one night in 1985. A night out at an icehouse quickly became a drink fest as they consumed about fifteen beers apiece before they decided it was time to go home. Most sales managers employed by CIC learned the hard way about drinking with Davis. Keeping up drink for drink with Davis usually ended with disastrous results, and that night was no different. Unfortunately for Hal, he pulled up next to Davis to say one more thing about his latest female conquest and how much he wanted to see her again and to say good night.

Talking through their car windows, they finished up the conversation, and Hal rolled up his window and punched the gas pedal too hard, which made the car react violently out of his control. He pitched the vehicle left, skidded through the gravel parking lot, and nearly hit Davis's car, which was moving right toward him. Davis was leaving the bar's parking lot too and, naturally, was drunk also. Hal made a drunken right turn to avoid hitting Davis, exceeding forty miles an hour, and suddenly, a tree appeared out of nowhere. Hal had no choice but to hit it head-on because his reactions were too slow, and there was no other place to go.

Davis stopped his car, and they both exited their vehicles to inspect the damage. "This wreck is going to be tough to explain to upper management," Davis said to Hal. "Let's get our minds to work, and we will come up with a great story by tomorrow or at least until a tow truck gets here."

The men began to formulate a report on how the damage could have happened. The best they could come up with was a hit-and-run situation, but they were both drunk and figured more sober minds could come up with a plausible story tomorrow. The car was in bad shape, but Hal coaxed it into starting again, so both men left the bar parking lot to go home and formulate a new game plan for tomorrow.

Hal obtained a rental vehicle while his company car was in the shop under repair, but the car wreck had been so violent that the repair shop reported to him the next day that the accident had bent the vehicle's frame. The car was a total loss, which would be difficult to explain to upper management since it had been a one-person accident. No police had shown up to the scene, so Hal decided to have the car repaired himself and pay the bill out of his pocket. No harm, no foul.

Unfortunately, moving a frame back into place was impossible to accomplish and expensive too. Hal paid the repair shop extra to repair the vehicle the best they possibly could because he had to turn in the car within a few short months. Once the mileage reached around fifty-five thousand miles, an employee would fill out the paperwork to order a new company vehicle. The maximum mileage time frame was fast approaching with Hal's company car. He could not let upper management discover that the frame had been damaged beyond repair, because totaling a company vehicle was unheard of, especially since it hadn't been reported to anyone. The fact that he hadn't reported the incident to the branch office personnel would be a firing offense, so Hal had to come up with a great story soon. The truth would be a big problem if it came to light.

The shop repaired the car as best as they could, but the bent frame was impossible to repair and a total loss. As the date for his car return came closer, Hal decided to check into a rehab clinic to buy more time and hopefully find another job because he knew he would be fired once the car failed an inspection by an auction house, where most company cars went after being turned in to the home office.

Hal was in rehab for only a few weeks, even though he tried to tell the rehab counselor he would relapse in no time to buy more time. Unfortunately, the target date to turn in his company car loomed closer.

Hal finally found a new job with a larger CIC agent located in the Houston area right after he turned the damaged vehicle in. The report to upper management, which came within a few short weeks after Hal left the company, said the vehicle had a bent frame. The frame damage was evident, and the resale or auction value was much lower than anticipated, so the problem existed without an answer.

The home office questioned Davis regarding the details of what had happened to the vehicle and what had happened to Hal during the accident. Davis laughed to himself and knew it was hard to call the wreck an accident, but given the drunken details, he played dumb and said he did not have an answer for home office.

The debacle put Davis in a bad light because his boss, Regional Vice President Tom Staben, was now calling for an answer. Davis knew it had to be a perfect story. When Tom Staben called, it was always a serious issue, so the story had to be believable, or Davis risked retaliation or censure. Due to his Wharton days, Davis already had formulated an excuse for how the company car had been destroyed and why it had not been reported, so he was ready for his call from Tom Staben.

Since Hal was no longer with the company, he could postulate something wild and unbelievable, because the wilder the story was, the more believable it became. The story couldn't be that Hal had been abducted by aliens or that a meteor had fallen from the sky and hit his car. He needed something a little more down to earth to submit to Tom. The story he gave to Tom Staben was a great story with a cast of characters.

Davis said, "A few months back, Hal was at a gas station, when two derelict men approached his car and asked for money and a ride. Hal indicated it wasn't his car to give anyone a ride in and said, 'Damn it, get a freaking job, you lazy bastards!' This approach didn't meet with the approval from the two derelict men, and they became angry. While Hal was filling up with gas, one of the derelicts decided to jump into his car and drive off, laughing wildly. Hal fought the other derelict off and had time to open the vehicle's door and grab the driver out of his car. When he accomplished that feat, the derelict hit the gas, and the car careened out of control and slammed into a pole. Both men ran off into the night, again laughing wildly.

"Given the fact it was a gas station, it could have been so much worse, with a possible explosion and possible loss of life if the gas pump would have ignited. All in all, it was wrong for Hal not to report it to you or the branch office personnel, but Hal felt no one would believe his story because the witnesses left the scene never to be seen or heard from again. He had the vehicle repaired out of pocket, and again, Hal recently resigned from the company, so we don't have him here to discipline him appropriately."

Davis had to put the phone on mute because he was laughing too hard, and he thought to himself, *And most people think insurance people are dull and boring.*

"The problem, I realized in talking to Hal recently," Davis said after he took the phone off mute, "is that he is currently employed with an agency that is one of our largest agents in the Houston area. We can't complain too loudly about this incident because it might affect business writings from the agency." Davis had thought up another good excuse, and he put the phone on mute again to laugh hysterically.

Tom accepted his explanation and asked Davis to keep a better eye on the company cars and institute a semiannual inspection of all company vehicles by the loss-control department to control the situation better. Davis felt that was penance enough for one day and said he would write Tom a letter regarding a new procedure for the branch or a new check-and-balance. The idea was for that type of nonsense never to happen again.

At the time, basic letters were written as a report or response to any questions or queries. Since Davis knew company cars, courtesy vehicles, and even golf carts were always fodder because they never lasted all that long, he felt it was a good idea to institute that new plan of action.

The sales manager job was now open in Houston, so a search began to find Hal's replacement. Davis figured he needed a more reserved sales manager. He wanted one who liked to drink as much as Hal did but who wasn't as crazy as Hal and was a little more responsible.

After several interviews, Davis chose a regional sales analyst located in Florida to take the helm. Art Hower was his name, and he was a seasoned salesperson. Art had owned a medium-sized agency near New York City and sold it to a national agency in 1984 and retired to Fort Lauderdale with his wife. Art had become bored with retirement, decided to go back to work, and landed a sales rep position with CIC to market the Southern

Florida area. Within one year, he'd received a promotion to Orlando's analyst position, and a year later, he interviewed with Davis. He then packed up with his wife and moved to Texas to be sales manager of the Houston branch.

A vast difference in venue was evident in moving from New York to Southern Florida to Houston. Still, it was Art's calling; he excelled at being a sales manager, and even though he was not a large person like Davis, he was the only one who could keep up with Davis in the drinking department. Most folks from the New York area started drinking while in the crib, so they were used to that atmosphere.

Art always found a way to win in any given sales situation. Much like when he'd been an agent in New York, the homes he wrote insurance on had to be protected by a fire department, and a fireplug would have to be near the residence. Art had an imitation fireplug in his trunk with a gray color on one side and a blue color on the other side. When he took a picture of the residence and submitted an image to the company with the application, it always passed through underwriting quickly because the imitation fireplug made it appear every home was protected. He reversed it to a different color every time. After a few months, he painted it two different colors to make it believable. Art was always thinking ahead and had great ideas, even if they weren't aboveboard and legal.

Art was also a colorful individual and dressed the same way, though not color-coordinated. He was an outgoing individual with a sales persona that people paid attention to and had respect for. However, for some unknown reason, Mondays were always bad days for Art because he was usually in a foul mood.

Employees usually complimented Art on or at least talked about his wardrobe, but when he walked away, they questioned why his wife let him leave the house dressed that way. A red jacket with brown pants or a pink jacket with red pants was the norm for Art. Everyone wore business suits, and the corporate standards, such as blue or gray pin-striped suits, were the dress for the times. Art always resisted the stereotypical pin-striped suits and wore his mismatched outfits because they caused a stir when people looked at his style of dress in the branch office. He caused even more of a stir while making agency calls; plus, his clothing always left a lasting memory with people, who wondered why he dressed that way.

Art was different from previous sales managers because he took his marriage seriously; plus, he had been married to the same woman since he was twenty years old, so he had class. Art was on the same page as Davis: interested in growth and having a good time while drinking heavily. Whereas Davis smoked big cigars in the office, Art smoked cigarettes. He enjoyed whiskey and vodka more than beer; however, he didn't really care what it was as long as it contained alcohol. Vodka and grapefruit usually followed morning coffee. It was not a nutritious breakfast for a New Yorker—or anyone else living on earth—but it always got him moving in the right direction. Art inevitably figured out how to exceed targets and always had a new idea about exceeding any production target assigned by the idiots in the home office. He gave the job his best effort and expected the same from everyone else.

Art, Davis, and Hal were all big golfers. Most sales meetings were held at the golf course, usually at Davis's home golf club. The sales meetings always included overflowing beer coolers in the golf cart or any other form of alcohol brought by any individual in attendance. Large amounts of alcohol were consumed on the course and more so on the nineteenth hole, where the party continued after the golf game finished. Planning meetings for the upcoming year were held at the nineteenth hole. All were ready to accept just about any target because of their condition at the time or because they were too drunk to argue. The biggest problem was remembering the agreements the next day after all the alcohol consumed the day before. There were great ideas shared at the nineteenth hole, but most were forgotten by the next day or lost to time. A few made it through on a golf scorecard due to bragging rights the next day or another official review of the results.

The 1980s were a great time to be in business, as the local economy was strong. Reagan was president, and money was cheap, so the usual market plan was to blow out expense accounts, have a good time, and grow the business. The Houston marketplace needed new and creative ideas to write business or a change in market conditions because the insurance market was soft up until 1988.

With a growing economy and growing business concerns, the annual independent agents' convention was always a street throw-down held at a ritzy hotel. The June 1986 convention in San Antonio, Texas, was no exception. At most conventions, the host branch opened up a hospitality room to attract future business and meet new agents who didn't represent CIC. Since Hal was still the sales manager at the time, the possibilities were endless with women, booze, and hanging out with his boss and drinking buddy Davis. One episode in particular involved tennis.

Davis was a better golfer than tennis player. Still, since he was an athletic individual, he could be good at just about any sport he tried, while Hal loved tennis more than golf. Their usual rants and raves about beating each other made their tennis matches a big ego trip. After a boring tennis match with Hal, which included the consumption of many beers because of the heat in San Antonio, Davis and Hal retired to the hospitality suite set up by T. J. and Susan for the night's festivities.

It was hot in San Antonio in June, and both guys were sweaty from the tennis match. Davis sat in one of the chairs, a leather chair, and proceeded to sweat profusely everywhere. He was a large man who sweated at the drop of a hat, so most chairs were ruined after Davis sat in them, and this day was no exception. Unfortunately, Davis had forgotten to pack underwear, so his balls were hanging out of his tennis shorts, which was a horrific sight to witness. Even the hotel staff were grossed out and traumatized over the visual as they helped to set up the room. The hotel cleaning staff and the CIC staff who attended the convention to help out could not mask their disgust. Everyone in the hospitality room was grossed out at the spectacle, especially since Davis was a large, hulking man, and his balls were the same way.

Susan, the sales tech, was in attendance for the convention and spoke about the incident for years to come because the visual was so bad that it left a lasting impression and probably some lingering mental anguish. Susan would place her hands over her eyes when the subject was brought up by the sales reps, because it was such a horrific thought. After someone brought it up in conversation, she always said, "I never want to see that visual again, and stop bringing it up!"

Davis decided to shower for the hospitality-suite festivities set to start at eight and find some underwear, so he left the leather chair in a sad state of disarray—completely covered in sweat. Since sweat was clear and leather hid so much, no one noticed or cleaned it up after Davis left the suite for his room. Everyone was still so traumatized over the incident that no one cleaned the chair or even wanted to talk about it.

Around eight, the hospitality suite opened up, with guests arriving in formal attire because there was a traditional mixer that night at the convention on the first floor. The first woman to show up with her husband was a petite, well-to-do upper-crust-type woman. As luck would have it, she sat in the disgusting leather chair with her formal gown flowing downward toward the floor and promptly placed a hand on the chair's armrest. Since the whole chair was wet from sweat still, she was disgustingly roused by what the chair had caked everywhere. For some reason, when people sat down in a chair that had a wet spot, they immediately smelled their fingers to figure out what substance they'd just sat in. The action was always comical to see, especially when they couldn't figure out what liquid they'd sat in. When the woman smelled her hands in horrific disgust, a deafening scream ensued, followed by a loud question of "Why is this chair wet?"

All heard her cry in the room and even outside. Davis had traumatized another woman without even trying to be disgusting. It was just innate at that point.

When Davis arrived at the hospitality suite and was informed of the leather chair debacle, he was nonchalant with his answer: "Well, damn it, she should have looked before sitting down in my filth." Davis spoke with his usual rough and gruff voice, but everyone knew that inside, he was laughing his ass off because she had to change clothes due to all the sweat she'd soaked up on her formal gown. The gown was ruined, but Davis didn't care in the least. All night, he told the story about destroying a formal gown without trying and laughed about it uncontrollably.

As the night wore on and the booze took effect, many jokes came to mind about the gown and how funny the woman's face had been as she smelled her fingers and hands. Jokes included

"That must have been a formal *ball* gown" and "I wonder if it smelled like Davis's balls even after it was dry-cleaned. Maybe she just trashed the gown because her husband couldn't stand the smell of another man's balls throughout their house."

The conventions were always a tremendous amount of fun, and everyone got lucky because they were huge events. It was the 1980s, and dresses floated off bodies quickly. It was like shooting fish in a barrel, and all attendees had a good time. The convention in San Antonio was also a future CIC employee's first convention. He enjoyed the benefits of being young in the business and meeting new people, including the women. In just a bit more than a year, this future new employee would land his dream job at CIC, begin a new career, and embrace a business philosophy that would lead him to great success in the future.

3
Chapter

Underwriting

*U*nderwriting or, more so, underwriters could be described as the bane of the industry. Commercially speaking, when an insurance agent submitted a commercial account to be considered by underwriting, a prayer usually went up to the heavens because no one knew what the underwriter would do or say. For instance, commercial accounts, such as contractors, manufacturers, and restaurants, all needed commercial insurance. Underwriters could be pegged into two categories: positive and negative. Some underwriters liked to write business and quote or price the account competitively, whereas some were negative and just declined everything submitted to them. An insurance agent couldn't make the underwriter angry, because it might affect future business.

In the independent agency system, agents represented many different companies and knew each company's appetite for business. It was the sales reps' job to push the agents to write more business with the insurance company in any way possible. Davis had known how to exploit the system when he was a sales rep but would generally go to the branch manager for assistance when an agent called about a declined account. He knew that most branch managers had sales backgrounds at that time in the industry, had been in his shoes at one time in their careers, and would sympathize with his plight and help out where they could. Later, most branch managers and CEOs of insurance companies were accountants and actuarial types with no sales backgrounds whatsoever, so it was no wonder that personal touches vanished along with most sales rep jobs a couple of decades later.

The underwriting managers were never likable people, and most were loners. Even their underwriters disliked them immensely. There was never a way to get to the right side of underwriting managers, because they were close to no one, not even their subordinates. They usually had large egos to go with their loner personalities, so no one ever got close to them, but they also were unapproachable because their decisions were final with no exceptions.

The underwriting manager in Houston who caused the most grief and had an unimaginably large ego was Marco Lozano, or just Marc. His ego was more extensive than his waistline, and he was a good ninety pounds overweight, so his gut walked into a room before he did. He was a Mexican national replanted to Houston from the Dallas office who always indicated he was from Spain. Everyone knew the truth, though, and even his subordinates and underwriters talked shit about him because they couldn't stand to be in his presence for more than a few minutes due to his massive ego. He was the brunt of a lot of jokes in the office. He was a real chickenshit type of guy who not only had the table manners of a goat but also could never hit his mouth when he ate lunch. Most of his lunch ended up on his tie. The joke was figuring out what he'd had for lunch that day, based on the stains on his tie. Buffalo wings? A hamburger? Chinese food? No one figured it out, but it was a gas to try to figure out the lunch menu from the ties he wore. He seldom wore the same tie twice, because the stains were so bad no detergent could get the spots out, so he usually trashed the ties after one wearing.

Marco was a self-proclaimed perfectionist, but he was fodder for people in the office because of his bad attitude, and his big ego did nothing for his reputation. Most people did not trust him, not even his underwriting staff. In addition to his ties being bad, he was so overweight he shuffled around like a rooster when he walked the office floor. Even the underwriting staff would chuckle when he walked by. He looked as if he had swallowed a basketball. If someone asked a question in a meeting, instead of saying, "I will address that question in a few minutes," he would say, "I will talk to that later." Everyone would just look at each other and wonder what the fuck he'd just said.

Marco's only redeeming factor was that he enjoyed playing golf, but since he had no friends, he would play either with his staff or with a sales rep and an agent who represented CIC. He was a terrible golfer but always kept score. It seemed he always brought a pencil with an eraser attached to even things out a bit. His score never matched his play, but no one questioned his scorekeeping, to keep things at an even keel.

Having five hours on a golf course with an underwriting manager usually built rapport, but that was never the case with Marc. Once he was off the golf course, it was business as usual, with no special business favors for an agent and no exceptions. The next day, he would always talk shit about the agents he'd played with, such as, "That is a shitty agent, and he never will write business for us. So taking him to play golf was a colossal waste of time and money." As that gossip circulated among agents, no one ever invited him to play again unless it was an entire branch management invitation.

As things went, the underwriting manager was an unapproachable individual, so if there was a problem with an account, a sales rep had to go to the sales manager or branch manager for help. These checks and balances were necessary but made it difficult to increase business writings. The insurance field had to do something in the future for a better way of doing business; however, the soft market would change in the blink of an eye to a hard market in less than a year, with disastrous results for some companies, though better results for other companies.

Davis knew Marc was a tough person to deal with, and they needed someone who could get along with the beast and make things work better, a kind of peacemaker. The current sales reps in the Houston branch did not work well with Marc and mostly had nothing to say about him except for what an asshole he was because of his massive ego and horrible personality. There was help on the way.

Even though the underwriting manager was unapproachable, some underwriters took it upon themselves to write business despite Marc, because they knew it was profitable for the company. They ambitiously wanted to make names for themselves. These underwriters were few and far between, but they did exist and were put into specific areas to underwrite business to grow a particular area in Texas. Austin and San Antonio were always growth areas but were also growth areas for every other company that existed at the time, and the competition was fierce in those areas. A fresh approach was needed, and new ideas were sorely in short supply. As luck had it, one of CIC's current sales reps applied for a sales manager's position in Atlanta and was hired quickly. A sales rep position in the Houston branch was open, and interviews were held to replace the position. Davis and Art looked for some fresh ideas and a person with a great attitude to increase business and fill in the gaps, but it was no easy task to find the right person. The person would need to have a fresh approach and new ideas to impress management, with an underwriting background perhaps, and get business past Marco.

The Interview and Sales Reps

Sales representatives were the lifeblood of companies but sometimes were man-whores too. In Davis's case, the latter was true. His idea was to meet the ladies, but his education from Wharton always brought him back around to finding ways to increase business writings. The ability was innate, because he was ambitious with everything he encountered and everything he tried to accomplish. Whether with sports, business, women, or otherwise, he was a competitive individual. To be successful in the business world, one had to be competitive and driven.

With the underwriting situation at the time, new ideas and fresh blood were needed, so the search was on for a new sales rep. The previous representative was now the Atlanta branch's sales manager, and he disliked Marco immensely, so the new hire had to be a perfect fit.

The convention from June 1986 was over and in the books as a great time with many stories to tell into the future. It had been the first convention for a sales rep who worked for a competing insurance company: Michael DeForest.

Michael was young but an ambitious type. He didn't have Davis's education but made up for it with grit and determination. At the tender age of twenty-four, his dream job was to work for a much larger insurance company for more money and, hopefully, future opportunities. He was a good-looking guy, stood five foot eleven, and weighed around 170 pounds. He was a gym rat in excellent physical health, but his current mood was living for the day he landed his dream job and mostly just living for the day.

The company Michael worked for was much smaller than CIC, called Commercial Standard. Commercial Standard—or CS, as it was known throughout the industry—was stocked with small thinkers and idiots who were counting the days until retirement. Michael knew there were better things on the horizon and better companies in the marketplace, but he figured languishing through the management bureaucracy of folks with corporate cancer and people touting the party line would be a decent enough job. Still, he knew a change of venue was in the future because of the idiots he worked with at CS.

Michael had been employed by Commercial Standard for almost a year and a half and was fed up with the small thinkers and flawed business model. He wanted to start winning in business and knew he had to start looking for a new job because CS was a dead-end job. Michael was ambitious but was still wet behind the ears due to his age and inexperience. Still, maybe a company would be looking for just that type of person to hire—someone to groom for the future and someone ambitious enough to get things accomplished.

Michael's first convention was the independent agents' convention in June 1986. He enjoyed meeting the many new contacts, and of course, like his future boss, Davis, he enjoyed the ladies. Since he was young and good looking, meeting the ladies was not a problem, but his good looks never went to his head, because he had humility. Even though Michael did not meet Davis or his crew at the convention, he heard stories about what went on during the conventions and was anxious to partake in the festivities.

While Michael was covering Commercial Standard's hospitality suite, two ladies walked up to introduce themselves as Darla and Wendy. They were interested in meeting Michael, as they'd heard a lot about the well-dressed kid in the suit. Michael had met one of them earlier at the trade show while working the booth, and he thought she was pretty good looking, but what a stroke of luck for her to show up with a friend who was even better looking than she was.

They stood next to a table with food for the incoming beasts, and the conversation was normal but soon turned to other decadent things, as it was 1986 and wide open for singles. A glass full of M&Ms became the conversation topic after the usual questions, such as "Who do you work for?" and "How long have you worked there?" Michael commented that eating just the green M&Ms provided a mental experience of euphoria and said they should be consumed regularly. His remark was greeted with loud laughter. It was a good come-on to two good-looking gals.

Michael excused himself for a second to greet two more guests who arrived at the suite. After passing off the two new guests to one of the other sales reps, he went back to the decadent conversation with Darla and Wendy. When Michael returned, one of the ladies had a coffee filter full of just green M&Ms and indicated they were ready to test the euphoric theory he'd mentioned earlier, with some assistance. Michael was interested in pursuing the ladies and tried to decide which one.

After they all laughed, it was time to get down to the brass-tacks details. "So are you two staying at the hotel?" Michael asked.

"Oh yes," Darla said. "So what time does the hospitality room close?"

"At eleven, so meet me at the bar downstairs at eleven fifteen if you guys want to continue the party," Michael said.

A quick wit always won the day and usually the women too. They all agreed. The ladies left the suite to find more free drinks at other hospitality suites and continue their rounds. Abundant free liquor flowed at the conventions like water from a garden hose, so it was a huge party every year.

The bar scene was just like at any other ritzy hotel bar, with comfortable seating arrangements, people having a good time and laughing a lot, and a massive bar with a quiet area to carry on private conversations. Michael, who had the sales thing down to an art form, had absconded with many green M&Ms to set the mood for the evening, and he offered them on the table after ordering drinks for everyone. His idea was to see who grabbed them first, and she would be the catch for the evening.

As it turned out, they both grabbed them as if taking poker chips from a casino table after a win. The conversation then descended into something Michael had never experienced before. It seemed Darla and Wendy were part-time lovers, but they still enjoyed the sausage, as they put it succinctly. After the surprise wore off—and, of course, Michael hiding a surprised look—it was time for a few more drinks. "Three more Cape Cods, please," he said, and the conversation continued until the glasses were empty. It then was time to adjourn to someone's room.

They decided to go up to Darla's room. The elevator ride up to the room was mind-numbing, as both women attacked

Michael with a vengeance. While all three were locked into kissing and groping, Michael looked out the elevator window to see if anyone was watching. He saw a few people watching from the bar area but not anyone he knew, so things were going smoothly. As they sandwiched in the elevator, he knew it would be a long night ahead.

The next morning, the sun flowed through the drapes in the hotel room to remind them it was time to get up and move for the day's events. They'd had only a few hours' sleep, but at the young age of twenty-four, Michael felt that rest was a commodity to be enjoyed on the weekends and maybe holidays.

He rolled over to see Wendy and Darla in the nude, both complaining of bad headaches but looking as hot as the morning sun. He guessed their ages were around the late twenties. Unfortunately, he knew he had to leave and get ready for the trade show, as it started in less than an hour. Kisses and hugs ended the morning, and after a quick shower and shave in his hotel room, he was back to the convention trade show.

The other sales reps greeted him with questions and comments.

"What did you do last night?" one asked.

"You're the opposite of the movie *The Picture of Dorian Gray*, in which the picture ages but he doesn't age," said another. Everyone laughed.

"You look awful," added one of his coworkers.

Michael said, "I feel terrible, but you wouldn't believe what happened last night, so let's leave it to your imaginations."

After lunch, Darla and Wendy showed up with big smiles on their faces and the freshly fucked look that only guys could recognize. The other sales reps present at the booth knew what the smiles were all about and questioned Michael about what had happened last night. Michael said, "Just use your imagination, but even your imagination will not be anything like it genuinely was last night."

It became tranquil, as the other reps were speechless, until one asked for Michael's autograph as they all laughed loudly.

On the drive home on Sunday, Michael thought, *Monday again and back to the same old grind.* It was a horrific thought, given that he was tired from the convention, and parts of him were still sore.

After finally arriving home, Michael opened up the newspaper he subscribed to, the local Houston newspaper. He always looked in the want ads for jobs on Sunday. Something caught his attention: a job at a company he always had thought was a great company and a market leader, the Cleveland Insurance Companies. They were looking for a sales rep to replace a recently promoted representative. The next step would be to fax a résumé, but that was a difficult proposition in the Commercial Standard office, as everyone watched others to see what they were doing or not doing.

The next day, with a quick trip to the fax machine when most employees were at lunch, the deed was done. Michael crossed his fingers and, having been raised Catholic and attended Catholic schools, said a prayer about the job. *Christians aren't perfect, just forgiven*, he thought. He had a healthy disdain for his current employer but was thankful to have a job.

The next day, Michael picked his phone up to answer a prospective agent phone call, as his secretary had announced to him. Michael answered his phone with the usual: "Michael DeForest speaking."

The person on the other line sounded familiar and introduced himself as Tony Diablo with a laugh afterward. Tony Diablo was Tony Delany, a former employee of Commercial Standard who'd resigned from CS to start his own insurance agency nine months prior. He had been with CS for more than ten years and was a beneficial person to know because of his long tenure, but Tony had had enough of the company's bullshit and decided to strike out independently. Tony was also a well-known woman chaser and partier, thus his nickname of Diablo, or Devil in Spanish.

After a few pleasantries, Tony said he was looking for a contract with Commercial Standard because things had gone well for his agency during the last nine months, and he wanted to add CS to his contracted companies. Tony knew what Commercial Standard's appetite was for writing business. He already had added his son as a perpetuation plan, or someone to take over the business if an agency principal died or retired—a necessity in the agency business.

Part of a sales rep's job was to find new agents for the company who qualified for a contract, so this was a natural appointment for Michael and CS. It also was an excellent excuse to hang out with a friend and toss back a few at a local haunt called the Hofbrau, off Shepherd Drive in Houston. They agreed to meet the next day to talk about an agency contract but more so to talk about recent female conquests and how much booze had been consumed at the recent convention.

The appointment was late in the afternoon, which was a good idea because a late-afternoon appointment allowed bar-hopping afterward or at least more drinking after an agency contract was discussed. Bar-hopping also added more opportunities to meet more women, which was a bonus.

During the meeting at the Hofbrau, there was the usual talk of women and booze. After the pleasantries and a few drinks, Michael indicated to Tony his displeasure in working for Commercial Standard. The company's paradigm was poor, and the company was honeycombed with small thinkers who couldn't have managed themselves out of a box. There wasn't much of a future with a company like CS because the business model was not aggressive in the marketplace, and the company had decided to decrease their premium writings in Texas. No growth, no winning, and no future. Furthermore, the regional vice president was a loser and was always bitching about expense accounts and increasing agency calls per day.

Michael shouted, "What the hell for anyway? The company isn't growing, damn it!"

Tony indicated that was one of the reasons he'd left: there wasn't much of a future for a sales rep, and there was way too much bullshit to contend with, especially from upper management. Tony said, "The company is lost anyway because most upper-management types have never been in the field competing for business and couldn't sell a life vest to a passenger on the *Titanic*, even after the iceberg was struck." They both laughed loudly.

After a few more drinks, the real questions opened up the conversation, such as how large Tony's agency was, which companies he represented, and so on. A good sales rep always asked those types of questions because they gave a better idea of whether or not CS was a good fit for the agency. Tony knew the drill, so he indicated he had bought a small agency and had increased premium writings by double but needed more companies to compete in the marketplace. Tony continued, he had recently contracted with the Cleveland Insurance

Companies but still needed more company representation to grow the business.

Michael was in shock at his statement, because he had just applied for a CIC job, though he had not heard anything back yet. Of course, he hid his feeling of disbelief and asked how things were going with CIC and whom Tony was talking with at the company.

Tony replied, "The sales manager is Art Hower, and we recently talked extensively about a contract with CIC. I was assigned a sales rep to do the paperwork: T. J. Martin."

"Ah, T. J. Martin. Everyone knows him, and he's a damn good sales rep because he always fights for the agents and their business. Plus, T. J. is well known for calling things the way they are, whether management likes it or not." Michael pointed out that T. J. had coined a moniker for most commercial underwriters: surviving brain donors. More laughter broke out.

"Okay, I've got a favor to ask," Michael said.

The booze had begun to affect Tony, so he wasn't all that surprised about the comments about CIC but was also curious about the conversation and the question.

"You cannot tell anyone about this, because it is top secret. In other words, I'll have to kill you if you tell anyone what I'm about to tell you!"

"Okay, okay," Tony said. "Top secret it is. I'll keep it quiet if you buy me another drink."

"Two tequila shots," Michael told the waitress.

After the shots went down, Michael indicated he had just submitted his résumé to CIC because there was an opening for a sales rep position at the company, and he probably needed some outside assistance with the process of being interviewed.

"Aha, I've got a good idea about the question now," Tony said. "You need someone to give you a reference."

"Maybe more," Michael said. "Maybe you could call the sales manager, Art Hower, tomorrow and give me a glowing review and say how much CIC needs a rep like me. Plus, this would also get back at Commercial Standard for treating us both like shit. Maybe talk to Art about how we conducted annual meetings together and talk me up. We could even teach those small-time-thinking bastards at CS a lesson or two in the process of all of this subterfuge." They both laughed loudly.

In true form, Tony said, "If you can get to work on the appointment process for my agency and make sure someone can finish it off at CS if you decide to leave, I'm fairly sure we have a deal here. You will owe me more drinks and a few introductions to your female cast-offs in the future if this works out, you know! Sounds like a plan—and a plan that will work soon if things go well."

With a laugh, Michael said, "So do we need to draw up a contract in blood, or will a paper napkin suffice?"

"A gentleman's agreement and a handshake will be enough. Plus, the fallout from CS will be fun to watch and hear about in the future." They both laughed. "CS will be squirming on the floor, trying to figure out where they went wrong with a fairly new employee leaving the company for a brighter future, and it couldn't happen to a nicer bunch of assholes." Tony continued. "I bet some other company will end up buying that chickenshit company anyway because it's poorly run, with no real prospects for the future."

"Great minds think alike," Michael said. "Let's get out of here; it's late. Do I need to call you tomorrow to remind you to do this favor for me, or can you remember?"

"I'll remember," Tony said. "I'm just worried about getting home without getting pulled over by the cops. We drank a shitload of booze, Michael, so the only reason you won't hear from me is if I'm in jail. But I'd be looking for someone to bail me out of jail, and that could be you, so stay near your home phone." They shook hands, stumbled back to their vehicles, and sped off into the night.

As the taillights flew off into the night, a feeling of excitement entered Michael's mind because he felt he was getting closer to landing his dream job. In the back of his mind, he hoped Tony would make it home without incident and make the call first thing in the morning. Tomorrow was just another day, but sleep would have been difficult if not for all the booze consumed. It was late when Michael pulled into his driveway and turned the lights off. He was anxious for sleep and felt confident Tony had made it home.

Unfortunately, someone was waiting for him in front of his condo on the Sharpstown Golf Course. Michael was dating a gal named Deborah Morgan, who was semicrazy but gave the best head in ten states, or so he thought at that time. They had been dating off and on for nine months but more off than on, so it was not a serious relationship to Michael and probably not to Deborah. He knew an argument would soon follow, because she had been busy ringing his doorbell most of the night, as he found out from an angry neighbor. Deborah thought he was in the condo, ignoring her and not answering the door, but he had been out drinking and making deals with Tony Diablo. The neighbors would be angry and bitch about all the noise tomorrow, but there never was a way to calm Deborah down. She was as crazy as a peach-orchard boar, and no amount of explaining why he hadn't called in the last week would make things better. His only idea was to soothe her with sex, because that was all she usually wanted anyway, and it was pretty good stuff.

Communication in 1986 was via a house phone with an answering machine. Most folks stopped communicating by just not returning a phone call after a message was left on the answering machine.

After Michael shut his car door, she stood up from the concrete in front of his front door and asked his whereabouts for the last week and that night, as it was twelve thirty, speaking in a harsh tone.

The best excuses came from a drunk mind, and sometimes they were the truth or at least sounded outstanding. "Deborah, listen. I was at a convention in San Antonio since last Thursday and got home late Sunday night, and I've been very busy with work and such. Please accept my apologies for not calling back."

Deborah asked, "Does that mean partying all night too and not taking five minutes to return a phone call?"

"Well, yeah, I was updating management about the convention because they were not in attendance; it was just the other sales representatives and me." This statement was a lie, because management loved conventions and would have missed one only in the case of an impending nuclear holocaust. In fact, even that might not have been a good enough reason not to attend a convention.

Michael continued. "So tonight I was visiting with management over a few drinks after work about the convention and how well the turnout was at the trade show and at the hospitality suite. It just got out of hand with management tonight, and damn it, they made me pay the bill."

"You are so full of shit," Deborah said. "Show me the bill!"

Since Deborah was beautiful, had a gorgeous figure, was gainfully employed, and possessed other handy benefits, Michael was ready to come clean. In Michael's mind, he felt her request was reasonable, and he had kept the bill. Michael always kept receipts because he would later input them on his expense account to get reimbursed. The bill he showed her was from the Hofbrau, which was a bar and steak restaurant, so it was harmless to show the receipt. He just would not show the receipt from the other night club they'd attended: the Colorado Club, off the Southwest Freeway at Hillcroft, a topless bar. That was out of the question. It was a usual haunt of Michael and his associates or friends and management types.

"Here. Look at the bill," Michael said. "It has the date and the time."

She took the bill, reviewed the receipt, and sheepishly said, "Okay, can we go inside your condo? I need to use the bathroom," which was a lame excuse to get inside and check around his condo to make sure no other women were there or had been there recently.

After going into his condo, using the bathroom, and checking around for anything unusual, Deborah was satisfied that nothing was going on.

Michael growled, "We both have to work tomorrow, and it's late, so if you're finished snooping around, please leave!" The comment was an excuse Michael used because he was still recovering from the craziness of the recent convention and was tired. He was nearly healed up from all the action at the convention, but hard dick had no conscience at twenty-four years old.

She followed him to his couch and apologized for being jealous. She immediately kissed Michael and grabbed his crotch, so there was no way to say no at that point. Things adjourned to the bedroom with a lot of wailing and gnashing of teeth, but Michael didn't care how much noise emanated from his condo; he was ready for some action since he'd struck out earlier. The Colorado Club dancers and all the booze he'd imbibed earlier made it necessary to take care of business, which he accomplished well.

Michael would find out soon that his condo walls were paper-thin, and the upstairs and next-door neighbors heard everything that went on in the condo bedroom, which became nicknamed the Man Whore Zone.

He was ready to walk Deborah outside, or kick her out of the condo, at two in the morning. Michael thought it was time for some sleep because he was exhausted from the last week and the debauchery.

Deborah was much happier and wasn't her usual crazy self after sex but was more relaxed and reasonable. She blurted out afterward, "I need a cigarette."

Michael answered, "Smoke it on the way home; I'm tired."

The relationship was toxic as hell but fun too. It was not going anywhere, but that was fine with Michael because he wasn't ready to settle down with anyone. The relationship was tolerable at that point, but there was much more to think about, especially since Michael was hoping for a banner day tomorrow. He expected to hear something from Tony soon or maybe even Art Hower about the new job. It was worth a shot.

The next morning was a regular morning with sales calls, but it was different because a new employee for Commercial Standard joined Michael on a few sales calls to brush up on his sales acumen. The individual was Rick Muller. He'd been hired months back to replace Tony Diablo, but Rick was still wet behind the ears and inexperienced. Management's idea was to get him up to snuff on his sales abilities and help him learn how to be a professional sales rep. Rick hadn't become as successful as Michael and needed some sales pointers.

This task shouldn't be all that formidable, Michael thought, but since Rick was younger than he was, everything was funny or had some sexual connotation attached to it. Michael didn't engage in any form of sex talk. It was unprofessional, and he engaged in the real thing so much that it wasn't all that interesting to talk about with anyone. However, when two twenty-something kids got together, there was always going to be a lot of tomfoolery happening, and crazy shit could ensue at any time.

The agency calls that day were off the Gulf Freeway in Houston. Michael had spoken with a few prospective agents on the phone who were interested in an agency contract. There were two calls lined up with prospective agents in the morning and a call on current agents in the afternoon.

It was a tough day because of the lack of sleep the night before and the anxiety Michael felt in waiting to hear something from Tony. Michael used pay phones to check his voice mail fairly often during the workday to determine if Tony had called and left a voice message. However, he'd received no messages or calls. *Pretty quiet*, he thought. *Maybe Tony didn't make it home and is sitting in a jail cell somewhere, being a girlfriend to some guy named Bruce Buster. Who knows?*

The company car pulled up to the first appointment at James Fenwick Insurance, a storefront agency with a few other business concerns in other parts of the strip center. Rick said, "Fendick, huh?" Both laughed.

Michael said, "Yeah, true, but let's get our game faces on because this might turn out to be a good agent who might need Commercial Standard, and let's be very professional. I met this agent at the recent convention, and he seemed interested in an agency contract but is an ultraconservative individual. So conservative I'm sure his dogs screw in the missionary position." Laughter ensued.

As they were about to walk into the office, Michael stopped and said, "Oh shit, what is that smell?"

Rick smiled and said, "Well, we are near the Pasadena paper mills, or maybe it was dinner from last night. Who knows?" Rick continued after he stopped smiling. "The Mexican food and beans were great last night. We went to a restaurant called Donraki's, off Richmond Avenue."

Michael considered canceling the appointment right then, but they were only a few steps from the door, and the receptionist had already seen them about to walk into the office. She called the agency owner, James, to say his appointment had arrived.

Michael barked, "We have already been noticed, damn it, so now we have to go in. Whatever you do, hold the farts in; it smells like a Pasadena paper mill on steroids, and we are only in the parking lot."

As most locals knew, Pasadena had a lot of paper mills and refineries, and it smelled downright disgusting when one drove in or near that suburb of Houston.

Rick smiled and said, "Hey, no problem, Michael. I've got this!"

The meeting was going well, with a lot of common ground found. Then Rick started asking questions out of the blue. "Mr. Fenwick, I see from your wall that you graduated from Texas A&M."

"Yes, Rick, a great school!"

As Rick asked a question about A&M football, the worst possible thing happened: he talked over his fart.

It wasn't loud but was loud enough that Michael could hear it, and he thought to himself, *Oh crap, if it smells like the last one, we have to leave immediately.*

As it turned out, the smell was atrocious and would have knocked out the current heavyweight boxing champion, Mike

Tyson, in the first round without one punch being thrown. The smell was like that of rotten cheese.

"Okay, Mr. Fenwick, here is the application," Michael said hurriedly. "Please fill it out, and call with any questions, because we have another appointment." Michael gave Rick a dirty look of disgust as they both stood up to leave.

Mr. Fenwick stood up and said, "Okay, thanks, guys. I'll get to work on the app, but—son of a bitch, what is that smell?"

"We are pretty close to Pasa-get-down-dena, so the refineries must have released some toxic fumes," Rick said with a sheepish grin. Pasa-get-down-dena was a well-known nickname for Pasadena, which was home to the honky-tonk Gilly's from the movie *Urban Cowboy*.

Michael thought to himself, *Toxic fumes is about right*, but they were pretty close to Pasadena, so it was a convenient excuse for Rick.

They shook hands with Mr. Fenwick, walked out of his office, and said goodbye to the good-looking receptionist. She had a question for the two young sales reps, though Michael was trying to leave the premises before Rick decided to let another one go. Michael was horrified as the smell seemed to follow them out of Mr. Fenwick's office. *Or*, he thought, *Rick struck again*. Unfortunately, the latter was true.

"Hey, guys, I'll probably be the one to fill this application out, so whom should I send this to?" the receptionist asked. "Gosh," she added, "I hate living near Pasadena; it always smells awful!"

Both salesmen tried to hold their laughter back. It was obvious Rick had let another go in short order from Mr. Fenwick's office to the receptionist's desk.

"Here is my card," said Michael. "Just call me with any questions. And you might get your septic system looked at; it's pretty bad smelling around here." Michael figured, *If you can't beat 'em, join 'em.*

Rick turned away, trying his best not to laugh out loud at Michael's comment, but there was no real way to explain the office's toxic fumes.

As they left the appointment and opened the car door, Michael looked at Rick and said, "You fucking bastard! How could you fart in their office? It truly smelled like a dead goat with a bit of Mexican food thrown in. Plus, the one you let go in Mr. Fenwick's office sounded like it was in B-flat." They both laughed hysterically as Michael started the car.

As they drove off to their next appointment, Michael said, "Don't do that again. I don't think I can stand much more of the smell, and neither can the agents, especially if it gets back to management."

Michael suddenly realized he had gone the wrong way to get to his next appointment, and he turned around to go back to the Gulf Freeway, which meant they had to pass Fenwick's agency again. They stopped at the stop sign and looked at Fenwick's office front, and Michael began to laugh hysterically.

Rick asked, "What the hell is so funny?"

Michael tried to catch his breath for about thirty seconds and then said, "Look at Fenwick's office door!"

Rick looked and roared uncontrollably after he saw the scene. He laughed so much he couldn't get his breath. The agency's front door was propped open with five large telephone books because the smell had permeated the entire office. To top it off, it was the middle of a Houston summer, which meant it was sweltering outside. Since the smell was so bad, the office preferred to sweat to death rather than to smell Rick's skunk smell for another second.

"That was the worst agency call ever made," Michael said after the roaring laughter died down, "and if management ever hears about this call, we both will be looking for a new job. We will be in a lot of trouble if they hear about it, and it will be impossible to explain, given the fact that bad farts on agency calls are hard to explain."

"Okay, okay, I'll do better on the next call, but you're going to have to pull over and find a bathroom because I have to go badly."

"Seriously?" asked Michael. "After all those farts you let rip at Fenwick's office? It smelled like you took a shit in his office, and now you have to go to the bathroom?"

"Yes," Rick said sheepishly.

"Okay, I'll find a hotel you can tear up without too much notoriety. In other words, we can get out of there before everyone starts to pass out and blame it on a terrorist attack." Laughter ensued.

After Michael found a hotel, Rick ran into the bathroom in a hurry. The hotel bathroom trip seemed to be taking way too long, so Michael stuck his head into the bathroom and said, "Damn it to hell, it smells awful in here!"

Rick said, "I've been trying to get your attention by calling your name. You didn't hear me?"

"No, and the last thing on my mind was to enter this bathroom," Michael said unapologetically.

Rick screamed out, "There are no shit tickets here!"

Michael laughed. "What the hell is a shit ticket?"

"Toilet paper, man."

"Okay, hang on. I'll go to the next stall and grab some." Michael took off the roll and threw it over the stall while holding his breath. "Okay, hurry up, please, before the police get here, because I'm sure someone phoned in a complaint!" They both laughed and left the scene of the crime.

After the day was nearly done, Michael dropped Rick at the office and decided to go home early. It had been a shitty day in more ways than one, and his voice mail had been quiet the entire day. He walked into his condo, happy that no one was waiting for him at his front door, and threw himself into his lounge chair.

The phone and answering machine were next to the lounge chair, and the answering machine was blinking with a message. *Could it be Deborah, Sheila, Ginger, Christy, Darla, Mary, or maybe an invite for more fun with a new gal?* It was none of those. It was a call from Art Hower from Cleveland Insurance Companies!

He played the message with anticipation: "Art Hower calling from Cleveland Insurance Companies. Hope you are doing well, Michael. I got your number from Tony Delaney; he said to call him Tony Diablo as an inside joke, whatever that means. I'm the sales manager for the Cleveland Insurance Companies, and when you get time, please call me back. Tony indicated you are looking around for a new job, and we are looking for a new sales rep, as the last rep got promoted recently. Hope to hear from you soon. If I'm not in, just leave a message." The message ended with Art's direct number.

Michael fell on the floor, laughing. "Oh shit!" The dream call finally had come. All his energy came back, and he let out a loud "Yes!" and played the message again. "Oh man, oh man, oh man! I'll have to find a pen and paper, damn it, and write the number down!" Michael screamed out. "What is the fucking time anyway?" It was 4:45, so the office wasn't closed yet. "Get your ass together, Michael," he said to himself, "and be fucking professional!" He was elated but hid his excitement as he dialed the phone number to Art's office.

The phone picked up immediately. "Art Hower."

"Art? Yes, Michael DeForest here. How are you doing, sir?"

"Doing well, Michael." He went right to the subject. "Heard through the grapevine you were looking around for a new job."

Michael said, "I'm thinking about it, but it has to be a good fit for all involved."

"The territory is Houston, Corpus Christi, and the Valley in South Texas, so the person chosen for the job will have some overnight trips about every five weeks. Does that sound like something you would be interested in doing?"

"Oh yes, very much so." Michael knew he couldn't sound too excited but at least had to sound interested in talking further.

Art asked, "So how many agents do you work with currently?"

"Oh, about three hundred."

Art was shocked. "You might have a maximum of about twenty-five to thirty agents in this job, so let's talk further. Hmm, today is Wednesday, so how about tomorrow after lunch, around one?"

Michael wondered why he was in a hurry but agreed to the time anyway. "Okay, sounds excellent. See you at one o'clock tomorrow." Michael tried to hold in his enthusiasm after hanging the phone up but was ecstatic about having an interview with the company and danced around his condo as if he'd just won the lottery.

A dream-job interview! Wow! Now how to prepare for this interview? Michael thought. He knew there was only one shot at this job, so he must dress the part and be perfect.

As he danced a jig in his living room, the doorbell rang. *Oh crap, I hope it's not the insatiable hose beast Deborah ready for round two*, he thought. But after mulling it around in his mind, he thought maybe some action would take his mind off the interview tomorrow—and of course, she accomplished other things well too. Michael had joked with her that the head was so good he had to pull the covers out of his ass afterward due to the suction power. She always laughed at that comment.

Michael thought, *Not two days in a row with Deborah*, but maybe he'd change his mind after a few steps toward the door.

He sheepishly looked through the peephole in the door, and to his surprise, it was not Deborah. It was his upstairs neighbor, Janet. Michael thought she was coming down to bitch about all the noise from the night before, with the constant doorbell ringing that had gone on for hours. He opened the door and greeted Janet, asking how she was doing.

Janet was about twenty years older than Michael, and he wasn't interested in her, even though she was divorced. "Oh, hi," she said. "I'm doing well. Can I come in and visit for a while?"

"Sure, what's up?" he asked.

"I have a favor to ask. I'm leaving town this weekend and wanted to ask if you could feed my cat once in the morning and once around six o'clock."

"Oh, sure, no problem." Michael was relieved to hear the request, as he'd thought she was going to bitch about the noise level from last night. Even though she didn't, after agreeing to feed her cat, he apologized about all the noise recently.

"Oh, I understand lady problems. It's so difficult to meet someone these days," she said. "But I'm not sure you know about this or not, but these walls are paper-thin."

"Oh really?" Michael said. "I never hear anything at all from any neighbors, so I thought the walls were pretty thick." Michael was speechless.

"I hear everything from your condo," Janet said quickly. "The doorbell ringing didn't bother me as much as the screaming from your bedroom afterward. I almost called the police, until I heard 'Don't stop' about fifty times."

"Oh, well, uh, yeah, sorry about that. She is pretty vocal." He laughed a bit. "I'll hold the noise down in the future. I promise."

"With the walls being paper-thin, I can tell you have a lot of company during the week and even more on the weekends. What's your secret?"

Michael thought, *Is she hitting on me?* "No big secret. As you know, I'm in sales, so talking to the ladies is no big deal to me, and how to make them comfortable around me is second nature."

"Hmm, okay, I was just curious because I have many single friends who never seem to meet anyone and are looking for advice on how to meet that special someone."

"It's not too tricky. Just be yourself, and ask more questions; it's incredible what one can find out during a normal conversation, and it will pay dividends in the future."

"Thanks for the advice," Janet said, "and I will leave a few beers in the fridge for taking care of my cat while I'm gone. My boyfriend is finally taking me to Palm Springs for the weekend—the cheap bastard." They both laughed.

It was a relief to find out she had a boyfriend, because he wasn't interested in Janet, but he was surprised she knew about all the action in his condo. "I'm preparing for a job interview tomorrow that I'm very excited about," Michael said. "The only problem about feeding your cat is I'm not sure what's going on over the weekend, but it really shouldn't be a problem."

As she left his condo, Michael figured he needed a new game plan for the gals that didn't make as much noise, but that issue was secondary because he had more pressing things to think about, especially the interview tomorrow.

Sleep was difficult because of the impending interview the next day, but rest finally came, and he woke up early the following day. Michael decided he was not going anywhere near his current employer's office, because something would get in the way of his going to the interview, such as a meeting or conference call that required his attention. He phoned his office and told his marketing tech he would be making calls all day but might be in later in the afternoon.

Okay, I can check that off the list. Now to get ready for the interview.

He put on his best suit, his hair was perfect, and copies of his résumé were located in his binder just in case they asked for one. The agency calls were quick and uneventful, with a few Houston agents close to his appointment at one o'clock near the Galleria area in Houston. After a quick bite to eat, 12:45 came quickly, along with some nerves he couldn't control. Being nervous was a good thing because it helped a person become sharp during a speech or interview, so Michael welcomed the nerves.

He parked his car; took the elevator to the third floor, where the reception area was located; and asked to see Art Hower for a one o'clock appointment. The receptionist asked him to take a seat in the waiting area, and as the tension built, he thought, *You've only got one shot at this, so make it good, asshole.*

He was given an employment application to fill out while he waited on Art and was done with that chore quickly. As Art appeared from the left side of the waiting area, Michael was a bit surprised at the way Art looked and dressed. He wore a red jacket with brown pants and an awful tie. Michael shook hands, introduced himself, and thought, *He looks around midforties but looks a bit older, as his hair is starting to thin out a bit, but a likable-looking person.*

After pleasantries were exchanged, Art said, "Hey, let's go back to my office."

As they passed by Susan Taggart's desk, she tried to look busy but wanted to size this kid up to see who was interviewing for the job. "He's young," she said to T. J., who was also at the office, after Michael and Art walked by.

T. J. said he wouldn't last long even if he got the job. "He's probably around just to get Davis laid more often or get more women, but who the fuck knows?"

"So tell me about yourself," Art said as the interview began.

"My past was in underwriting, but in the last year and a half, I've been a sales representative for Commercial Standard here in Houston."

"Okay, good. So why are you looking for a change?"

"My goal is to work for a company like CIC and help make it a more prominent company and increase premium writings to whatever you and the home office would like in production results. Unfortunately, though, Commercial Standard is not an aggressive company, and the truth is, I'm spinning my wheels working there."

"Do you play golf?"

Michael said quickly, "I've made my home on the Sharpstown Golf Course for the last year and play every weekend, so yes, I do."

This comment was met with a big smile from Art without any further analysis. The interview continued for a couple of hours, with basic banter going back and forth between Michael and Art regarding the territory's agents. Davis was in the corner office, waiting to hear something from Art, and couldn't control his curiosity. Davis figured he would go to Art's office to see how the interview was going with the kid. He extinguished his foul-smelling cigar, walked to Art's office, knocked on the door, and walked in.

Michael stood up and introduced himself and shook hands with Davis. Michael immediately recognized the northern accent and the fact that Davis was the boss and a big boss too, all 320 pounds of him. Right away, Davis made it known who the boss was and who called the shots in the Houston branch office.

So this must be the branch manager, Michael thought.

Davis could tell the kid was aggressive enough to be in sales and a good fit for the job. Besides, he would also attract new women because he was a good-looking kid, and in hanging around with someone like this guy, Davis would have new choices of women available everywhere. Davis was always thinking about a new female conquest, but he also recognized the kid would provide many new faces for his boss if given the opportunity. It was getting late, so Davis suggested getting a pop somewhere close by—not a pop as in a soft drink but a beer.

Michael said, "Great. Where to exactly?"

Art suggested the Cellar Door, off Stella Link, about ten minutes from the office. Davis thought it would be a dark, quiet place to finish the interview and see if the kid could hold his booze.

"Okay, sounds like a plan; see you guys in ten minutes," Michael said.

Michael left the branch office and drove toward the Cellar Door, excited because the interview had gone well without incident. It had been a lively interview with Art, so now it was time to impress Davis. Michael thought as he pulled into the parking lot of the Cellar Door, *I need to close this deal here and now, or I'll work for the idiots at Commercial Standard for the rest of my miserable working life.*

Michael was familiar with the Cellar Door because he'd imbibed there on many occasions in the past with great success. It was a great place to get better acquainted with someone, due to the quiet ambiance of the bar and the dark atmosphere, but mostly, Michael used the bar to break in new female prospects with alcohol and some smooth-talking. Because of his history with the Cellar Door and because he was in familiar surroundings, Michael was at home when Davis and Art arrived.

Davis ordered two beers; he always ordered two because he never knew when the waitress would be back, and he hated waiting, so his logic was to order two at a time. He always guzzled them down quickly due to his size and was always on the lookout for a waitress to order another few beers.

After the first round appeared, Michael's first question to Davis was "What type of business does CIC target for writing business?" He already knew the answer, but the question would get Davis talking, and it would show his interest in working for the company.

"An excellent question," said Davis before Art had time to formulate an answer or even think of one. "We write many contractors at CIC, and yes, it's a very competitive atmosphere. Still, under most circumstances, the incumbent agent renews the account every year without fail, so it's basically down to the relationship a company has with its agency force that renews the account with the current company. We are looking for a person who keys on relationship building with his or her assigned agents and will increase business."

"Okay, got it," Michael said, "but what about the company's plans regarding growth in the future?"

"Another good question," Davis said. "The company has been looking for the states with the best political atmosphere or, more so, a legislatively friendly state to increase business. Texas is almost there, but a few problems still exist. I'm not waiting on the home-office idiots to develop a plan or make a decision, because they never will, so it's up to us to take the bull by the balls and run with it to the bank. The CEO of CIC is a friend of mine, and the cards are stacked in my favor on this deal, but what we need is the right people below me to make it all work. Do you think you are the person for this job?"

"I am for many reasons, Davis."

Davis listened intently for the answer. He was a rough, gruff, tough-sounding person with a large ego, so this was the time to give the right answer.

It was now or never. Michael wanted to make his answer straightforward and to the point but spot-on for the question. "Let me start my answer by saying every one of my agents knows my name and phone number and trusts me with their business—one of the many reasons I'm successful at Commercial Standard currently. Secondly, I'm young, I'm very ambitious, and I want to make a name for myself in the industry. My current employer is lost in a quagmire of bullshit because they do not know whether they are coming or going and couldn't make a good business decision if it came up and bit them in their ass. The company's current market plan is for zero growth this year, and that doesn't make any sense to me, because I'm not a status-quo rep. My agents want to grow with Commercial Standard and increase premiums' growth, but they are hindered by current management. My contacts are ready to grow and kick ass and take names. I'm under the impression that it is not what will happen this year or in the future either.

"If you're looking for a sales rep who is aggressive, takes direction well, doesn't get tired of making sales calls, has new ideas, and doesn't mind the travel, I'm your man. If you're looking for the status-quo rep, I'm not your man. That is my current situation, and it's a very boring existence, and I'm looking for a more challenging position, if you know what I mean."

Michael's answer showed he was interested in working for CIC, and Davis understood his statement but wanted to probe for more answers to see if he was the right fit for the company. Davis picked up that Michael was comfortable at the Cellar Door, so he asked Michael if he had visited the bar before.

"Yes, I have," Michael answered. "I sometimes bring dates here because of the ambiance."

The answer piqued Davis's interest, so he asked, "So you're not married?"

"No, I'm not, and I don't plan to get married anytime soon because my life is fun, and I enjoy hanging out with many friends." Michael thought, *Don't talk much more about having too much fun, or risk being tagged as a partier.* He didn't know that Art and Davis were big-time partiers and were looking for a good sales rep and someone new to party with in the future. Even though Davis and Michael were on different ends of the women spectrum, they both were after the same thing: a lot more women in the future.

Davis had just ordered the fourth round of drinks, when Michael said, "Guys, I'm thinking that is probably enough for me." He wanted to make a good first impression, but Davis and Art wanted to see if he could hold his booze.

Davis said, "Ah, bullshit, have another because Art is buying tonight," and all three men laughed.

They laughed so loudly they got the attention of some of the women present at the Cellar Door. To add even more fun to the situation, Michael pointed out a table of four women, walked over, and asked about everyone's marital status—a ballsy move at a job interview. He indicated he was on a job interview but might join them afterward if they hung around.

Michael reported to Art and Davis about the ladies and asked them to stick around after the interview. They declined but wanted to continue the interview process. Art was married and had been since he was twenty years old, and Davis indicated he was separated. He was not legally separated, as Michael found out later; he'd just left his family in Kansas City and made up many excuses to his wife about not bringing her down. Plus, his kids were still in school, and they didn't want to move, so he took the kids' side. That was a genius move by Davis. Things always went his way during any discussion or any problem that came up; he was brilliant and lucky. He always had the perfect answer to any question posed—another benefit from Wharton.

After the tenth round showed up and the discussion had deteriorated to talking about women, Art talked about his plans for the branch and what a sales rep's responsibilities included. Davis was the macro, or the forest, in his conversations, while Art was the micro, or the trees, and it seemed to be a great working relationship and made sense. Michael liked what he heard, even though the booze was beginning to take effect. He at least made eye contact with one of the ladies at the other table and winked. It crossed his mind to go to the bathroom and hand the best-looking one his business card, but he felt it might interfere with his successful interview, so he just smiled at them when he walked by their table.

The table got quiet as he walked by, but a loud burst of laughter filled the room as he unzipped his pants in the bathroom. He almost pissed all over himself because he knew the conversation and laughter were directed at him, but he had to stay focused.

When Michael returned to the table, Davis asked him if he would join the ladies—probably another test. Michael said no and indicated this conversation was much more critical, and he was interested in working for them. Art and Davis were surprised by his answer, and Art indicated it was about time for him to go home.

"I'll walk you to your car," Art said.

As they approached their vehicles, Art said, "We want you to come work for us and CIC. What do you make at your current job?"

"Around thirty-five thousand."

Art said, "We could pay you thirty-eight thousand a year, but take the weekend to think it over. It's a big move, so think about it, and here is my card if you have any questions."

They shook hands, and Michael pulled out of the parking lot.

Art came back and indicated he'd offered the job to the kid, and Davis said, "A good job, but I wish he would have stayed and helped me out with the table full of women. It's been a while since I got laid, and those gals are gorgeous; however, a wingman would be needed in this situation. Too bad you're married, Art!"

Art said, "There will be plenty of time for that, especially if the kid takes the job. I just hope Michael's employer doesn't try to talk him out of leaving."

Davis and Art finished their drinks and left the Cellar Door, hopeful they had a new sales rep hired.

After he left Davis and Art, Michael went by to visit his parents to sober up some, as he was a bit drunk and stressed over the interview. His folks heard the back door shut and walked into the living room to see Michael on their couch with his arm over his face. His dad said, "Oh gosh, you didn't get the job, eh?"

"No, I got the job, but these guys are serious partiers. I'm supposed to get back to them on Monday with an answer. I'm just here to relax for a bit before heading home."

"Congrats," his mother said. "This job sounds great and like what you were hoping for, so congratulations."

Most parents would have said the same thing to their children, but it was gratifying to hear it from them.

After about an hour on the couch, he locked the door and drove home. Michael was excited that he had his dream job, and tomorrow was Friday, so it was a great double-dip. He was beyond tired and just wanted to get some sleep but was concerned there might be an intruder waiting outside his condo, because he hadn't talked to Deborah in a few days, and it was time for her weekly feeding. Speaking of feeding, he thought, he had to feed Janet's cat!

Michael drove around the block a few times near his condo entrance to make sure the coast was clear in the parking lot, and then he pulled into his parking space and killed the engine. He took one more look around his condo's front door, and no one was hiding near his door. "No one there," he said to himself, "and now better go feed Janet's damn cat and go to bed."

He went upstairs first to feed the cat and relax for a few minutes after a busy day and night. He opened the door, and the cat greeted him with a loud meow. She was hungry but a friendly cat, so he proceeded to open up the cat food and sit down on Janet's couch. After he sat down and closed his eyes for a few minutes, tired from the busy day, he noticed something immediately when he opened his eyes again. There was a huge dildo across from where he was sitting, on the other end of the couch. He laughed out loud, wondering if it was a message or an honest mistake. Maybe the cat feeding was a setup to get him into her condo and make him ask her about the massive dildo on her couch when she got back from Palm Springs. *So how does one question an enormous dildo on the couch anyway? Does it have a name? Most women call their vibrator Bob, an acronym standing for "battery-operated boyfriend." So how is Bob doing? Have you been taking care of Bob? Does Bob ever talk back? Does he ever get a headache?* If she'd forgotten about Bob on the couch, she was probably worried about it in California and wondering if Michael had run across Bob yet.

As much fun as it was to think about it, Michael was exhausted. He went downstairs to his condo and ate a corn dog before bed. He was delighted with the day's outcome and even meeting Bob the dildo, but he was exhausted. Michael would find out a week or so later that Janet was going to pack Bob in her suitcase but forgot to pack him, so he spent the whole weekend alone in her condo—poor Bob.

As Michael left Janet's condo, he thought, *Hell yeah, I'm going to quit that chickenshit company for my dream job on Monday. Might as well make it a banner weekend of golf, sex, and booze.*

The condo Michael lived in had a pool and hot tub at the end of the entrance driveway, basically at the other end of his condo unit, which was about 150 yards away, a short walk. Michael went to work as usual on Friday but left Commercial Standard's offices early because he knew he would quit next week, so why work himself to death for the lost chickenshits at Commercial Standard? Since it was a beautiful Friday, he decided to hang out at his pool, and while he was sunning in a chair, he thought about a friend he had run into recently. About a month before, Michael had been walking back to his condo after sunning and swimming at his pool, when someone had honked a car horn at him. Michael had given a dirty look to the driver and had been surprised to see it was an old friend, Dave Millet from high school, when the driver rolled down his window. Dave had moved to a condo close to the pool recently, but they'd lost touch years ago. It had been a pleasure to run into an old friend in the same condo complex.

"Oh wow, Dave Millet, how the hell are you?" Dave had been a good friend at one time, but his folks had moved halfway through their senior year in high school to a suburb of Dallas. Dave never had said any goodbyes to anyone; he'd just left one day never to be heard from again. After he'd graduated high school, he'd returned to Houston the next day and, soon afterward, gotten married. It had been the wrong thing to do, because he'd gotten divorced in less than two years. As it turned out, Dave was an avid golfer like Michael, and they both lived on the Sharpstown Golf Course, so they rekindled their friendship on the links every Saturday or Sunday. Michael had been amazed to learn that Dave's girlfriend worked for one of his agents he conducted business with, but he never put two and two together.

Since Michael had taken the afternoon off, he went to the gym and then sunned by the pool on the sweltering, sunny late-summer day in Houston. Dave had taken the day off too, so they hung out by the pool. They talked about what time to play golf in the morning, when a gorgeous blonde came out to the pool.

Since Dave was living with his girlfriend and was not a cheater, Dave ignored the lady.

It was natural for Michael to say, "Hey, come on over, and have a beer, because there is plenty."

She approached their chairs and said thanks. Her name was Angela, and she was the sister of the condo manager. Angela was nearly six feet tall and gorgeous, with a killer body, so Michael turned on the charm big-time. She was going through a divorce currently and had a young daughter around five years old.

Who on earth would divorce this beautiful lady? Michael questioned to himself.

After everyone was introduced properly, it was time to get down to brass tacks. Unfortunately, Angela indicated it was much too soon for her to be dating, because the divorce papers had just been filed, and her attorney had advised her not to get into any relationships yet. But Michael was happy to meet someone new and always had a business card in the gym bag he brought with him to the pool, so he gave her his card.

After she hung out for a bit and listened to the music playing and had a few beers, Angela excused herself to finish some laundry, and everyone exchanged the usual "Nice to meet you" parting pleasantries.

Dave and Michael were in shock that she wasn't dating anyone and that there was a new conquest so close to home. Michael looked at Dave and said, "I'll save that one for a future date or a future draft pick," and they both laughed loudly.

Michael updated Dave on all the goings-on with his new job and the old job he was about to leave next week. The plan was a tee time tomorrow around ten.

Later that night, with several phone calls to some old college and high school friends, Michael and his friends decided to meet at Face's, a crazy nightclub in Houston, to start the night off correctly. They'd go bar-hopping from there. The next bar was Cooter's and then a new bar called Confetti's, which had been a country-western bar called Cowboys a few years back. The club had gone from country music to top forty overnight. All the nightclubs were located in the Galleria area, where everything was happening in Houston, Texas. It was a great time to be single in Houston, with a lot of fun, dancing, and craziness and many women to be had if one had the right story to tell.

Michael handed out a few business cards to the prettiest gals at each club, which was his standard procedure for meeting new gals and dancing the night away; however, he decided to go home earlier than usual because of his tee time tomorrow with Dave.

On Saturday, the golf game was the usual stuff of betting on putts, drinking, and trash-talking. Dave and Michael enjoyed each other's company, and it was always a lot of fun. Tomfoolery usually ruled the day, including throwing golf tees as the other person was trying to drive off the tee box and running over the opponent's golf ball to make it harder to find. With all the craziness going on, it was easy to forget about the upcoming week. Michael had to write a resignation letter and finish other tasks, but an exciting week lay ahead.

Saturday was the same old stuff: finding the prettiest gal in the bar, talking a bit, and handing out a business card but mostly just acting stupid. Usually, the next week, someone would call to go out for the following weekend, but sometimes they did not call, so it was good poker to keep handing out business cards and keep dancing until the phone rang.

Monday rolled around, and Michael made a quick call to Art Hower from his desk at Commercial Standard. "Yep, I'll take the job, Art! I'll resign today, and you can expect me in two weeks unless they decide to let me go sooner, okay?"

Art said, "No problem. Just stay in touch, and by the way, you have made a great decision about your future."

Michael's sales manager at Commercial Standard, Sam, was flying in that day from a Boston meeting, and one of the other sales reps was assigned to pick him up that afternoon. He had stayed in Boston over the weekend. Michael told the other sales rep, Rick, he was resigning that day for a better job, which caught Rick off guard, but he was happy for Michael. Michael asked if he could ride along to the airport to pick up the sales manager.

Rick said, "You know he will figure out something is up if two sales reps are in the car when we pick him up at the airport."

"Good," said Michael. "No problem. They won't have me to kick around much longer."

At the airport, the sales manager walked up to the car, saw two people in the vehicle, opened the door, and laughed and said, "Two reps to pick me up? I must be important, or one of you guys is about to resign from the company."

Rick pointed to the backseat, where Michael was sitting.

"Oh shit, you're quitting?" asked Sam.

"Yes, I am, but I've enjoyed my tenure with the company and your help over the last year and a half; it was truly a learning experience." Michael handed his resignation to the front seat.

Michael was surprised when Sam said, "Wow, Cleveland Insurance Companies, eh? Very difficult to compete against those guys. Okay, I'll be back in touch with you this afternoon about the future, but I'm very disappointed to see you leave the company."

Michael thanked him again, and they drove back to the branch office.

Commercial Standard could not compete with Cleveland Insurance Companies in pricing accounts or employee retention because CIC was a much larger company than Commercial Standard. They allowed Michael to work his two weeks, which was good in a way because Michael didn't do a whole lot during those last two weeks. Why kick ass and take names when one was leaving a company? He wanted to go on good terms and at least showed up for work during those two weeks, but he didn't do much more and had drinks with friends after work to relax before the new job started.

After about a week, a letter came to his mailbox at home, addressed from CIC. It was a letter from the HR department with the offer for employment. What stuck out was the fact that the offer was contingent on verifying his salary at Commercial Standard. Of course, after his jaw hit the floor, he thought about the outcome when they discovered he'd lied about his salary at CS. It had not been a bad lie, just a white lie, because he'd added in his expected bonus for that year. Michael needed to call Art and did just that.

After he explained the situation to Art, Art asked, "Are you still going to be here in a week?"

"Sure am, Art!"

"Let me handle those dumb fuckers in HR; you just be here next week."

"Well, that kind of brings up another problem: my company car has to be turned in on my last day of employment at Commercial Standard, which is this Friday. Should I just take a cab ride into the office on Monday or find a ride into the office?"

"No, I'll pick you up next Monday at eight o'clock at your condo."

"Okay, thanks, Art, and thanks for offering me the job." As he hung the phone up, Michael was relieved. Everything was still on; it had been just another scare.

Friday arrived with a going-away party with a few friends. It was a good excuse to party and have a good time. Having a good time was second nature to Michael, and he chose a club called Midnight Rodeo to party at, because it was a club Michael went to often.

Everyone consumed a lot of beer and shots. It was a great send-off for Michael. After the festivities were over, Michael was already making plans for the next night because he had received a surprise phone call from a gal he'd met the previous weekend. *It seems if one distributes enough business cards, someone will call*, he thought as he laughed to himself.

The gal's name was Breanne, but she went by Bren. She was a small-framed lady with a nice body and was hot looking but a reticent type. That was not Michael's type, but he made exceptions at times.

He picked her up early on Saturday, around seven, and went to dinner at Paisano's, his favorite restaurant. Since nothing good was playing at the movies, Michael suggested going to his hot tub with a bottle of fine Italian wine from the Tuscany region he had at his condo. She greeted the plan with delight, and Michael decided he would give the neighbors some rest from the screams that emanated from his bedroom every weekend and take care of business in either the pool or the hot tub.

Bren didn't have a swimsuit, so she borrowed a business shirt from Michael's closet. She put on the shirt with just her underwear on underneath. He poured the glasses full of wine, walked to the pool area, and got into the hot tub, but Bren had other ideas. With her glass in one hand, she jumped on top of Michael, pulled down her panties, and went to town.

For about thirty minutes, the action went on with only a few breaks for a sip of wine, when Michael heard someone call out his name in a low voice. He looked at Bren, but it wasn't her; she was still bouncing on top of him. He looked over his shoulder and saw his golfing buddy Dave with his girlfriend, Kathryn.

"Hey, what's up, dude, and why are you calling my name out in the middle of the night?"

"Probably because I want to be doing what you're doing in the hot tub," Dave said, and they both laughed. "The reason is,

Kathryn and I just got engaged! So when are you going to be done anyway?" Dave and Michael laughed again.

Bren was embarrassed, and she stopped bouncing on Michael for a bit and hid her face while Dave and Michael talked and laughed about the situation.

Michael said, "Give me a few more minutes, and I'll finish up at home. My neighbors have slept enough anyway." Everyone laughed again. Michael added, "Congratulations to you both!"

Michael thought, *Well, the neighbors will not get a break after all, so back to the condo we go.* Bren was ready to lie down anyway after all the cardio in the hot tub.

Monday came fast like a bullet train, and Michael started his first day at Cleveland Insurance Companies. His dream job came with better pay too. He needed to soak up a lot of information and learn a lot in his first few months on the job.

Where the hell is Art anyway? he thought. It was already 8:45, and Art had said he'd be there at eight.

Art finally showed up at nine, and they went to have breakfast at a Champ's off the Southwest Freeway. Art indicated many training areas that included about ten pages of expectations or, as Michael put it, shit he would have to learn in a short time.

"Thanks for breakfast, Art," Michael said.

Art seemed to be in a bad mood and said, "Don't get used to it; this is a one-time thing."

The other sales rep, T. J., would comment in the future that Art was in one of his Yankee New York moods whenever he acted that way, which generally was on Mondays.

When they arrived at the office, Michael was introduced to Susan, the marketing tech, and T. J., whom Michael had heard a lot about during the last few years. Michael thought Susan was gorgeous. Later, he found out she had many different problems, but she sure was a lot of fun to hang out with and loved drinking White Russians.

He next went to the human resources department to finish up the paperwork crap and then went back to the sales department.

Michael spent the rest of the week meeting other department heads, meeting different folks in underwriting, and going over the training bullshit. He knew he had to learn everything quickly. Michael was a sponge of information and learning procedures, so it wasn't that tough, just time-consuming. There were always a few meetings on Mondays, as well as a few conference calls with the regional home office, but nothing different from his last job. He felt that part of the job would be a breeze.

Susan indicated she was having a birthday party for her husband at her house in Katy, a suburb of Houston, in about a month and invited the sales department to attend with a significant other. Michael thought it was another test, one to see whom he would bring to the party, and it was. The test was to find out what kind of taste Michael had in women: gorgeous or just okay. If his date was beautiful, everyone would think Michael had high standards; if not, maybe he had not been such a good hire.

The first week was in the books. Nothing fascinating had happened except for a party invite, but it was Friday and time to party it up because he had his dream job and wanted to make it work. The party was like any other party, but there was a lot of booze, and everyone was getting better acquainted. Michael walked in with his date. He'd brought Deborah because he couldn't find anyone free on such short notice. Besides, he hadn't talked to her in a few weeks, so he thought she would be ready for her bimonthly feeding.

When Davis saw them walk in, he was stunned by Deborah's good looks and figure. Susan had a Polaroid camera, and at Davis's request, she took a few pictures. Davis put his arm around Deborah while Susan took the photos, and he asked how she'd met Michael. They'd met at a nightclub in Houston, but she was a bit afraid of Davis because of his hulking, titanic body, and it appeared from the conversation he was well educated.

After the pictures were taken, Davis went over to where Art was standing with his wife and said Michael had good taste in women. Art agreed. Deborah went to the bathroom, and Michael went over to Davis and Art and proceeded to tell a joke he'd heard the day before. Michael said, "How does a deaf gynecologist communicate with his patients?"

They both said, "I don't know."

Michael said, "He reads lips."

They both fell over laughing.

Deborah walked up and asked what was so funny. Michael said, "The next task is, we need to carry Susan's husband to his bed, because he drank too much."

Davis said, "Yeah, too many tequila shots, I think."

A few Polaroid pictures later, Susan's husband was in his bed, snoring away, so the party broke up, and everyone left Susan's house. Michael knew it would be a late night with Deborah around, and it was feeding time, so they went back to his condo to fulfill his obligation.

The next morning, Michael told her he was playing golf with Dave, so she needed to go home. She reluctantly left, angry as always.

The next weekend, Michael had dates on both Friday and Saturday, but he still had time to play golf with Dave and hang out with friends at various clubs, even with the dates he lined up. They went to a new club called the Metropole, near downtown Houston, on Saturday. Friday's date had gone well with Bren, but when Saturday rolled around, the women at the Metropole were drop-dead gorgeous. Michael figured he would come back without a date next time. Besides, his birthday was coming up soon, and his birthday parties were legendary and crazier than hell, with champagne, bourbon, limos, friends, and crazy gals. Anything went, but a stop at the Metropole would be necessary because the women were out-of-this-world gorgeous.

After seeing Bren on Friday, he broke down and called Deborah for Saturday so he didn't get a surprise guest at his doorway in the middle of the night again. He also disconnected his doorbell to cut down on at least some of the noise from his condo and hopefully prevent neighbor complaints.

A month later was his birthday celebration with all the bells and whistles, including a limo; all kinds of booze; and, later in the night, invitees throwing up everywhere. The first stop was the Metropole, where all the gorgeous gals Michael had come across the previous weekend were. The club did not disappoint. The women seemed to be at every end of the bar, so it was time to hand out some business cards to prospective females and let them know it was his birthday. That usually tore down the walls of snobbery, even with gold diggers. These arrogant women loved shots and limos, and the party revelers began to increase substantially. Tomorrow was not going to be a good day, but no one gave a shit. Everyone was young, having a good time, and slamming tequila shots as if they were free-falling from the air. Michael didn't like the arrogant types, because he knew they were high maintenance, and that took all the fun out of the chase; however, it was his birthday weekend, so he made exceptions to have fun.

That type of partying and living had been going on for many years. It usually left Michael with an empty feeling on Sundays, but it sure as hell was a lot of fun. *Probably the reason most guys get married*, he thought, *is that although the partying and good times are enjoyable, there truly is no redeeming factor when the party is over, and one encounters an empty feeling of wondering what's next.*

Marriage was not on the horizon or even on Michael's mind. The only thing on his mind was making his tenure at CIC a success. That would be a tall order with Davis and Art because they both utilized the sink-or-swim concept with new employees, and Michael needed help to make his tenure successful. This help would come from a particular individual who was unexpected and much appreciated.

Both Davis and Art were demanding in their management styles, and they gave excellent direction but wanted production and results immediately. The weekly large-line meeting on Monday was always tricky because Davis wanted updates on every large account submitted to the branch to either quote to the agent or decline to quote. No one said anything to Michael about being prepared with answers for each large account submitted to the company, but he never made the same mistake twice. His first few large-line meetings were a bust, but he quickly figured out the system. Michael also figured out that Davis loved large accounts, so the more submitted to the company the better.

Given that it was a competitive marketplace, it was challenging to write large accounts, but that would change soon. There were storm clouds in the future that would make or break an insurance company. A few would fold and go out of business in Texas, mostly due to the market conditions in the late 1980s. A company would either react to market conditions or start packing up their desks. Texas's future market problems would be devastating to some insurance concerns but an opportunity for others.

Market Conditions

After learning a tremendous amount of information and procedures regarding CIC's way of doing business during the first year, Michael felt he had a good handle on what he was doing, and he had increased production but not as much as he would have liked. He hadn't yet convinced his managers he was an asset to the company. The jury was still out on that for several reasons. A couple of times, he hadn't known if he would make the next week, because of some different choices he made regarding business and agent appointments, but Michael never stopped trying to succeed.

It was a complicated learning process, but there was some leniency regarding a new hire. However, with the management style Davis and Art utilized, a new hire never knew if he or she was doing the right thing until the wheels fell off. By that time, it was too late to fix things. The employee could do damage control at best, and Davis never forgot about the incidents and would bring them up on certain occasions just to show who was in charge of the branch, mostly to benefit himself or make himself look better in a crowd—it was an ego trip. In office politics, Davis and Art were the masters of their destiny because of their experience in the business world. They always had an answer for just about every question but no solutions for dealing with the underwriting department. When an account was declined by underwriting, there was no check-and-balance at that point; it was a dead deal. If a sales rep complained about the account or elevated the account to the underwriting manager, it fell on deaf ears. Some fresh ideas and a new approach were needed to deal with the underwriting department and make things work better.

During his second year with CIC, Michael began to enjoy a newfound comfort level with his assigned agents and better understood CIC's direction and target markets. The company wanted a particular type of business from the agency force, and Michael keyed on that type of business to push on agency visits. There was still a problem in dealing with underwriting, but Michael could always sell his way through any debacle and did so on a few occasions. Underwriting was a problematic department to deal with, and Michael knew he could overcome the problem with a few suggestions in the future.

Since Davis expected immediate production results, the relationship between Michael and Davis had deteriorated since Michael started with the company. An increase in production was not easy for any sales rep to accomplish. Davis was a taskmaster and wanted significant increases in production yesterday—not only premium increases but also more women, because one of Michael's unwritten expectations was to get dates for Davis. It was not an easy task to accomplish but not impossible. Davis was a big man, and most women saw that as disgusting, but Davis was the branch manager, so his job made up for any unlikeable characteristics.

Michael still enjoyed the same personal life and partied most of the time but decided to distance himself from Davis until production increased. Michael disliked people with large egos and overbearing personalities; plus, he was not an ass kisser. Davis liked to have his ego stroked and his butt kissed, and that was not how Michael rolled in business. He worked mostly with Art, the sales manager, which was the way most sales departments worked anyway. The biggest problem was that since Davis had a sales background, the sales department was his baby, and he understood the sales department was the lifeblood of all companies.

When Michael went to happy hour and Davis showed up, the employees had to watch everything they said in front of Davis. No one wanted to bruise the massive ego of Davis. Davis ran most of the ladies off due to his size and personality when Michael ran across new ladies to introduce him to, so Michael decided it was time to distance himself.

Davis noticed the distance and acted upon it in a short period. Instead of talking to Michael about it, anytime Davis saw Michael talking to any lady in the office or outside the office, he started rumors that Michael was having sex with her. It wasn't always the truth. Art would bring it up to Michael and ask why he was interested in a particular woman who wasn't Michael's target market. Everyone, including Art, was used to seeing him out with blondes with gorgeous figures, so it didn't make sense to see him out with a regular-looking lady. Michael was taken aback when asked about a lady he never went out with or even looked at funny. Michael asked Art, "Who said that?"

"Davis said that because he heard you were banging that gal and a few others in the office."

"Well, not that one, but yes, there are a few I'm currently banging who are not on your list of ladies you mentioned. Hell, if anyone lived up to Davis's idea about banging every gal in the branch, my knees would have bandages around them, so just take those comments as him stirring the pot in the office."

Art always weighed both stories or both sides of any situation and came up with his own opinions because he was a level-headed guy and never jumped to conclusions. He was a grounding factor for Davis, because Davis always jumped to conclusions and also made up his own stories to fit the situation. Art would think about the situation, say to himself that it was all bullshit, and make his mind up because he knew Davis was full of shit most of the time.

Michael continued. "The real truth is, I'm trying to set the office record in the parking garage out back. I kind of have a bet with myself to see how much the record can increase as a bar for future generations." They both laughed.

"What office record?" Art asked.

"How many times I have sex in the garage out back after work. I'm up to three and probably will have number four soon. I'm talking to a gal on the first floor who doesn't work for the company, but she is a hottie. I've heard Hal did a lot of that sort of thing in his company car, but no one said he kept score."

"Okay, but don't get caught, because I can't bail you out of that situation," Art said. "And oh yeah, we have a meeting in ten minutes regarding market conditions. Find T. J. quickly. Usually, at this time, he's asleep in the second-floor break room."

"Okay, I'll find him."

The quick talk with Art adjourned, and Michael knew Davis's plan to start bullshit stories about him was not going to work, but still, he wasn't ready to rekindle the friendship again. Michael's new plan was to talk to every lady in the office during the next few weeks and make sure Davis saw the conversations just to add fuel to the fire. In other words, he would make it difficult for Davis to make up more shit, because Michael couldn't have sex with every woman in the office. Who could have?

The meeting was a big one in the branch manager's conference room, near his office, and included sales and underwriting managers, underwriters, and sales reps. Since smoking hadn't been banned in the office setting yet, Davis walked in with his cigar lit and started bitching about the home office and the three-hour conference call he'd just had with them to try to figure out the Texas marketplace. He slammed the door to produce an air of authority and to make sure he had everyone's attention. He did. "We just received our workers' compensation assessment from the state, and it's twenty million dollars. Home office just shit an egg roll, and they want a new game plan as soon as possible."

The workers' comp law in Texas stated that the more you wrote, the more a company would pay in assessments, which would support the state pool. The state pool was the market of last resort. It was a lousy law and unprofitable for all insurance companies. The unprofitable atmosphere was about to worsen because a loophole had been discovered in the law, and different entities were taking advantage of it. The price was about to go up astronomically to purchase workers' compensation insurance. CIC decided to stay in the marketplace, but most companies ran for cover and stopped writing workers' comp altogether and just keyed on the other ancillary lines of coverage because they were profitable and had no assessments.

Davis said, "If we are to stay in the marketplace and continue writing workers' compensation, we need some new ideas. Does anyone have any ideas?"

Michael felt it was a bit premature and wasn't ready to show his original ideas, but he raised his hand and said, "Let's key on a workers' comp to the ancillary line of coverage ratios. We have the automation to figure each agent's work comp to package or ancillary coverage policy ratios. Once they give us enough of the less-risky coverage areas, we can write a work comp policy for any given agency."

Davis stood up and said, "Great fucking idea. Get to work on it. This report needs to be on my desk by each agency by the end of the week—Monday at the latest."

Davis really meant Monday, because he would be playing golf for the rest of the week and didn't want to be disturbed by office shit or even home office shit. The meeting adjourned with different employees' assignments to formulate the new game plan as soon as possible. Davis left the office to play a round of golf with one of CIC's largest producing agents. Golf was king in the 1980s, especially at the Houston branch office of CIC.

Art walked into Davis's office before he left for the golf game and said, "That was a pretty good idea from Michael. I'm glad he took the job we offered, and I'm assuming this is just the beginning of a stellar career here."

"It was a good idea, but the jury is still out on him, in my opinion," Davis said.

"Why?" asked Art. "Because he hasn't gotten you laid enough with all the women he's been fucking?"

"No, that too, but it seems like he avoids me most of the time, and I can't figure it out yet."

Art replied, "Seems like every time one of his agents writes a big account, you always say, 'That bullshit didn't happen,' or someone is full of shit. If it were me, my feelings would be the same, and I'd avoid you too, so why do you have it in for him?"

"I don't have anything against him. I'm demanding of all my employees and just want the best performance."

"Oh yeah, kind of like the new gal in the file room, Davis?"

"Damn it, Art, she's not only gorgeous, but I've never seen an ass that small on a woman before. It's like the size of one of my thighs," Davis said as he pointed to his sizeable right leg.

Art responded, "Yeah, and firmer too." They both laughed.

Davis said, "Yeah right. Wait just a minute! Fuck you, Hower!"

After Art left Davis's office, he went to Michael and said, "When something big happens or one of your agents writes a big account, make sure you let me know about it afterward. Just so my report can include that information to the branch manager."

Michael said, "No problem. Something big like the fact that the parking garage record increased recently, for instance?"

Art laughed and said, "No, just when your agent writes a big account, okay?"

Art walked into his office to return a few phone calls. Michael talked with T. J., mostly about weekend plans. T. J. asked Michael how many dates he planned to have for the upcoming weekend. Michael had built a good relationship with T. J. over the last year, becoming friends with him. T. J. had helped Michael out on numerous occasions over the last year with questions regarding how to be a successful rep at CIC. He'd made one of his first calls with T. J. in a small town near Houston called Santa Fe, off the Gulf Freeway going toward Galveston. The agency call had been on one of T. J.'s older agents he had worked with for an extended period and had a great relationship with due to the familiarity of working together for so many years.

The call had been quick but ended up at a topless bar called Heartbreakers, near the agency in Santa Fe. Not a lot of business had been accomplished that day, but Michael had observed T. J.'s perspective on sales calls.

Heartbreakers was not an upscale place, such as the Colorado Club or even Rick's, but a place to have a few beers, relax, and enjoy the scenery. One dancer in particular knew T. J. because he was a regular, and she danced for him often. She had a nice figure but imperfect teeth. T. J. called her Super Chops, but she didn't seem to mind, because she would dish out as much as she took. The dancers had to be well endowed by Mother Nature or by surgery to interest T. J.

The drive back to the branch had seemed more extended than the drive earlier. They'd talked on the way about how a new rep should act and how to master office politics. T. J. told Michael to make sure he treated Susan with respect because she could get a representative fired quickly and had before. T. J. had taken a liking to the new hire and figured he would help him out; T. J. was a useful resource for information on how to do the job correctly.

T. J. had married young and stayed married. He did not fuck around at all, and he was proud of that fact. T. J. never became close to anyone, but he and Michael both loved women's breasts. Michael was more of an ass man, but hell, who didn't like women's breasts?

T. J. had become a great friend and resource and a running buddy because they had a lot in common. Both were aggressive in business situations and loved talking about women. T. J. and Michael had lunch together on Mondays at their favorite Mexican restaurant and talked about Michael's latest conquests and how much booze they'd consumed over the weekend, mostly just guy talk. They enjoyed each other's company. Michael was a city boy, and T. J. was a country boy about twenty years older, but opposites attracted.

T. J.'s favorite joke was about a senior bull and a younger bull talking on the mountain while looking down at the valley. The younger bull said, "Let's run down and fuck one of those heifers!"

The older bull said, "Why don't we walk down and fuck them all?"

T. J.'s business advice was always right, except for matters concerning women, because he had been married since he was twenty years old. He was inexperienced in 1980s women. He did try to occasionally give advice when Michael ran into a woman problem, but Michael relied on his own gut instincts to solve the problem. Some of T. J.'s advice would come back to bite Michael in the ass within the year, but he trusted T. J. and his advice because it was always sound and usually worked well.

T. J. enjoyed seeing the ladies in the office come by the sales department to see how Michael's day was going and to entice Michael with their good looks, especially after a crazy weekend involving one or more of the ladies who worked in the office. Women talked in the office, and T. J. got a charge out of Michael's being scolded about the women by management too. Art would say to Michael, "Please get rid of the women hanging around the sales department, because they interfere with business and getting things accomplished!"

Michael would call them on the phone and say, "You're banned from the sales department because you're hanging around too much and pissing off my sales manager."

The scolding usually made matters worse, because the women would wait until Art left the office and then hang around even more. Art was angry not just because he was an excellent, efficient manager but because he wanted to partake in the festivities and was jealous of all the action Michael enjoyed.

Art, many years later, admitted to that fact. He was married and didn't fuck around on his wife but was still a bit jealous.

T. J. was older than Michael by twenty years and was a weekend peanut farmer near Schulenburg, a small town west of Houston. It was a quiet existence, so T. J. enjoyed hearing about the who, what, and where of Michael's crazy lifestyle. T. J. occasionally met some of these ladies, mostly if the woman was beautiful and had big floppers. They would sometimes meet out for dinner over the weekend.

T. J. had been with CIC for more than ten years by the time Michael was hired and had seen a lot while working for CIC with different sales managers, other sales reps, and many branch managers. He always had a story about someone or something that had happened in the branch office. T. J. had a wealth of knowledge about how CIC had changed over the years and how to get ahead.

When Davis, Art, Michael, and T. J. got together, it was always a crazy meeting, party, or otherwise, primarily if it was at the Hofbrau on Shepherd Drive, an icehouse, a golf course, or a topless bar. Trying to carry on a sales conversation while getting a lap dance was challenging but not impossible. It was tough to comment on production numbers when the meetings were held at the Colorado Club or Rick's, off Richmond Avenue in Southwest Houston. It was a vintage 1980s business atmosphere.

Into Michael's second year at CIC, things were going well but not as well as Michael wanted. The business was up, and he had located some outstanding producing agents who were beginning to pay off. Davis called a meeting to talk about his recent visit to the home office. There was some nominal growth in the branch but not the dramatic growth Davis wanted. Something else was brewing within Texas's marketplace, and it was not a positive atmosphere for growth. The CEO of the company, Ed Daniel—better known within the sales department as Dead Ed because he looked very old—called for a meeting with Davis. A one-on-one with the CEO of CIC in Cleveland was a scary thought for Davis and everyone else, as one-on-one meetings did not happen often and seldom had good outcomes.

Davis returned a few days later and called a sales meeting with Art and the reps—not the usual meeting in the conference room but one at an icehouse in the late afternoon. Davis ordered his standard two beers to start the discussion at the icehouse, which was located off 59, or the Southwest Freeway, at 610, near the Galleria area. It was a late meeting, so they could continue drinking into the night and not go back to the office.

Davis started the session off by saying, "We just got our assessment from the State of Texas, and it was forty fucking million dollars. As one might imagine, Ed Daniel, the CEO, was not only pissed off but wanted an explanation as to the future of CIC writing business in Texas. I used Michael's idea of property to workers' comp ratios, and that was well received, but we need more useful or even useless information to update his unhappy ass. This assessment could turn catastrophic in the future, but damn it, we are writing a shitload of business, and I want to keep it that way. We have grown at eight percent in the last few years, and I want to grow more. We have the right people at the right time and can grow the business if given the opportunity, and we need stronger growth as soon as fucking possible."

His statement was a small compliment aimed toward Michael, T. J., and Art, which did not happen often. It felt good and was motivating to hear. As the rounds of drinks continued, the conversation turned to the real problem: legislative activity and the fact that the Independent Agents Association had a political action committee, or PAC, that was underutilized.

Davis continued. "We need to meet with the PAC to see what we can develop legislatively speaking, but we don't need another meeting with Ed like the last one! Let's put our heads together and come up with a game plan because the more business we write, the more difficult it will be for the home office to shut us down. Any other ideas?"

Michael spoke up immediately. "I have been working the Rio Grande Valley and Corpus Christi agents recently, and we can grow there if we assign aggressive people to underwrite the territory. We currently have two underwriters who are just waiting to retire and do not write any business, because they don't have to write any business. The territory is virgin territory, and I'm sure we have never grown in that territory. The underwriters assigned to that area are just counting the days until retirement. If we assign some aggressive underwriters to work the area, we can succeed there and increase business.

"We have about a million dollars of total business in Corpus and the Valley areas, and it should be around twenty million, given the right attitude and game plan. The bottom line is, these territories are currently underutilized, and my research shows they have always been underutilized. Give me the tools needed to grow, and business will increase exponentially. Several prospective agents would love to have a contract with CIC and have committed to large amounts of premium volume. Since we have never instituted a game plan for the territory, the excuse given on my recent calls in the area was 'I'll run my game plan by management to see if something sticks to the wall.'" The table laughed out loud.

Michael continued. "If we make Corpus and the Valley a target area for growth, we can increase our writings there quickly because of the poor market conditions; plus, most competitor companies are running for cover in the territory. What do you think?"

The table became tranquil as they all chugged their beers, and then Davis blurted out, "Do it, and make it work, Michael. I'm counting on you, and I'll have a meeting with the underwriting manager next week to instruct him to get on board with the game plan, which is not an easy thing to do with Marco. I'll need a report on agents we have and agents you're going to appoint and estimated premium volumes, so get to work on that as soon as fucking possible."

Michael was ecstatic to hear the news but hid his excitement. He didn't want to look delighted about his game plan's positive reception in front of anyone at the table. Art looked smug but also proud of his hire and wondered how and when Michael had thought up that game plan.

After everyone else left the icehouse, only Davis and Michael remained, chugging beers. Davis asked, "When did you think this up anyway?"

Michael said, "It has been in the back of my mind since my first few months at the company. My thoughts had to be presented at the right time, as timing is everything." They both laughed.

Michael continued. "The other reason for my game-plan introduction was that there are a few new lady friends in the territory. There is a necessity to investigate these opportunities. It also seems it will take some time to close these deals."

Davis laughed and offered his assistance in any way possible. They both laughed as they left the icehouse.

Michael was currently hitting on a receptionist on the first floor who worked for another company in the office building and had caught his eye the week before. They had walked in together from the parking garage one morning, and naturally, Michael had introduced himself. Michael always checked out a woman's left ring finger to make sure there was no jewelry on her hand. It was always good to be safe, especially if he was interested, and Michael was interested in this new find. She was a hot blonde with a kick-ass body, about five foot five, and she seemed to be interested in him. Her name was Sheila, and she was easy to talk with, so he walked down during the day to visit with her and find out all he could in a short period. She was in the process of a divorce and had four kids, so she was not his target market, but he was thinking about adding to the parking garage record. It was hard to believe she had such a hot body after four kids, but she was young and swamped with work, it seemed, so it was time to close the deal.

Yesterday's meeting was on Michael's mind, along with the game plan for Corpus Christi and the Valley, but this was way too good to pass up. There was a concert in town, and Michael had tickets to attend, so he figured he would invite Sheila. What woman would not have wanted to go to a George Strait concert? The parking garage record looked like it was about to increase.

He took the elevator down to the first floor and asked her to the concert tomorrow, and she readily said, "Yes, I would love that, and I love George Strait!"

Michael was ecstatic and indicated he would call her in a few hours to set up everything, because he had to get back to his office on the third floor. "So we should just meet here tomorrow to go to the concert?"

Sheila said, "Yes, that would be perfect, but we can get it all carved in stone when you call later."

"Okay, great. We will chat soon."

Michael went back to the third floor to continue his market plan for the Valley area. When he stepped off the elevator, he ran into Davis.

Davis immediately asked, "How is the Valley game plan coming?"

Michael had known Davis would ask about it, so he gave his well-prepared answer without hesitation. "I'm halfway finished, but the call of nature was more robust than the call of business."

Davis laughed and said, "What the hell does that mean?"

"Well, this receptionist on the first floor has a killer body and is gorgeous too, and tomorrow is the George Strait concert, and my date canceled on me. The reasonable thing to do was to find another date."

Davis laughed loudly. "Ah, okay, I understand that notion, but finish the report as soon as fucking possible, okay?"

"Of course. It will be on your desk by midmorning tomorrow. The other thing is, I'm working on adding to the parking garage record, and the date tomorrow lines up perfectly. After the concert tomorrow," Michael said with a grin.

"What's the total as of today?" asked Davis.

"Four is the current number, and tomorrow should be number five if everything goes according to plan, and it appears things are looking good, because she is meeting me downstairs before the concert. She does work on the first floor."

"Oh shit," Davis said. "*That* receptionist on the first floor? Damn, she is a hottie and ripe for the picking, you lucky fucker." Davis knew Michael was an aggressive sales rep, so he knew he had to step up his game when he ran across a hottie like Sheila, because the competition was fierce, especially with Michael sniffing out every gal within a ten-mile radius. The idea Davis had instituted to calm the ladies down and increase his chances was to spread rumors about Michael's conquests and make even more crazy stories about him. Davis told people that Michael was sleeping with everyone in and out of the office. The rumor might slow Michael's conquests down in the future, Davis thought; he didn't know the rumors made things even better for Michael. Like men, women talked about their conquests, so the more rumors Davis started around the office, the better things got for Michael, which was not what Davis wanted to accomplish.

The stage was set for a fun evening the next day. Michael had already finished the Corpus and Valley game plan, as he'd worked on it off and on for two weeks when he heard about Davis going to Cleveland. He had known there would be a bunch of shit from the meeting, and it was always better to be lucky than good in business, as well as a bit intuitive about the future. Michael was very intuitive.

The next day arrived quickly, and Michael turned in his game plan for the Valley and Corpus Christi to Davis and Art. A meeting was called with the triumvirate in attendance, and the ambitious report was well received by Davis and Art. They could expect a $20 million increase within three to four years, given aggressive underwriters to underwrite the area, plus ten new agency appointments with names of the agency and contact names if they felt the need to check on the game plan's validity. Michael had prepared well for the following questions, but his mind was on his date later in the evening and breaking the current parking garage record.

"Are you sure you can accomplish this game plan?" asked Davis.

"I'm confident with the premium increases if we can get the underwriting department's cooperation and commitment."

"It's aggressive, to say the least," Davis said.

Michael continued. "While I was visiting with the prospective agents located in Corpus Christi and the Valley, the agents committed to a large block of business within a short time frame, so it's based upon those assumptions. Our current agency force has also committed to premium increases, so even though it is an ambitious marketing plan, we can have the plan up within a month."

Davis and Art were convinced this was the way to go and gave the go-ahead to implement the game plan. Michael was delighted when he left the meeting but was surprised when Davis and Art went into Davis's corner office to talk about a few items of interest.

Art started off the conversation. "So are you still up in the air about Michael, or are you still sitting on the fence?"

"He's doing better," said Davis, "but let's see what happens when he implements this game plan of his. Anyway, I'm tired of him fucking all the women around here, and he never throws a cast-off my way."

"Ah, do I sense a hint of jealousy? Yeah, no one gets as much action as he does, but he is young and good looking. It makes sense he has so many conquests to brag about, and yes, I am a bit jealous."

Davis said quickly, "Not jealous, but ten years ago, he would have been catching up to me."

Art laughed and left Davis's office to enjoy his win. Art knew Davis's comments were bullshit, because Davis was jealous and envious of Michael because of all the female conquests and his parking garage record. Since Michael held the record and was planning to add to it, Davis didn't ask much more about it, because he knew no one was going to get close to the record, not even himself.

Michael felt it was time for a celebration since business was profitable and his Valley game plan had been approved and well received. He went down to his car at five o'clock and then changed clothes in the bathroom and met Sheila in front of her office on the first floor. She looked hot in her jeans and red pumps, so Michael's parts were already applauding his later success in the parking garage. Since she had kids and the concert was close by, he knew he would add to the parking garage record that night; there was no other place to go except a hotel. Maybe she had an open mind about having sex in a car. Who knew?

She threw him a curveball, though, and suggested she would drive. Michael was okay with the idea, but he hadn't expected her to drive to the concert. She drove a Jeep Cherokee, and it was bigger on the inside than his shitty company car. He currently drove a Chevy Celebrity, which was a positive departure from the Chrysler K-cars he'd driven in the past, but taking her Jeep was a relief of sorts. Maybe she had some plans too for after the concert.

They arrived at the venue and drank fairly heavily, and after the concert, they dropped by a Bennigan's on the way back to the branch office. They were having a great time, and the conversation was laid back, with talk of work and how her divorce was going. The booze began to take effect on her, and things started to get friendly. It was getting late, so Michael suggested going back to the branch office and ending the night. In his mind, he thought the night was just beginning, especially if the parking garage was involved. Michael was a planner and always thought ahead. He had parked his company car on the top level of the parking garage because no one ever parked there, and it was a private location with one way in and one way out.

Sheila entered the parking garage and asked where he'd parked his car. Michael replied, "It's on the top floor because there were no other parking spots on the lower floors."

She drove to the top floor and turned off the ignition, which was usually a good sign.

The moon was bright on the cloudless night, and Michael moved in for the kill. After a few moments of talk about the concert and how close the seats had been to the stage, things began to heat up in the vehicle. Things progressed to the Jeep's backseat.

Sheila's jeans were tough to get off, because they were skintight, but that was not a problem for a skilled tactician like Michael. Things were going well after the oral activities finished. It was time to break the current record and put some distance between himself and the rest of the bunch at CIC.

After about an hour of loud noises and the Jeep shaking in every direction, the deed was done. Michael backed out of the backseat, opened the door, and was surprised that his pants were still on but down at his ankles. Since Michael was young, he was still turned on even after the deed was done, because it took a while for things to relax. After he exited the Jeep, he looked around to make sure no one had noticed all the action in the Jeep. Michael looked up at the branch office building, which was about eight stories tall and all glass windows. As Michael stood there with his pants still at his ankles, he noticed someone on the seventh floor, looking down through a window. The person watching waved at Michael.

Michael about shit an egg roll. "Ah fuck, we are busted; someone just noticed us getting out of the car, and my pants are not on yet, and they are waving at us!"

Sheila screamed out, "This might not have been the best idea!"

Michael gave her a quick kiss good night, and they both started their vehicles and drove down five floors to the first floor of the parking garage. It was a stress-filled two minutes as they went down each floor, hoping no one would stop them and ask what they had been doing on the top floor.

No one showed up on the drive down, and no one was at the office door entrance, so they both sped off into the night, feeling relieved, but Michael was worried he might get some grief about it the next day in the office.

Michael thought on the drive home, *Another successful night, and a new record, number five, but who was the person waving at us from the seventh floor?* It could have been a maintenance worker cleaning out the trash or vacuuming the carpet. The mystery would not be solved until someone brought it up in a future conversation. *Hopefully it wasn't human resources or, worse, the services department.* The services department was more like a Nazi death patrol or the SS. They would take pictures of an employee's desk after the office closed and turn them in to that person's manager or supervisor the next morning, especially if it was messy or dirty. They were known as the after-hours gestapo and needed to be dealt with in the future in some form or fashion to get them off their high horse. The gestapo went through employees' desks to make sure there were no harassing materials or bad jokes—of course, there were always bad jokes in people's desks. Art instructed everyone to always lock his or her desk before leaving for the day. It was a sales department, for crying out loud.

The next day was a bit scary for Michael because he was waiting to see if anyone would approach him to ask about the parking garage activities from the night before, but nothing was said. It was Friday, so everyone's thoughts were elsewhere.

Michael went to Art's office to ask for his advice about the situation. "Hey, Art, I've got a problem." Michael shut the door behind him. "To get to the brass tacks, I broke the record last night in the parking garage," he said, and Art laughed and congratulated him for his efforts. "That's the good news; the bad news is someone was waving at me from the seventh floor when I exited her car, and my pants were around my ankles at the time."

"Oh! You banged her in *her* car? That's a big change for you, right?" Art began to laugh uncontrollably.

"So you're saying I should not worry about it then, right?"

Art said, "If it had been HR or the gestapo in the services department waving at you, they would have already been in my office, bitching about it, so no, don't worry about last night. Just concentrate on the Valley and Corpus Christi areas and your game plan. Make sure you tell Davis about the new parking garage record because it will burn his ass big-time, and we both know he can't catch up at this point." They both laughed even harder. "Start with that big account you wrote in the Valley recently, the grocery store chain, and end it with the new garage record, and make sure you come back to tell me how it went. It is Friday; we should end the week on several positive notes, right?"

Art had a great relationship with Davis, both a working and a nonworking relationship, and he knew how jealous Davis was of Michael. He figured he would poke some fun at Davis and give him some shit at Michael's expense. The conversation with Michael would make Davis come down to Art's office to talk about it some more and get the scoop on everything, especially the waving incident.

After Michael updated Davis on the recent goings-on, Michael walked by Art's office, gave him a thumbs up, and went to lunch with T. J. Soon afterward, Davis was in Art's office doorway. He said, "Wow, a new large account, a new game plan for the Valley, and a new parking garage record in one week. I may have to change my thinking about the kid after all."

Art laughed and said, "I assume you're talking about Michael?"

"Hell yes, who else?" Davis tried not to sound too pleased with the excellent performances over the week, but it was too late. He was not big on compliments.

A compliment for the kid had been Art's game all along, even before Michael had walked down to Davis's office. Art was always thinking ahead. Davis tried to change the subject, but Art could see he was burning up on the inside. Art decided to stay on the subject for a while and twist the knife a bit more. "Michael was the right person for the job, so you could congratulate me on an excellent hire," Art said with conviction.

Davis said, "I'm not one hundred percent convinced, because he has yet to implement his Valley game plan."

"He just came up with it this week!" Art shouted.

Davis continued. "There is also an opening in the regional home office for a sales analyst position. Dr. No is looking for candidates and a new victim to brainwash." Dr. No, the regional sales manager, was a real asshole. If Michael was coaxed into taking the job, Davis could again reign over the ladies in the Houston branch. Always thinking ahead was Davis's methodology too.

Dr. No, nicknamed after the movie with the same name, was coming to Houston in a few short weeks to check on the sales department and be on the lookout for new hires because no one wanted to work for the regional home office. Dr. No had gotten his nickname also because *no* was his favorite word whenever someone asked him a question. CIC's regional job was like being condemned to hell, or at least that was what T. J. had indicated on many occasions, and Michael took those words to heart.

Dr. No's real name was Dave Schmidt, and he was another egomaniac. His first and final answer regarding any business decision was no, whatever the question might be.

Davis always had nicknames for everyone. His nickname for Michael was the Whoremonger, but secretly, he wanted the name for himself because he wished he was still in his twenties. Being a large man in his early forties didn't help his cause, but he was the branch manager, which gave him some status. So Davis's plan was afoot, even though he knew Michael was a great hire and probably would be hard to replace. Since Davis was a member of the River's End Golf Club, he would set up a golf game with Art, Michael, and Dr. No to seal the deal and Michael's fate in the Houston branch. That was Davis's technique to win in business and everything else.

Michael wasn't aware of the situation, but Art was mindful of the plan, so he tipped Michael off. Art was an excellent boss and didn't always believe or agree with Davis or his methods. Art decided to create his plan to let Michael determine his future with the company. He left room for Michael to make up his mind, because that was the kind of person Art was: a great sales manager and person.

Everything was going so well for Michael at CIC that Michael was curious why Davis would even think of doing such a thing and involve Art too, but he figured it was just office politics. Maybe it was all the action with the females he was involved with, so maybe it was time to tone it down a little or not talk about it. It seemed the office was full of rumors about him anyway, and shying away from that kind of talk might ease the tension between himself and Davis's giant, bruised ego. *It's Friday*, Michael thought, *so time to step up the game, mostly since the week went so well*. He felt it was time to celebrate, even though storm clouds were forming in the distance.

That weekend, like every weekend, involved bar-hopping on Friday and Saturday, searching for new conquests, handing out some business cards, and golfing with Dave on Sunday. The clubs were always the same, and even with new faces, occasionally, the club scene got boring, so maybe it was time for a different approach, Michael thought.

Or maybe the next week's golf game with management and Dr. No was weighing heavily on his mind. The kind of betrayal Davis initiated to get rid of someone was not unheard of in the business world but was a disappointment to Michael.

The weekend was like most weekends, with a lot of fun but with no one beating his door down. Deborah might have finally gotten the hint after a month without a phone call, so there was no sneaking around his condo to get home.

Monday raised its ugly head with meetings and work. The only respite was lunch with T. J., when they could hold court about all the crazy goings-on during the weekend. During the conversation, Michael asked T. J. what he thought about the regional position, genuinely seeking his advice on the job and what to do in the future. There was only limited time to talk about all the new females he'd met over the weekend.

T. J. said with conviction, "You know how most underwriters are surviving brain donors? The regional analyst job is even worse because most are dumb fuckers who couldn't analyze their way out of a box. The standard answer from Art is 'Don't go,' and you are much too good a rep to be shipped off to the regional home office for some brainwashing. The plan would be to determine why Davis decided to suggest this job to you, because he hates everyone in the region, especially Dr. No."

Michael said, "He is pissed off because I'm banging all these women, and it's cramping his style. He is the alpha-male type." They both laughed.

"That is true. So what are you going to do about this job then?" asked T. J.

"My first reaction would be to play dumb and say I'm still learning about this job, and I'm not qualified enough."

"Not a bad angle, but you don't want to look too dumb in front of Dr. No or the others, so figure it out."

"I've only got another day to figure it out, damn it."

T. J. said one more thing as the food arrived. "They are always looking for fresh blood in the regional home office because no one lasts there very long, and Dr. No is an asshole. The next step is a promotion to the first sales manager's position that comes open at any given branch office, but that never happens, because most branch managers hate the region and do not want a sales manager from there, and it's a dead-end job. The guy you replaced is now sales manager of Atlanta, and he didn't go to the regional home office. Davis told the Atlanta branch manager he was ready for the job, and he got it. It's a waste of time and talent. Just concentrate on getting promoted in the branch, as there are two more levels to shoot for in the branch: sales specialist and sales consultant. I've already attained the specialist title, so I'm shooting for the consultant position. I'm always talking about it to Art when he does my annual chickenshit review. The branch is growing, and it could prove to be the best job decision you ever made to work here.

Davis will cool off in a bit; he is in a dry spell and needs to get laid more often or find something steadier."

They both laughed and finished lunch.

On the way back to the branch, Michael said to T. J., "I've got an idea, and it will work if everything goes as planned."

T. J. said, "I'm sure you do."

"I'm just going to play dumb as long as they allow me to, but the one thing I'm going to do is beat the shit out of Davis on the golf course tomorrow and teach him a lesson, damn it."

T. J. laughed.

Michael continued. "The key to tomorrow will be to come up with a perfect excuse for why I'm not interested in the region, but I'm also going to make Davis look bad in front of Dr. No to teach him another lesson."

T. J. said, "That might not be the best idea or to go that far, because Davis not only looks like an elephant but also has a memory like one. Don't forget that point."

"I'll try not to, but I'm not going to be treated like shit and roll over and ask for more bullshit in any situation. If the situation permits and things go as planned, no one will bother me in the future about going to the regional home office in Orlando, damn it."

The next day came fast, and no talk of the regional position came up during the eighteen holes, but Michael knew that was just a ploy to ease his mind. Then Dr. No would swoop in for the kill on the nineteenth hole. It was the oldest trick in the book.

Davis led the foursome off after putting some sunscreen on his face, because it was a sunny, hot day in Houston. Davis always acted like it was an awful thing to put on sunscreen, so he would dab some on his nose as if it were aftershave and then say in a loud voice, "All right, let's go!" That action was his way of being the alpha male in the group, but he looked stupid when he put sunscreen on his face and started shouting afterward.

Davis and Art were pretty good golfers, and Michael was better than both of them. He was a scratch shooter, meaning he could always get close to shooting par golf but always laid back so everyone could catch up. Michael was long off the tee box and usually hit his drives three hundred yards or more, and as the day continued, he would screw up on purpose because in golf etiquette, one never beat the boss, whose massive ego could not stand to be beat on the golf course by a rep.

The first few holes were uneventful. They played wolf, a fun golf game in which one picked a partner due to his drive off the tee box, or if one was the wolf, the person could go it on his own against the other three. Michael was a master at the game because he could always see an opening in the game to go it alone, especially on a par three. Par threes and par fives were the best bet to go it alone in wolf, and the bet would double if someone scored a birdie on any given hole.

On the sixth hole, a par-five hole, Michael hit a drive in the middle of the fairway about two hundred yards from the green and indicated that he was playing alone, or lone wolf, against the other three. Dr. No was a shitty golfer, so Michael didn't give him a second thought while playing, and neither Davis nor Art was long off the tee box. Michael knew he had the advantage. Michael's five iron was his best club in the bag, and he knew he would eagle this hole, as he was so close to the green.

Davis always started the trash talk when things were not looking good for him or his team—and they weren't looking good at that point. He yelled out taunts such as "It's not how you drive but how you arrive," "I'll bet you wish your dick was that long," and "Employee reviews are coming up soon, but don't let that affect your play." Everything under the sun was mentioned to damage the other person's confidence. Davis would trash-talk whenever he was down in a golf game.

Michael was angry with Davis and thought, *Expect no quarter*, which meant to take no prisoners. Michael knew Davis was a poor loser in golf and thought, *I'm kicking everyone's ass today, and I might as well finish this hole strong.*

His second shot was about five feet from the hole. Everyone in attendance was in shock because an eagle would triple the bet. At that point, the bet was a pretty large amount of money. Everyone had a look of disbelief on his face, except Michael.

As the foursome approached the green, more trash talk continued from Davis because he knew he was in trouble and was looking for a way out. Unfortunately for Davis, Wharton, his alma mater, didn't teach a student how to lose a round of golf properly.

Michael looked at his putt and began to talk some shit himself, aimed at everyone. "We haven't talked about what happens if my putt goes in and I score an eagle this hole. Doesn't it triple the bet?" Michael began to line the putt up. It was an easy one straight in, but he figured he would relish the moment and also give them a bunch of shit for what they were about to do after the golf game.

"Yeah, it triples the bet," Davis said. "Hurry up and miss it, so we can putt out."

The rest of the foursome were already putting for par, and Michael knew he had their fucking asses in a bind and kept the thought *Take no prisoners* in the back of his mind. Before he finished the hole, Michael asked, "Any side bets before I putt?"

It was as quiet as a nun in church. Art said, "Nope, just putt, damn it."

Michael hit the ball, and it went right into the middle of the cup for an eagle. Everyone in unison said, "Fuck!" as loudly as he could.

Michael said with a laugh, "I'll take a credit card, by the way, if anyone is low on cash." He laughed to himself again, but the only one who laughed out loud was Dr. No for whatever reason.

The golf game continued in about the same way. The big winner of the day was Michael because he was motivated to win and wanted to teach a hard lesson to Davis, but the real lesson was about to happen. After all the bets were added up, Michael had won $752 dollars total. Being the gentleman he was, he didn't ask for the money and figured it was all for fun anyway. Everyone was shell-shocked by Michael's play that day. Motivation and anger were a deadly combination when it came to Michael's personality. He was ready for the second round on the nineteenth hole, because he knew what was coming next. As all golfers knew, the nineteenth hole was in the bar at the golf course, where jokes were told, business was conducted, and just about everything else was talked about. Mostly, though, the nineteenth hole involved a lot of drinking one's favorite libation and playing poker.

Dr. No started off the conversation with a compliment on Michael's golf play that day as drinks were served. Dr. No was curious how he'd gotten to be so good on the links.

"Easy answer," Michael said as he took a big sip of his bourbon. "My condo is located on a golf course. I play a lot on the weekends, in between my many dates with the lady types." Everyone laughed.

"Ah, okay, that makes sense." Dr. No went right in for the kill after the golf question, mostly because he was an egomaniac. "You know, Michael, we have an opening in the southern region for a sales analyst position. I would like you to apply for the job, because many people think you would be a great addition to Orlando's staff, including myself."

Apply for the job? Michael thought to himself. *Seriously, what a crock of shit.* He didn't even want the fucking job. Dr. No had proven he was an asshole, but he also had no tact in his approach to sales. Michael hadn't been ready for the question that quickly, but he already had formulated an answer for Dr. No.

"I've worked with the analysts in the region before," Michael said, "and my qualifications are not good enough for this position." Michael wanted to say, "The position is a bunch of shit, and I'm not interested," but he couldn't say that out loud.

Dr. No did not like to hear the word *no* from anyone but himself, so he continued. "Whatever qualifications you're lacking, we would teach you in the region to become an expert in the field."

Michael wanted to say, "Becoming an expert asshole?" But he didn't; he just said with a smile, "My interest is in making the Houston branch office a much larger branch, which is my expertise currently. Sitting in a chair all day is not a job that interests me in the least."

Dr. No replied, "Why not? Also, the next sales manager's position would be yours when it came up, just an FYI."

It was an actual selling point from the asshole. Sales 101 said to provide a benefit when one received an objection, and Dr. No had done just that. But it fell on deaf ears because Michael had no intention of ever interviewing for the shitty job.

"Dave, listen. I'm originally from Houston, I grew up here, and my family is here, so please take my name off your list, because I'm not interested in the job."

Dr. No was not happy with his answer, and neither was Davis. Davis was trying to sit back as an innocent bystander but was fuming on the inside.

Michael read into that quickly and was excited on the inside. Many emotions went through his mind: thrill, excitement, and happiness. He was commanding the conversation. Michael was not interested in the job or the regional home office in Orlando under any circumstances and had made it clear to everyone present at the nineteenth hole. The conversation didn't even make it to what kind of money was involved.

While Davis and Dr. No were fuming because of the golf game and Michael's answer, Art was relaxed and didn't say a word; he just drank his straight bourbon. Art often stayed silent to see where everyone was going with a conversation and to be ready to pounce, offer advice, or give his two cents' worth if asked to do so. He knew when to keep his mouth shut and when to speak up. At this juncture, Art decided to keep his mouth shut and watch for any opening to end the evening.

The evening ended with Michael thanking everyone for a great day of golf, and Art said, "I'll walk you out."

As they headed toward the parking lot, Art said, "You know, that could have been better."

"Oh, I know it could have been better and even answered better, but my demeanor was to show Dr. No and Davis there was no interest in the job. My idea was to let them know now and in the future to stop talking to me about this job. My method was to make sure this does not happen ever again in the future. With those two giant egos in that one room, do you think their conversation right now is the same one we are currently having? I bet they're saying, 'That didn't go well or as planned.' I'm sure Dr. No is pissed off and Davis too. I'm sure they will think twice about offering me another job in the region.

"The answer came to me at lunch with T. J. yesterday. To please everyone is a complete waste of time. To do my job to the best of my ability is what I'm truly shooting for, and the plan is to do that in a short period. That would solve the Davis problem, and I don't give a shit about the region, because languishing in an office five days a week is not what I'm looking for in a career. There's probably more money involved but not enough to make a difference in the overall scheme of things. After doing my due diligence about the regional home office and talking with some different people about the job, it all came down to the same thing. Everyone hates the region, and there is no future for me there. Can you imagine sitting at a desk from eight to five every day?"

"Yes," Art said, "I did it for a year and a half, but please tell me you didn't talk to T. J. about the region's job."

"What if I did?"

"Oh fuck," Art said. "That is the real reason you weren't interested in the job—because T. J. painted you a picture of the region you didn't like, right?"

"Well, T. J. is no Picasso, but he gave me the facts about what he knows about the regional home office, and I'm truly thankful he told me about the job. No snap decisions were made, which is obvious, but my position was to get the fucking region off my back for the foreseeable future, and soft-soaking the situation wouldn't do the trick. If you could, pass it on to Davis how truly disappointing it was that he thought this job would be a good fit for me. My old method of just ignoring his ass most of the time will start over again, because this day was truly disappointing to me. Thanks again for the heads-up about this horseshit regional crap, because it is truly appreciated. At least there was time to plan for this meeting and get ready for the onslaught from Dr. No."

"You know, I'm going to take a lot of shit off of this meeting," Art said.

"I'm sure you will, so accept my apologies for it now, okay? I'm sorry, but we will do great things together and write a shitload of business in the future. Agreed?"

"All true, but at least come up with a better excuse in the future, please. This one will hurt for a bit," Art said.

"I'm not married, so I will put my mind to work on a better excuse, but there shouldn't be any more bullshit from the region in the future about me working there, so you can thank me later."

Art laughed and said, "See you tomorrow."

Michael drove off and wondered about his future but was pleased with the day's events.

Michael covered his tracks as best as he could and hoped to do some damage control after the nineteenth-hole meeting and his kicking the shit out of everyone in golf that day. Things had not turned back to normal with Davis, but he didn't want them to go back to normal. Michael implemented his ignore-Davis approach again, which had worked in the past. He did not see any improvement in the relationship, but that was not what Michael wanted currently. He tried to do his job, ignore office politics, and get laid as much as humanly possible, but ignoring Davis was difficult. Davis was his boss's boss, so their paths would cross eventually. Currently, he saw Davis only during the occasional meeting, which was the norm in the office. Michael had other plans for happy hours when Davis and the bunch were attending. He figured it was better to let a sleeping dog lie than wake it up and listen to a bunch of barking bullshit. Michael called on his agency force most of the time outside the office. It was a convenient excuse not to be around except for a meeting or two on Mondays.

A few weeks went by, and it seemed the Dr. No debacle had disappeared into thin air. Michael made a trip down to the Valley to implement his game plan and to appoint five new agents in both Corpus Christi and the Rio Grande Valley. Market conditions had worsened, and the new agents were ready for some new blood or a new company to represent in their respective agencies.

The norm for working that area was always the same: drive to McAllen, Texas; set up home base at the Embassy Suites on Monday; make appointments to visit with agencies in McAllen, Harlingen, and Brownsville; and set up golf games for Monday afternoon and Tuesday afternoon. Each agency had its own set of personalities Michael always enjoyed when he called on them. The calls were positive, mainly due to the poor market conditions.

In McAllen, the Insurance Place Inc. agency was owned and operated by a few ex–Hartford Insurance sales reps. The relationship with this agency was great because of the familiarity the agency principals had with being sales reps. Years later, this agency would become one of the top-producing agencies for CIC, and Michael always enjoyed his calls on the agency, because they were fun calls. Two of the owners whom Michael met and played golf with were Bill Divvy and Don Oxnard. Bill and Don were both ex–sales reps too, so they had a lot in common with Michael and knew his plight as a sales rep.

Don was what Michael called a repeater. He drove everyone crazy in his office and outside it by repeating the same sentences over and over. He would complain about a few things regarding doing business with CIC and would start and finish with the words *type situation*. For instance, Don would say, "I've got a problem with this account, and it's a tough-type situation, and I've talked to your underwriting department, and they feel it's a tough-type situation, so do you think you can help me out with this type situation?" Bill Divvy and Michael would jokingly create sentences with nothing but "this type situation." It was overkill, but it never stopped. Even Don's daughter would tell her dad to stop saying "this type situation," as Bill told Michael on one agency visit.

When he met with Don, Michael would use "this type situation" against Don in every conversation, saying, "Don, I want to thank you for your business, but are there any tough-type situations we need to talk about currently?" Bill usually left the room because he couldn't help bursting out with laughter at the inside joke. In the CIC office in Houston, the underwriters assigned to underwrite this agency didn't call Don by his name but called him This Type Situation. They said, for example, "I talked with This Type Situation today, and he submitted a new account." The joke always generated lots of laughter in the CIC office and the Insurance Place Inc. office. The joke even was utilized on the golf course when Don, Bill, and Michael played golf, especially if someone hit a lousy shot. The next comment would be "Oh, that was a bad-type situation." When Don caught on to people imitating his way of talking, he usually just said, "Fuck you guys." Of course, everyone would laugh uncontrollably for a while, until the next shot happened. The joke lasted for years.

The agency in Brownsville was a great producing agency but had no prominent personalities to speak of, but the agency in Harlingen had several characters Michael always enjoyed calling on. The agency's name was April and Associates, named after the original owner. The agency's president was a nice guy by the name of Stephen Danaher. Those in the agency played a lot of golf, mostly when Michael was in town and called on them. It was a good-ole-boy type of agency. One producer for the agency was Mark Trajan, an outstanding producer, who always talked about his female conquests. Mark and Michael would either play golf or go to South Padre Island for the day to enjoy the bikini-clad women. It was a great time to work in the Valley area, because it was a lot of fun. The area was taking off production-wise and would be a feather in Michael's cap because the Valley and Corpus Christi game plan was already beginning to pay dividends for the future.

The business trip always wound up with Michael being in Corpus Christi on Wednesday, which, coincidentally, was ladies' night at a club called Shuffles. Michael always stayed at the Hershey Hotel in downtown Corpus, which was a great place to stay. It was a nice high-rise hotel with a great view overlooking the bay of Corpus Christi. Since it was ladies' night at Shuffles, Michael always checked into the hotel, took a quick nap, wolfed down some food, and headed over to the club. He would invite some of his agents in Corpus to meet him there, but they rarely showed up, because most of them were married, but Michael did his best work alone.

Shuffles was an excellent place to have a drink and meet the ladies. Michael got there early, and the best-looking ladies were at the club early. Arriving allowed for an early night too. He could meet a gorgeous lady, go back to the Hershey Hotel, take care of business, and not stay out too late, because he had appointments the next day. Over the years, Shuffles always paid off handsomely because it seemed there was always a glut of single women on Wednesdays. The ladies' night didn't hurt the cause either, because ladies' drinks were cheaper and more affordable. Since most folks had to work the next day, there weren't many guys around to compete against, so picking up women was almost as easy as shooting fish in a barrel.

In 1988, Michael met a breathtaking blonde by the name of Darla. She was a bit older than he was, but a few drinks and shots later, they ended up on the elevator, going to the twenty-fourth floor, where Michael's room was located at the Hershey.

The elevator ride seemed longer than usual, as they were locked in a kiss that would have made Hugh Hefner jealous. There was always a problem with getting a woman's tight-fitting jeans off, but that was nothing compared to the marathon that ensued after the clothes came off. After a lot of noise and a call from the front desk about all the loud noise coming from the room, the deed was done two hours later. Michael was sweaty and out of breath but was relaxing, when Darla got up, turned on the light, and started to put her clothes back on.

"Why the rush?" Michael asked. "You don't want to stay the night here with me? We can have round two tomorrow morning if you stay," he added with a smile. "I'll even buy breakfast tomorrow."

"No, I have work tomorrow," she said. As she grabbed her purse, a photo fell out. It was a picture of Darla and a guy.

Michael picked the image up and asked, "Who is the guy in the picture?"

"I'm sorry you saw that picture. That is my husband," Darla said.

"What the fuck? You didn't tell me you were married! Why in the hell did you go home with me then?"

"Well, the marriage was great initially, but my husband works all the time and goes on hunting trips regularly, and I'm tired of being alone. As a matter of fact, he is bird hunting this week in Mexico, and a woman has needs too, you know."

That never had happened to Michael before, and since he was Catholic, he felt guilty about the situation, even though she was drop-dead gorgeous. He was at a loss for words, which was unusual. Before she left, he asked, "Was this a one-night stand?"

She said, "Yeah, probably, because I'm not ready to give up on the marriage yet. I just needed some attention, and you were in the right place at the right time. You're a great-looking guy, Michael, and a great lover. The right gal will come along one day. Just don't give up."

After she left, Michael lay in bed thinking about the craziness of his life and the craziness of that day and the night before. He got out of bed, went to the balcony, watched Darla drive away twenty-four floors down, and felt empty. That was probably the best sex he'd ever had, but he still felt like something was missing.

He laughed to himself. *Well, at least my wallet isn't missing.*

Michael didn't believe in love at first sight or even love at first bang. This lady had put the hook in him big-time. She was not only gorgeous but also soft-spoken and in a bad relationship, so he felt sorry for her, as if she were a princess who was locked up in her room with no way out and needed help. It was late, and he figured he needed to get some sleep because he still had one more golf game tomorrow before heading back to Houston on Friday.

The trip wound up being fruitful, and the Valley game plan was in full swing. All the agents he called on were producing nicely, and production was way up in the area already. Since it had been such a crazy week, Michael didn't feel much like going out. *But what the hell?* he thought. It was Friday. Maybe with a quick nap and a few phone calls, things would begin to look up.

His answering machine was almost full, and he listened to several messages indicating the game plan for the weekend and where everyone was going. He had a message from Deborah too, but he would ignore that one for most of the weekend unless he didn't get lucky, and then maybe he'd make an emergency call to her for some action Sunday afternoon after golf with Dave.

The weekend turned out to be good, as Michael heard from an old high school buddy named Chuck Kemp, who'd moved back to town recently. Chuck and Michael had been best friends in high school, and they picked up where they had left off a few years ago. Chuck had moved to Breckenridge, Colorado, but had moved back recently without Michael's knowledge and was anxious to catch up.

Of the thousands of stories about Chuck, almost all were crazy as hell, starting with one involving the infamous St. Thomas High School hill next door to the school. Chuck always brought up the incident, asking if Michael wanted another try at the peak, because the hill had won the first time around. In 1980, Chuck drove a 1977 Chevy Impala practically the size of a boat, which his wealthy dad let him drive to and from school. After having a few beers after school one day at the local stop-and-rob, Chuck decided it was time to take the hill. Back then, everyone had a fake ID, so beer was easy to come by even at that age. Michael got into Chuck's Chevy and drove to St. Thomas, located at Memorial and Shepherd Drive, near downtown Houston. They were not too far from the school and got there in record time—one of the few times a high school kid was in a hurry to get to school.

Chuck stopped a good two hundred yards from the hill and punched the gas pedal down. The car got up to about sixty miles an hour, became airborne, and quickly hit the ground after taking the hill. They both had a beer in their hands, which also became airborne when the vehicle became airborne, so the beer spilled everywhere in the car. The car landed with a loud thud, and Chuck hit the brakes when the vehicle landed. The sound of shrieking tires cut through the neighborhood's silence as the car landed at a four-way stop sign and finally came to a halt about forty feet later. Chuck had forgotten about the stop sign located at that small intersection, but thankfully, no one was in the intersection at the time. It would have been an impressive sight.

They both exited the vehicle, laughing hysterically, and went to the stop sign to inspect how much damage there was to the asphalt and the Chevy. When the car had landed, the undercarriage bolts had made a two-foot-long hole in the asphalt. More laughter ensued.

They talked about doing it again, but unfortunately, they were out of beer and time. Chuck ended up totaling the vehicle a few weeks after the hill incident, but that was Chuck. He went through a few more vehicles and finally decided to take better care of a new car that he talked his dad into buying him.

That had been seven years ago. They rehashed the incident over a few beers at a club called Confetti, which was a hot spot of the time. Chuck usually called things like they were, and he had several nicknames for Michael. Most frequently, he called Michael a male slut, but it didn't bother Michael; he thought it was a compliment.

Chuck always had great New Year's Eve parties too, and Michael was glad Chuck had returned to Houston, because he missed attending them and was looking forward to the next one. It was late Saturday night, and Michael was tired, so they bid each other good night until the next time. The next time would probably be the following weekend. Michael always enjoyed Chuck's company and all the craziness that came with it. Monday was beginning to raise its ugly head; he had one more day of solitude, and then he had to go back to the grind.

The regular meetings happened on Monday morning and afternoon, but Art wanted to know how the Corpus and

Valley trips had gone and how the game plan for the area was proceeding. Michael never tooted his own horn but figured it was time to do just that, because business was up, and he wanted both Davis and Art to know about the increase in production. He told Art everything, from the golf games to Darla, and noted that business was booming in the area in a brief period. Art wasn't aware that Michael had been working and planning his game plan for two years and had counted on making the area a success way before anyone thought of the plan.

"Good job!" Art said. "This news will piss off Davis." They both laughed.

"Correct," Michael said, "and after doing some calculations for the future, I believe these areas could turn into a twenty-million-dollar territory if everything stays the same."

"That's a bit ambitious," Art said, "but I like the way you think. I'm going down to Davis's office to boast a bit; we will talk soon."

Art walked to the corner office to talk to Davis and gloat over Corpus and the Valley's growth. Mostly, though, he just wanted to piss Davis off again. This approach was a game they played, the back-and-forth about an employee or regional person or production, to figure out who could give the other more shit. It was just the usual banter with friends and coworkers.

Art couldn't wait to tell Davis, "The business we are writing must be great production, because it met with Marco's underwriters' strict underwriting process."

Both of their minds were made up about the underwriting department, who were, as T. J. said, surviving brain donors. Since Davis had it in for Michael at the time for different reasons, Art had a lot to boast about regarding the game plan's success.

Art walked into Davis's office and said, "Hey, what's up?"

Davis said, "I know what you're in here about, and I just printed out a report on the production for Corpus and the Valley, so I'll save you some time because I'm aware of the production in the Valley and the shit you're about to talk about extensively."

"My opinion is that Michael is way ahead of schedule on his game plan." Art started to crow.

"Yeah, I know," barked Davis loudly. "Tell him I said good job."

"Why don't you tell him yourself? A little praise never hurt anyone." Art laughed.

"Yeah, maybe that will happen one day, but I've got some great news to pass on to the sales department," Davis said, changing the subject. "Dr. No left the company for a competitor, so no more listening to any of his shit, and Michael can breathe easier since he pissed him off last week on the nineteenth hole."

"Seriously? Wow, what a surprise, but that is good news for a Monday and good news overall. Do you know his replacement yet? Maybe I'll apply for the job." Art laughed to himself again.

"Nope, not yet, but you would hate that job, and you fucking know it. The region is a piece of shit to work for, and you did that job before as an analyst. Are you thinking of going back to that work environment?"

"No, not really. It was just a thought, but I'm pretty happy here. I'm just concerned about who will replace Dr. No. Probably another dumbass. It seems like it always gets worse when the replacement is announced," Art said.

After the gloating was finished, Art was on cloud nine with all the good news. He called a quick sales meeting with Michael and T. J. to pass on the good news and even invited Susan to enjoy the announcement. She hated Dr. No too, but who the hell didn't?

As Art shut his door, he exclaimed, "I have good news today! Dr. No left the company. No replacement has been announced yet, but one probably will be soon."

There was a big sigh of relief in the room because T. J. hated Dr. No and felt his departure would make for a better working environment. He looked at Michael and said, "Always listen to your elders," and everyone laughed.

In Michael's mind, he breathed a sigh of relief too and felt his gamble in turning down the job had been the right thing to do; plus, he knew how much he'd pissed Dr. No off and knew it would bite him in the ass one day in the future.

Art congratulated the sales department on the production increases and said, "Keep up the good work," after the laughter died down. It was an unusual Monday with all the good news following a banner week last week and a great weekend.

"Any idea about the replacement?" Michael asked.

"Nope, not at all. I just hope it's not as bad as Dr. No. Usually, they pick a sales manager in or sometimes out of the region, so we will see." Art loved to give everyone shit, and he thought it was Michael's turn since there was so much good news. Art looked at Michael and said, "I sure as hell don't want the job, and by the way, your hair is looking especially poofy today. Is it big-hair day?"

The quickest way to piss Michael off was to talk about his hair, because there never was a hair out of place, and he took pride in the way he looked.

"What the fuck is that all about, Art?" asked Michael.

"Well, it almost looks like there is a butterfly in your hair." Art laughed. Since Michael never took a lot of shit off anyone, it was Art's turn for some retribution.

Michael said to Art, "I'll bet you didn't know there are serial numbers on condoms."

Art said, "No, I didn't know that fact."

Michael said, "That is because you've never rolled one out all the way."

The entire room broke out into laughter for about five minutes. The laughter was so loud that after Susan got her composure back, she opened Art's door to see if anyone was around the sales department, listening to all the noise. Art had been bested at that point, and there was no reason to continue the meeting. He learned a lesson that day about giving too much shit to anyone, especially Michael.

The Audit

A new regional sales manager was named within two weeks. Unfortunately, it was another egomaniac, named Jim Morgan. Jim was a seasoned sales manager from the Northeast and was ready for a venue change because of the horrific winters that happened every year in the North. They were so bad that it seemed like heaven to go to Orlando, Florida, so a promotion and a relocation package to sunny Orlando was a perfect fit for Jim.

He was divorced, so the bikini-clad beach women living in or near Fort Lauderdale were a strong attraction. A mere hour's drive from his home near Orlando, the beach was a convenient distraction, and it was Jim's favorite place to go and a favorite topic of discussion at sales meetings. Jim always talked about the beach and all the scantily dressed ladies he was surrounded by most of the time. No one knew whether it was true or not, because he wasn't the best-looking guy in the world, but he did hang out on the beach a lot, it seemed, because he had a great tan in no time, a significant change from the dreary Northeast.

He said the bikinis the women wore were like anal floss, and the nickname stuck. Always, the first question to ask Jim was "How are all the anal-floss-bikini-clad ladies looking these days?"

The question was met with a big grin and the standard answer of "They are just downright gorgeous. Florida is lovely, and so are the women."

T. J. and Jim had been hired at the same time ten years before and roomed together while attending a home office sales rep school for new hires in Cleveland. During that time, one always had a roommate when going to a home office school. Some hit it off, and some didn't, but soon, the home office ended the rooming-together bullshit because of the many complaints about snoring, late hours, and guys having sex all night with women.

When Michael had gone to the new-hire school, his roommate had been Mike Grant, and they'd hit it off fabulously. They would have farting contests in their room after each day at the school. It was tough to hold the farts all day, and it was usually a farting melee after class disbanded. Mike Grant's and Michael's paths would cross again shortly but under different circumstances.

During school in Cleveland and many happy hours, T. J. and Jim had hit it off too, but they'd lost touch. T. J. had no intention of becoming a sales manager, because he loved being a sales rep and had no future ambitions of going up the corporate ladder, as Jim was doing. T. J. understood office politics and would use his past relationship with Jim for any advantage he could. He also understood he needed to rekindle the relationship if possible, which would make for a smoother transition.

Art called a sales meeting after the announcement was made and shut the door behind everyone in attendance. "Jim Morgan accepted a promotion to the regional sales manager's position in Orlando. Does anyone know this asshole?"

T. J. spoke up immediately. "Yes, I know him. We went to the new-hire sales rep school in Cleveland ten years ago."

Art was surprised but happy to hear the good news. "Do you think you have an inside with this guy?"

T. J. said, "Oh, hell yes, I'll rekindle the friendship again when he comes to the branch for a visit."

"Well, you will have your chance because he is coming to Houston in about two weeks."

"Okay, that is a bit ahead of schedule, but I'll make myself available and see if he has time for some after-hours beers while here," T. J. said. "He was a big beer drinker last time we met and roomed together, and I'm sure nothing has changed in ten years."

Michael asked, "Did he say why he is coming to Houston for his first stop? There are other branch offices to hassle. That is a very suspicious thing."

"I'm not sure why Houston is his first stop," Art said. "I'll try to find out why, but you work on that question too, okay, T. J.? Maybe call him to congratulate him on his recent promotion."

Michael asked, "What should I do?"

Art said, "Don't worry about it; you pissed off the last regional manager. Try not to make a habit of that in the future."

Michael laughed to himself and said, "Okay, boss, no problem."

As everyone was leaving the room, Art said, "Michael, stay here for a bit. We need to talk about a few things."

Michael shut the door. "What's up? I don't think I've done anything wrong recently or fucked up," he said with a grin.

"No, you haven't. I just know Jim will probably talk to you too about going to the region, and you need a new excuse or at least one better than last time, okay?"

"Not a problem at all. I will put my mind to it. We do have a few weeks, right?"

"Yes, you do, and by the way, Davis said an excellent job on the Corpus and Valley game plan results. He was impressed."

"Why doesn't he tell me himself?" asked Michael.

"Well, you know Davis—not very big on compliments. Over the last two weeks, we received three new commercial large-line quotes from the Valley and one from Corpus, so production is going well. Just keep doing your job, and things will pay off in the end."

"Is that it?" asked Michael.

"Yep, keep kicking ass, and make sure we write those large accounts," Art said.

The weekend was fast approaching, and Michael had been out with Sheila a few times since the parking garage incident. He kept most of his conquests to himself, except for telling T. J. T. J. liked to hear about his liaisons but had no animosity for the outcomes, as Davis did. T. J. and Michael had become good friends over the last few years, mostly because they enjoyed each other's company. The next day, T. J. and Michael were driving on Richmond Avenue, looking for a restaurant at which to eat lunch and talk about Jim Morgan. T. J. always had a coupon for lunch because he bought large coupon books, and they were searching for a particular Mexican restaurant on Richmond, near Loop 610. It was a dreary day. It had rained for many days, and the streets were flooded but not entirely underwater. There was a lot of standing rain everywhere, especially near the storm drains.

T. J. was driving his company car and was in the far left-hand lane as Michael commented on how much fun the clubs on Richmond Avenue were as they drove past them. In Houston, one always saw many folks standing near a bus stop to try to find work—basically day laborers. Usually, there were between two and twenty people, especially near a stop-and-rob convenience store, just waiting for someone to pick them up for a day's pay. While Michael was midsentence, T. J. made an illegal two-lane change from the far-left lane to the far-right lane.

Michael yelled out, "What the fuck?"

T. J. had spotted a large puddle of water near where the day laborers were standing and figured they looked pretty sweaty because of the hot day. His idea was to cool them down a bit. As the vehicle plowed through the flooded storm-drain area of water, a massive tidal-wave effect rippled across the curb toward the laborers. As the tidal wave lurched toward the unsuspecting laborers, one of them with an umbrella quickly noticed the massive wave coming at him and panicked. In a split second, the laborer opened his umbrella to stop the wave, but the wave hit all three men standing there and drenched them with water. Even the guy with the umbrella opened up was soaked because the water had so much force behind it. T. J.'s vehicle was doing about forty miles an hour, so the tidal wave of water went over the umbrella, and all three were soaked head to toe with water.

When Michael figured out what had just happened, he laughed so uncontrollably he almost pissed his pants. T. J. laughed as well, and the crazy laughter went on for about ten minutes. T. J. had to pull the vehicle over about a mile away because he was laughing so hard. He found it difficult to control the steering wheel.

As they exited the car after locating the restaurant, they finally got ahold of themselves, and Michael said, "I wondered why in the hell you made a two-lane change out of the blue." Since T. J. and Michael were both competitive individuals, Michael added, "We have a new competition."

T. J. laughed loudly and said, "What competition?"

"You're ahead one to nothing, and I'm thinking we can start this competition on who can wet down the most individuals with standing water on the side of the road."

T. J. laughed again and said, "It sounds like the biggest tomfoolery competition in the history of man."

Michael laughed too and agreed, and they shook on it. "Okay, it sounds like a bet. One rule, though: women and children are excluded from the competition. If women and children are within a group of individuals, no soaking them down."

"I'll agree to that rule," said T. J.

The competition was on, but unfortunately, they had other things on their minds, such as Jim Morgan, the new regional sales manager. Michael asked T. J., "What do you know about this asshole?"

"Just that he is an asshole and likes to drink beer, smoke cigars, and belch and fart a lot."

"Wow, a very likable, gross, and magnetic individual," Michael said. "Maybe I've found my soul mate." They both laughed.

"Yeah, he farts even more than you do, and I should know; I roomed with him in Cleveland years ago. You will get along with him fine; he reminds me of an older you."

"An older me?"

"Yes, an older you because of all the bad habits you have with women and drinking." They both laughed again.

"I guess we will see him in a few weeks, but I feel like there is a more massive shit storm coming and possibly another invite to the region, because they never filled that chickenshit analyst job. I'm already working on a new excuse not to interview for the job, but according to Art, it has to be more creative and not just 'Fuck that job,' like it was with Dr. No."

They laughed again, ate lunch, and headed back to the branch office.

The next few weekends were the same as any other weekend, with clubs, ladies, friends, sex, and booze. Michael liked to go to dance clubs, especially country-and-western dance clubs because the women were gorgeous and liked to ask the guys to dance. One in particular, Midnight Rodeo, located at Longpoint and Gessner, was always a favorite. It was not the best part of town, but there were always gorgeous gals with tight jeans. The staff at Midnight Rodeo called Michael at the office about every three weeks to give away a free party at happy hour on the weekdays to generate business. During one weekend visit, Michael had put his business card into a fishbowl with "Free happy hour" inscribed on it. He'd figured, *What the fuck? A free happy hour after work.*

The happy hours usually happened on Thursday—or Thirsty Thursday, as it became known—and a good time was had by all who attended. Michael even invited several agents in his territory to attend the happy hour, and some showed, but some didn't. It was a good idea to load up potential ladies or a future conquest because there was always a gorgeous lady Michael was interested in at any point in time, and some worked for his agency force. Michael always made new friends at the happy hours. However, a few friends in particular were man-whores and competition for Michael. A friendly contest was set into motion, starting on Thursdays, when things usually began to heat up for the weekend.

One Thursday in particular, Michael was with five of his friends, including his old friend Chuck from high school. Of course, the subject at hand was women because it was after happy hour at Confetti's on Westheimer, and the night crowd hadn't shown up yet. The meeting started around a round table as Chuck said, "You know, I'm thinking of spicing things up. We need some friendly competition."

"What do you mean?" Michael asked.

"Okay, here are my thoughts." He raised his voice because the music was so loud. "The competition starts every Thursday, and the person with the most scores—that is, who gets laid the most—by Sunday wins. The others all have to chip in to buy the winner drinks on Sunday."

Everyone agreed, so the competition was on, and of course, Michael knew he would win every weekend. He usually had at least three new gals over each weekend, so this was going to be easy money, he thought. Michael always liked some competition anyway, and it sounded like fun. "Okay, a few questions," Michael said. "What happens if one of us shacks up all weekend with the same gal? Does that count as four? And does it have to be different women each night?"

They all thought about it as they ordered another round of drinks. "Hmm, that is a good question," Chuck said, "so let's do it the democratic way and vote on it together. All in favor of different gals each night, say yea, and all against, say nay."

There were all yeas and no nays, so the motion was passed for a different gal each night. Michael asked one more question. "If we have carnal knowledge of a gal, how does one prove it happened? We can't have one of us standing over a couple having sex to prove it happened and announce a winner."

Everyone laughed, but it was an excellent question. "Okay," Chuck said, "we will have to do the honor system, but if we are all at the same club—and we usually are at the same club—it should be undeniable what is about to happen. Especially if they leave together."

They all agreed. Chuck announced he would be the keeper of the score tally because he enjoyed that sort of thing, and everyone could report the results every afternoon during the competition.

The competition went on for close to a year, with the clear-cut winner being Michael, but sometimes he would fudge his total to allow someone else to win that week. He was just that kind of guy—he didn't have to win all the time.

At the beginning of the competition, one lady he met while at Confetti was a pretty blonde but dressed like a guy, with a black tie over a white shirt. It was a different look he hadn't seen before. Her name was Chelsea, and he gave her his business card and danced with her a few times. She seemed pretty drunk but was coherent enough to carry on a conversation. Chelsea indicated she had just graduated from Texas A&M, Michael's alma mater, but it seemed she wasn't smart. Michael made a comment about his friend being as drunk as a skunk and not up to snuff, and she didn't understand what the common phrase "up to snuff" meant. After he tried explaining, he changed the subject and asked if she wanted to hang out later that night.

She said no but maybe a movie tomorrow if he didn't have plans.

"Nope, I sure don't."

The club was about to close, and everyone said good night and went home.

Chelsea called the next day and wanted to get together that night, and Michael quickly agreed. He picked her up that night, and she dressed in all denim. It was shitty-looking denim, and she didn't have a lot of makeup on, so during the date, he kicked himself for not paying more attention to what the gal had looked like the night before and her lack of intelligence. Unfortunately, she hadn't gotten any smarter overnight, and Michael figured, *I'll just lose this weekend's competition and live with it, but I need to get rid of this gal as soon as fucking possible.*

He dropped her off and called Chuck when he got home. "Yep, only one this weekend, and if anyone did any better than that, I lost this week's contest."

The Fab Five, as they came to call themselves, met up every Sunday night at a sports bar on Westheimer to brag, pay up in alcohol, and go over the weekend's festivities. It was fun, but everyone was so tired they always called it an early night on Sundays, especially with work the next day.

Everyone had left to go home one Sunday, when Chuck said to Michael, "Hang around a bit. I've got a story. You're not going to believe what happened to me last night."

"What?" Michael said with a laugh.

"I got home a bit early, but I was drunk and figured I would clean out the water in my water bed because it looked filthy. I plugged in the hose and emptied all the water from the bed. Then I plugged the hose in to the water intake, started to fill it up with water again, and sat down to watch TV. Unfortunately, I fell asleep on my couch. I woke up right when the clock changed from two fifty-nine to three o'clock, and immediately, the thought came to me: *The water bed!* I looked behind me, and the water bed was so full of water that it had become round instead of the regular rectangular, flat shape of a water bed."

Both Chuck and Michael laughed, and Michael knew where the story was going.

"You've been to my house, and I rent the upstairs from this older couple who live downstairs, right?"

"Yep, I'm aware of that," Michael said, still laughing.

"When I stood up to go to the kitchen and turn the water off, the bed exploded, and a rush of water came out at me like a tidal wave. It was like a damn movie—kind of like when a ship is sinking, and water is coming from all directions, you know?"

"Oh fuck," Michael said, laughing loudly, "what did your downstairs neighbors say?"

"There was so much fucking water everywhere that it started leaking through their downstairs ceiling and fucked up their chandeliers, and of course, it woke them up because they were soaking wet too."

Michael had known Chuck since high school, and this was a vintage Chuck story, a classic. They both laughed hysterically at the thought of the water bed exploding and knocking Chuck off his feet.

"What was the bottom line?" Michael asked. "Did they tell you to get the fuck out?"

"Yeah, basically, they did, but I'm paying for all the damage and repair to the house. I'll revisit the lease with them again after it is all finished, and hopefully, they will have forgiven me by then."

"Wow, what a story," Michael said. "Almost as bad as the time we drove down to Laredo for Mark's wedding." Mark was another friend from high school. "I'm still not sure how we made it back from Laredo with only three hours of sleep the entire weekend." They both laughed loudly at the memory. "All right. Let's get the hell out of here; I'm beat," Michael said.

Monday reared its ugly head again the next day. On Tuesday, Dr. No's replacement, Jim Morgan, was flying into town and would be at the Houston branch to check on the sales department.

Art called a quick meeting and said, "Make sure everyone is here on time tomorrow, because Jim will be here bright and early."

"Do we know what the fuck he wants?" Michael asked.

"Nope, probably to meet everyone, so don't be late." Art asked Michael, "Do you have your new excuse ready?"

"Yep, the latest excuse is carved in stone," Michael said. "If he offers the usual bullshit about going to the regional home office, I'll use the old standby of 'I just got engaged to be married in six months, and she doesn't want to move anywhere currently.' That should throw his fucking ass off for a bit."

"Ah, very good," said Art.

Michael continued. "So if the fucker brings it up again and asks how the wedding is coming six months from now, the excuse will be the bitch broke up with me because of my partying habits. I've got another lady I'm planning to propose marriage to in the future."

Everyone laughed about his new story and figured it should appease the region for a bit, at least until Jim got another promotion and a new egomaniac was hired to replace him. Then the excuse could start over with a new fiancée for Michael and a new story.

One of the few times Michael's alarm clock did not go off was on the wrong day: the day Jim was in the branch. Michael got ready in record time, called Susan before he left, and desperately said, "I need an excuse, please!"

She said Jim wasn't there yet. "But stop off to get some doughnuts, and I'll tell him the doughnut shop was ultrabusy when he arrives." Susan could make or break a good sales rep.

"Thanks so much for the excuse, Susan. You rock!"

Michael arrived at the office about thirty minutes late, and Jim was behind closed doors with Art. Susan knocked on the door and, with a smile, offered some doughnuts that Michael had brought in, so Art knew everyone was in the office. They both took a few doughnuts, which were still hot and fresh.

Jim said, "Wow, still hot even. Who bought these?"

"Michael. The doughnut shop was ultrabusy, but they are fresh, though!" Susan exited the office, and they began their discussion again.

T. J. was upstairs in the life department, talking with the life department manager, Ted O'Rourke. There existed a great relationship between the life insurance department and the sales department, mostly because of Ted. Ted was a tall, good-looking guy. He'd been a college basketball star at the University of Houston, was married to his college sweetheart, and had a mess of kids. He probably was the perfect dad and husband but never talked a lot about his family. It was apparent he was a happy guy. Secretly, perhaps he was an ax murderer but was never caught, a few agents suggested. He had a great sense of humor and always had a good joke or story to tell. No one could have been that perfect, but it seemed Ted was the all-American type of guy.

One story about Ted involved his vasectomy. His wife mandated he get one because they had six children, and they were finished having kids. Ted said that getting a vasectomy wasn't all that bad, but the doctor told him to stay off his feet most of the weekend and said the swelling should go down by Monday. Unfortunately, he picked the wrong weekend to get a vasectomy, because that weekend was Halloween. He spent most of Saturday night getting up and down to answer the door for the trick-or-treaters. His kids were out with his wife, so he was the only person home. Ted said that every time he got up, which was a lot, he cursed the damn doorbell because of the vasectomy pain.

T. J. had explained to Michael when he started with CIC that working with the life department wasn't necessary, but the two departments helped each other out in many different ways. "Ted is a great guy. Do the right thing, and work with the life department whenever possible."

T. J. finished his conversation with Ted and returned to the third floor, when he ran into Michael with the doughnuts in hand. The elevator door opened, and Michael said to T. J., "A doughnut or a thunderous fart?"

Before T. J. could answer, Michael put a doughnut in T. J.'s hand and let loose a loud fart, and they both laughed hysterically. Farting always made a stressful situation somewhat less stressful, and they both rode the elevator for their next meeting, which would be with Jim.

T. J. hadn't been at his desk when Jim walked into the office. When Jim exited Art's office, Michael and T. J. were at their respective desks, trying to look busy. Jim said, "T. J.!" speaking very loudly. "How the hell are you?"

T. J. said, "Doing great," and asked him how he was doing.

After the pleasantries were done, T. J. immediately started in on Jim. "So, Jim, are you still smoking cigars, belching, and farting all the time?"

Jim let out a big laugh and said yes, things were still the same. He then introduced Michael to Jim, and they shook hands.

Michael said, "I've heard a lot about you from T. J."

Jim said, "Nothing good, I'm thinking."

Michael said, "No, but I only believe about half of what I hear, so you're okay in my book." They both laughed.

Jim was going down to Davis's office to talk with him for a bit, and when Art came out of his office, both reps asked how things had gone with Jim. Art said, "It was no big deal; he just wanted to meet everyone and talk about the beach and bikinis. Since my home was in Fort Lauderdale for five years, we talked a lot about the beach and the anal floss the women wear these days, especially in Florida."

They all laughed, and everyone picked up where he'd left off, looking busy.

The visit was no big deal. The sales department went to lunch with Jim, which was uneventful, and the next day, Jim was back on a plane to Orlando. Afterward, Art, talking with the reps, said, scratching his head, "That was very weird, but knowing the region, some shit will come out of this visit, so prepare yourselves for some serious bullshit. They usually wait until they are safely back in their territory or office and then come up with a bunch of shit later."

So it was back to business as usual, they thought.

Business as usual was how most folks wanted their jobs to be. Still, in the insurance business, most companies were always trying to reinvent themselves and create more busywork than necessary because someone wanted to make life miserable for everyone with more reports, more bullshit, and someone always breathing down your neck. With Michael, though, the approach was currently to kick ass and take names, especially in the Valley and Corpus Christi areas. The four new large accounts his agents had sent in recently were all quoted and written by the company. Even Davis was surprised about a 100 percent hit ratio on these large-line accounts.

The territory and Michael's game plan had taken off big-time. Still, he received not even a "Good job" or "Congratulations on the game plan," but that was Davis. At least the relationship was improving, not only because of the new business but also because Dr. No was gone, and a new regional sales manager was in place, so there would be no more bullshit about Michael's nineteenth-hole incident with Dr. No.

The business was booming in the Valley and Houston, so Art called a meeting to go over a few new items happening around the company, and even Susan attended the meeting. Art was a master of laying traps so people would fall into them, and then he'd laugh his ass off about it for years to come. This meeting was one of those times.

Art started the discussion off with a question. "In everyone's opinion, who is the best sales rep in Houston?"

Without delay, almost before Art finished his sentence, T. J. said, "Well, me, of course, by far!" T. J. always tooted his own horn and always said "by far."

Art said, "Excellent," and stated he had received a communication from the regional home office to send the best sales rep to Orlando's five-day sales meeting. "I guess it's you, T. J."

Everyone but T. J. broke out into laughter. It was so loud that even with the door shut, the rest of the office wondered what was going on in Art's office. T. J. hated going to meetings in the region or home office. Art had baited the hook, and T. J. had fallen for it big-time.

After T. J. yelled out the word *fuck* loudly, he looked at Art and said, "That was very unfair what just happened."

The laughter died down after about five minutes. The meeting in the regional home office was in one week, and T. J.'s ego was in check for a few days or at least until quitting time that day. T. J. learned a big lesson that day: it was okay to toot your own horn, but there was a time and a place for everything, and you never should speak until you knew the whole story.

The meeting in the region came and went and, according to T. J., was a complete waste of time and energy. His report to Art was the same thing but watered down in case someone else read the information.

T. J. and Jim went out a few nights to have a few beers and catch up more on their lives, but Jim asked some strange questions regarding the Houston office. T. J. met with Art about the items that were not in his report, because he wanted Art to know something was amiss.

Art asked, "What questions?"

"What it's like to work for you and Davis and how the branch was run. What Michael was like to work with."

"Oh fuck, you know what that means, right, T. J.?"

"Yeah, but the kid has a pretty good excuse for Jim that probably will work out unless something crazy happens."

"Crazy as in he wants the job?"

"Yes," said Art.

"I've already taken care of that situation because he is a good hire, and everyone likes him, especially the womenfolk," T. J. said. "Don't tell him I think he is a good hire, because it will go to his head."

They both laughed, but something was brewing, and Art was a bit concerned about it. Whatever bullshit the region had in store for the Houston sales department was concerning.

A week later, the answer came. A regional home office communication and a phone call indicated the Houston sales department would be audited within a few short months. Art nearly shit an egg roll. The Houston branch had not been audited ever in its illustrious history.

Since Art had been around CIC for a while, he knew the situation could turn ugly if things didn't go well. Art went to Susan and said, "Find the reps, and call them in for a meeting immediately. If not today, set one up for tomorrow or as soon as possible."

The next morning, everyone huddled in Art's office, including Susan.

T. J. spoke up immediately, asking, "What is so crucial for an emergency meeting?"

"The region and home office called about auditing the sales department," Art said, exasperated.

"Are you fucking serious?" T. J. had been with the company for a good number of years before Art. "I don't think the Houston sales department has ever been through an audit before."

"Exactly," Art said, "so we are in a bit of a conundrum."

"Why is that?" asked Michael.

"I'm not sure we will pass an audit, and if they find something—or what they in the home office call a finding—my job would be in jeopardy over a situation like this," Art said.

"Okay, we all understand, so when is the audit?" T. J. asked.

"A month from today. We need serious help in going over all the files we have on each agency contracted to conduct business with us. Susan, we all know you do a great job, but you will need help going through each of the files, because there are more than a hundred. So any volunteers?"

Michael spoke up. "I'll help out. We need to know what each agency file is supposed to have in it exactly."

Art gave Susan and Michael the communication from the home office, plus all the information needed in each agency contract file. That information was the key to passing the audit, and they had a cheat sheet to go by while looking over each file.

"It's okay, Art. We've got this. Don't stress about it," Michael said. "We will have each file in perfect working order shortly because we all want you around for a good while. I guess the home office and the region don't give a shit about writing business or exceeding targets, because this will take a lot of time to accomplish."

Art said, "They don't, but production is up currently, so let's get to work on this shit as soon as possible."

The meeting adjourned, and Michael met with Susan afterward, saying, "No one wants to see Art get into trouble or, worse, get fired, because he is a great boss. Let's bust our asses to get this shit done quickly and, more so, get it done by the book." They agreed, but since Friday and the weekend were approaching, they would get to work on the task Monday morning.

Late on Friday, the competition with his friends and the hordes of women to meet were the only things Michael was thinking about, not the audit. His parking garage record was now at six because of another employee on the fourth floor who'd needed some attention. Michael had been unable to say no, but he kept this fact to himself because he didn't want to hear any more shit from Davis. The only person who knew was T. J., and he could keep a secret but would pass it on to Davis if he asked about the current record, because he liked giving Davis shit too. Who didn't?

The weekend was another great weekend in Houston, with wine, women, and song, mostly rock and roll but also some country music at the Midnight Rodeo. Michael's old hangout had been another country-and-western bar called the Diamondback, from 1984 through 1986. The crowd had moved from the Diamondback to Midnight Rodeo. Michael always followed the groups and always seemed to meet new friends.

When he pulled into his driveway after work, where the gate was located to get to his parking spot, he recognized a car with no one sitting in it. Michael knew the car well: it was Deborah's vehicle. "Aw, shit," he said to himself. He knew she was hiding in his doorway again, ready to pounce and give him shit because he hadn't called her in more than a month. His first thought was to call the police, but a cooler head ruled the day. His decided to wait her out. Maybe he'd drive to the closest bar, drink a few beers, and then circle back and try again in an hour. The nearest bar was a Friday's, and he headed in that direction.

Unfortunately, Deborah saw him driving away when she peeked out of his doorway, and the race was on. In Michael's favor was the fact that the gate was slow-moving when it opened, so he had a good head start.

Michael had talked his dad into buying him a 1977 Pontiac Trans Am when he was sixteen years old and had driven it for three years. He knew how to handle a car, even though his current car was a piece-of-shit Chevy company car. A few traffic lights and several turns later, he felt that he was in the clear and that it probably was safe to go home, change clothes quickly, and get the hell out again.

Surprisingly, it worked out in Michael's favor. He hoped Deborah had given up on finding him and gone home. He thought, *She knows my regular hangouts but isn't familiar with Midnight Rodeo, and I'll find a pay phone to alert my buddies to meet me there tonight.*

After a quick phone call and a rapid change of clothes, he was out the door, peering around to see if anyone was watching. There were two entrances off Bellaire to get to his condo and the Sharpstown Golf Course, and he took the one less used to ensure his escape, which went well. As he drove west on Bellaire to get to Gessner—at which, after a quick right turn and fifteen minutes more, he would be at Midnight Rodeo—his thoughts turned to the last few weeks. He thought to himself, *I've only gotten laid twice in the previous two weeks, so maybe running Deborah off wasn't such a good idea after all.* He knew what she wanted, and he was in the same boat but didn't want to settle for the same thing. Maybe he would meet someone that night, or maybe Deborah would be waiting for him when he arrived home later, to take care of business.

Unfortunately, neither happened, and Saturday was a bust too. Sunday rolled around with his regular golf game with Dave. "Can you believe I'm in a drought?" asked Michael.

Dave said, "In what way?"

"Drought women-wise. I've only gotten laid twice in the last two weeks, and it fucking stinks."

"You know that will change soon; just be patient. You get laid more than anyone I know currently or in the past, so quit bitching."

"True, and thanks for being my psychologist, Dr. Freud. It's your shot. You are two hundred fifty dollars down on this round, and you'd better catch up, because we only have two holes left to play," Michael said.

"Thanks a lot, asshole. You never forget anything, just like an elephant."

Sunday was ending, so Michael figured it was time to get ready for tomorrow and call his buddy Chuck to report his results. "I got blanked this weekend, dude. How did everyone else fare?"

"About the same. I'm thinking it was a draw this weekend, or all the single ladies had a meeting about keeping their legs shut tight this weekend," Chuck said, and they both laughed. "Well, there is always next weekend."

Since it had been a shitty weekend, the meeting was canceled for Sunday, and it was a good thing too, because Michael had to get to work on the sales files in the office. He knew Susan would be in one of her bad moods since it would be Monday, and she would be broke again and would bitch about it the entire day because her husband wouldn't find a job.

Michael was at the office earlier than usual on Monday and started reading the audit information and what was needed to pass the damn thing. He didn't just want to pass; he wanted it to be a stellar audit and make everyone look good, especially Art. That was the kind of guy he was: he not only wanted to make himself look good but also wanted all the people around him to look good.

Susan walked in and was surprised to see him already at his desk. She exclaimed, "What the hell? You are already here?"

"Yep, and ready to rock and roll."

They went over the first few files together to make sure they were all put together correctly and had all the necessary information and signed contracts per the home office's guidelines. "This bullshit isn't all that formidable," Michael said, "but it sure is time-consuming."

Susan agreed and added, "Try doing it full-time." She had been the marketing tech for eight years by that time and had the job down well, but CIC always taught that two heads were better than one. The philosophy was "Always get a partner when completing a challenging project or making a tough decision. Never go it alone, because two heads are harder to cut off than one. Just ask King Louis XVI."

Michael found out many years later through DNA that he was paternally related to the House of Bourbon king, so it was no wonder he hated cleaning fish or cutting their heads off.

"All right, this isn't all that tough, so let's split up and start kicking ass!" Michael exclaimed.

The process went on up until a few days before the actual audit. Art took Susan and Michael to lunch at the Hofbrau on Shepherd Avenue to ask about the files and everything else found in the guidelines the home office had sent.

Michael said, "Art, we are in the kill zone; in other words, everything looks great, but I couldn't have completed this task without Susan's help."

Art said, "I truly appreciate both of your efforts and the hard work put into this exercise of bullshit. Let's keep our fingers crossed that everything goes well. By the way, Davis wants a meeting with the sales department this afternoon. Let's get back to the branch reasonably sober."

T. J., Sue, and Michael were in the conference room when Davis showed up for the meeting he'd called. He was always late, even to his own meetings. That was typical Davis.

"Okay, guys and dolls, the audit team will be here on Monday. Is everything in place?"

"Yes, Davis," Art answered, "everything looks great."

"Okay, one more thing. The audit team will consist of the regional sales manager, Jim Morgan; a home office puke named Bill Stephens and one of his cronies; and the Atlanta sales manager, Mike Grant. Does anyone have a relationship with any of these guys?" Davis asked.

Michael spoke up immediately. "The Atlanta sales manager, Mike Grant, and I roomed together a few years ago for the new-hire school. We had a great time in Cleveland for a week and have kept in touch over the last few years." Mike was already a sales manager for CIC after being a rep for only a couple of years and quickly climbing the corporate ladder.

"So the bottom line is, we have someone we can trust on the inside, right?" Davis asked.

"Yes, we do," Michael said.

Davis told him to get updates from Mike every day to find out if there were any problems, or findings, as the home-office idiots called them.

"Okay, no big deal," Michael said.

"And lastly," Davis said, "make sure you take out the audit team every night to party and keep them out very late so they will be worthless the next day."

"Good idea," Michael said, "and I'm the perfect person for this job."

"Okay," Davis said, "meeting adjourned, and good luck!"

Monday came around quickly, and so did the fucking audit team. Art was in his office and thought, *My job could be over if there is a finding.*

It was just his imagination, because he was in great hands with Susan and Michael. They had done a great job on the files or completed all the tasks. The audit team walked in and went directly to the conference room, where a meeting was held with Davis and Art. Susan already had the files stacked in the conference room, ready for inspection, and they were prepared for the audit to start immediately. Michael saw Mike Grant walk in, but they only shared a glance and a smile because they didn't want to give away the fact that they were friends and knew each other from the home office school.

Near quitting time, Mike Grant walked out of the conference room to go to the bathroom, and Michael followed him into the bathroom. They shook hands before they got close to the urinals, and Michael asked, "How the hell are you, and how are things going in the conference room, fucker?" They both laughed.

Mike said, "Nothing to speak of yet, but it is the first day."

"Okay," Michael said, "are we going out tonight?"

"Nope, the team want to unpack and unwind after traveling early this morning, but the plan will be tomorrow night. Who is the host?"

"The host with the most, or me, dumbass. Hell, everyone else is married in this office, except for a few gals. The parking garage record is up to six now, so what do you think of that shit?"

"Not bad, but it seems like you're always getting laid, and I'm always getting promoted. It sounds like an even trade," Mike said. They both laughed.

Michael said, "True, but I would rather get laid than get promoted. Too much bullshit at that level; besides, it would fuck up my social life with all the extra hours."

"Correct," Mike said. "Let me get the team together, and we will see you tomorrow."

"Okay, see you tomorrow."

Michael immediately went to Art's office and told him the first day was done with no findings. Art was thankful and appreciative. Art asked, "Are you taking them out?"

Michael said, "No, but tomorrow is another story. We will go out every night until they are finished with the audit, and Mike Grant is working on that as we speak."

"Where are you taking them tomorrow?"

"The Colorado Club on Hillcroft, near the Southwest Freeway."

"Oh yeah, I think we have been there." They both laughed. "All right, see you tomorrow."

During the audit crap, Michael met up with an old friend he used to work with named Clarissa Spader, and she brought a much younger friend with her. Clarissa was a good twenty years older than Michael, and her idea was to introduce Michael to her friend and hope they hit it off—basically a blind date. She had called out of the blue recently after she'd found out from T. J. that Michael worked for CIC.

Their meeting was at a restaurant and bar called Houston's, off Westheimer and Fountain View in the heart of southwest Houston. It was one of Michael's favorite places to eat, because a club called Studebaker's, another bar at which to meet new ladies, was a block away. Michael walked in the door at five thirty and saw Clarissa talking to another woman. He quietly approached Clarissa from behind, put his hands over her eyes, and asked, "Guess who?"

Clarissa said, "I know that cologne; it's Michael!"

They hugged and exchanged pleasantries. Michael looked at her friend and introduced himself.

She answered, "Hi, Michael. I'm Alicia Berry."

Michael's jaw almost dropped because she was the spitting image of Victoria Principal, who played Pam Ewing on the TV show *Dallas*, which everyone watched at the time. Everyone had a crush on Victoria Principal because she was beautiful and played a character who was a bit vulnerable on the show. "Very nice to meet you, Alicia. So you work with Clarissa?"

"Yes, for the last couple of months, and I've learned so much from her, but I've got a lot more to learn."

Michael couldn't take his eyes off her because she was truly the spitting image of Victoria Principal and was drop-dead gorgeous. She had the same long brown hair, big tits, small frame, and great ass. They not only hit it off, but Michael ignored Clarissa for about fifteen minutes while trying to find out more about this person.

When he got his wits about him again, he apologized to Clarissa and asked how her family was doing and how the job was going. The agency she worked at represented CIC. T. J. was her sales rep, so she said a few things about working with him. She'd been surprised to hear Michael worked for CIC.

Michael spoke of the audit currently happening and how stressful the week had been but indicated things were going well. They all ordered drinks and sat down at a table that had just become open. Michael was quick to sit in the middle to visit with them both and talk business and any other things that came to mind.

After the second round, Clarissa excused herself to go to the ladies' room. Michael figured it was time to go in for the kill. "So are you married, or do you have a boyfriend?"

He was shocked when she said no to both questions, but he pretended not to be surprised, because he didn't want to seem too interested. Michael was getting close to his twenty-sixth birthday and asked how old she was, because he knew she was young.

She said, "I'll be twenty in a few months."

Wow, Michael thought to himself, ***all those attributes and only nineteen years old.*** Michael indicated that the audit would finished on Friday, so maybe they could go out, because he would be ready to blow off some steam.

Alicia quickly agreed and asked, "Where do you live?"

"I live on the Sharpstown Golf Course, in those purple condos backing up to the ninth hole."

"I know where that is located. Why don't we hang out at your house and make plans?"

Michael was shocked again. *Wow, she wants to come over to check out my digs to make sure I'm not a serial killer.* He agreed, and they exchanged phone numbers.

Clarissa returned from the bathroom. They ended up hanging out at Houston's until about eight, and then the party broke up. It was Monday night, and everyone had to work tomorrow. Michael gave Clarissa a big hug goodbye and hugged Alicia too and said it had been a real pleasure to meet her.

Clarissa and Alicia talked while going to their vehicles. "What do you think?" Clarissa asked.

"He's gorgeous, and we are going out this Friday."

They both laughed, and Clarissa said, "Mission accomplished!" Clarissa had hoped they would hit it off, and they had—big-time.

The audit continued Tuesday morning with serious facial expressions coming in and out of the conference room. Everyone in the sales department was a bit concerned.

Finally, Michael knocked on the conference room door, walked in, and announced it was quitting time and also beer thirty. Everyone agreed, and since they were all at a stopping point, they were ready for a drink, especially since everyone was rested up from going to bed early the night before.

"Where are we going?" Jim asked Michael.

"An old haunt down the street and close to your hotel, called the Colorado Club."

It sounded harmless, so everyone packed up and left the branch office. They followed Michael to the Colorado Club parking lot and exited their vehicles. They walked into the club and were immediately attacked by two scantily clad women next to the pool tables. The two said hello to Michael as if they'd known him his whole life, gave him a firm hug, and asked who the friends standing there looking bewildered were. Michael said, "Oh, just some business associates."

One dancer, Jasmine, saw Mike Grant and said hi to him while leaning against a pool table. It seemed most, if not all, dancers were named Jasmine. She proceeded to pick Mike up with a hug and throw him on top of the pool table. Then she got on top of him and initiated a dry-humping action as if fucking him with his clothes on. Mike's face lit up like a firecracker, and with a massive smile on his face, he exclaimed in a loud voice, "I love this place!"

The evening started off on the right foot, with everyone laughing his ass off, and it ended up being a night full of tits, ass, bourbon, and pool playing. The night went well, with no one but Michael shelling out the money, but he wasn't concerned about the big bill because Davis had told Michael to blow it out. When the bill was nearly a thousand dollars, Michael figured it was time to call it a night; plus, everyone was tanked up big-time. The mission had been accomplished.

The next day, they all tried to act as if the night had been no big deal and as if they didn't have hangovers, but everyone felt like shit.

Mike Grant walked by Michael's desk and said, "Hey, good job last night. Everyone is worthless in the conference room and won't stop talking about all the tits and ass last night."

"Ah, very good. During my next review, maybe I'll get a pay raise for last night's activities." They both laughed.

"Where are we going tonight?" Mike asked.

"I'm thinking about taking us to Rick's, which is now a publicly traded company on Wall Street."

"Another topless bar?" Mike asked.

"Well, yeah, it seemed everything went well last night, so maybe a higher-class bar, because the gals at Rick's are better looking and classier too."

"Okay, I'll run that by the hangover team in the conference room," Mike said, laughing.

"So any news on the audit, Mike?"

"All is going well, but I'll get back to you regarding tonight, and thanks for a great time last night."

Michael laughed and said, "Just doing my job."

Since there was a lull and he felt like shit, Michael figured he would call Alicia to see how her day was going. Since Clarissa and Alicia worked at an agency that represented CIC, he found the number quickly and called her office. "Hey, how are you?"

Alicia said, "Great. How is the audit going?"

"Pretty good, and we all stayed out late, per instructions from management." They both laughed. "Looking forward to seeing you on Friday. Are you still coming over?"

"Oh yes, I'm familiar where the Sharpstown Golf Course is located, but where is your condo exactly?"

"The second building on the left. There is a security gate, so if you can't follow someone in, just call on the telephone located in the entrance. I'm in B103."

After a few more pleasantries, he went back to work. Michael thought it was time to call Deborah, because if she showed up on Friday, she would screw up his date with Alicia—or, in his mind, Pam Ewing. *Better to head off a problem than to ignore it any longer.* He called Deborah's office. She picked up the phone, and Michael asked how she was doing.

"Okay, but you have a lot of balls calling me after your Indy 500 bullshit the other night. Maybe I'll forgive you if you say the right things."

Michael laughed in his mind and said, "Listen, things haven't been that good between us in a while, so let's agree to disagree."

"That sounds like a bunch of shit, Michael. We've been going out for over a year, and I'm marriage-minded because I'm not getting any younger, and neither are you."

Oh fuck, not the m-word, which is worse than the l-word: love. Michael said seriously with no inflection in his voice, "I'm not getting married anytime soon, and the thought hasn't crossed my mind." He wanted to say, "I'm not interested in being married to a psycho hose beast or, at this point, dating one either." He laughed to himself. "Anyway, I'm sorry about the situation, but I'm moving on. Hopefully this doesn't come as a big surprise, and please accept my apologies for springing this on you today."

She hung up on him. He figured the problem was taken care of and checked it off his list of shit to do that day. He did feel a bit bad about saying goodbye to Deborah, but how often did one get to go out with Pam Ewing?

Rick's was located off Richmond Drive and just a stone's throw from the office, so it was easy to get back to the audit team's hotel. Even for a Wednesday, Rick's was busy, but it was always busy every day, except Sunday because the club was closed on Sundays. The guys were in awe of how gorgeous the women dancing at Rick's were. They made the Colorado Club look like a dump with toothless women.

The guys all agreed not to make it a late night like the night before, but Michael had instructions to keep them out as late as possible with an unlimited expense account budget. Davis had approved the plan of action without Michael saying a word. Under most circumstances, everyone cheated on his expense account anyway, so it was no big deal. Art wrote his mortgage and boat payment on his expense account monthly. The expense account was more of a perk than a reimbursement.

The first gal at Rick's walked up to Bill Stephens, grabbed his ass, and said, "You look like you could use a dance, sweetie. Why don't you sit down and let me take care of you?"

Bill didn't know what to say; he just sat down and let the gal work on him while the song "Thriller" played on the loud stereo system. It was a pretty long song, so it was a long dance for Bill. It was the first time that tight asshole didn't have anything to say except "Yes, ma'am." Mike and Michael stood off to the side, laughing their asses off. It was funny as shit because he probably came in his pants. It was evident Bill had never been to a topless bar with gorgeous women, and he was a fish out of water.

The night went well, but they decided to call it a night earlier than the night before. It was a good thing because Rick's was a lot more expensive than the Colorado Club, and Michael was starting to get a bit worried about the bill being so large. They all exited the club and went their separate ways. After one more night of this, Michael would be free of the extra baggage. Rick's was not as much fun as the Colorado Club but more entertaining because of the gorgeous women.

The next day's consensus from the audit team was the same when Michael asked their thoughts on the two clubs. Everyone had been pleased with the festivities.

Michael made a few calls on agents the next morning because it would afford him some much-needed extra sleep and some fresh air without all the office stress because of the audit. One more night was left until his date with Alicia, and he figured he'd call her when he returned to the office, to make sure nothing had changed.

She picked up her extension, and Michael asked, "How are you doing?"

She answered, "Wonderful now that you have called!"

Her answer gave Michael the warm fuzzies, which he needed because of the hell-audit week. "Are we still on for tomorrow?" he asked.

"For sure, and I'm excited."

Wow, Michael thought, *Pam Ewing is excited to be going out with me!* He was excited too.

They talked for a bit, and Alicia said she would be at his house around six thirty. Michael tried to hide his excitement and said, "I'm looking forward to it," and they hung up.

T. J. had been listening to the conversation, because his desk was right behind Michael's desk. "Clarissa told me you are going out with Alicia. Is that true?"

"Hell yes," Michael said with excitement. "She's gorgeous, with a great body, and she looks just like Victoria Principal. Who the hell wouldn't want to go out with her?"

"Yeah, true," T. J. said, "but tell me you're not going to treat her like you treat most women."

"We haven't even gone out yet, but if you're talking about my past, the reason for lousy treatment is because they are about to start mistreating me. That is what dating is like these days—just who gets screwed first."

T. J. retorted, "I wouldn't know anything about that, because I've been married so long, but maybe try a different approach with Alicia. She's young and inexperienced, so cut her some slack. Besides, she is pretty hot, and it might lead to something in the future."

"Okay, T. J., you have a deal. I'll be on my best behavior, and the treatment will be stellar, but if this turns to shit, at least I know whom to blame. I've booked a happy hour tonight at Midnight Rodeo, off Longpoint and Gessner, to finish off the audit team. Are you game for joining the party too?"

T. J. said, "Hell yes, because I'm low on rum at my house, and it seems a lot of folks from the branch are going tonight."

"Yeah, correct," Michael said. "My happy hours are legendary. Since it's the last day of the audit, let's end it with a bang."

The night was crazy, and most of the branch office attended the happy hour. Most left early, but it still was a lot of fun. Mike Grant updated Michael on the audit, which seemed to have gone well. Management showed too, which was unusual. It was even more enjoyable with all of their stories about the good old days, including motivational stories about writing more business, so everything went smoothly. Michael did his best to keep the audit team from leaving early, but they were tired from the audit and the week, and they left around nine o'clock. Everyone else left early too. Michael spoke with Art and Davis about the audit and told them his inside guy, Mike Grant, had indicated nothing had been found, but the official results would soon come. Everyone left the party drunk as hell, but all had a good time.

The big day with Alicia arrived without fanfare. The audit was complete, and the audit team met with Davis and Art to go over some results but indicated a full report would be mailed out next week. That was alarming news for Davis and Art, but they figured they could wait and not worry a lot about it until Monday.

Michael was relieved the week was over, and he decided to leave a bit early to get home and shower for his date. He had done his job as best as he could to keep Art around as sales manager or at least until the next horseshit from the home office came up.

Before Mike started toward the door to go to the airport, Michael asked if he could ride down in the elevator with him. The audit team were in the conference room, packing their shit.

"Well, what happened?" asked Michael.

"They found a few things. I don't think it would be a firing offense, but we have to wait for Bill Stephens's report. I think everything is okay for Art, so pass that on, please."

"Okay, have a safe flight. We will talk soon."

The audit team left after shaking hands with Michael, who was talking to Mike Grant near the rental vehicle. They all said they'd had a great time, so another mission had been accomplished.

Michael left the office after they pulled out of the front parking lot, and he took a few shortcuts to get home as quickly as possible. He took a shower and went about his condo to tidy up a bit, so Alicia wouldn't think he lived like a pig. He was relieved that Deborah wouldn't be beating his door down either.

The doorbell rang, and Michael held his breath. Thankfully, it was Alicia. She looked even more gorgeous because she was all dolled up. They hugged and talked about the audit and how thankful Michael was that it was successfully finished. He offered Alicia a drink, and they shared a bourbon and Coke and spoke about where they wanted to go. Michael suggested Pappadeaux's, off I-10.

Alicia said, "A great choice." She told Michael she'd worked there in the past and loved the food. It was seafood, and who the hell didn't like seafood?

They left the condo, and Michael, as he'd promised T. J., was on his best behavior. He opened her car door for her, carried her drink to the car with him, and put it in the drink holder. The date was going well, and Michael was in awe of how gorgeous she looked and how she talked like someone much older than her age. Of course, her looking like Victoria Principal didn't hurt the date either, but a connection happened quickly that night, which was unusual with Michael. Most of his previous dates had been crazy as hell.

They finished dinner and went back to his vehicle. "Just a thought," Michael said, "but it's past ten o'clock, and all the late movies have already started, so do you want to watch a movie at my place?"

Alicia said, "Another excellent idea!"

Michael turned on his favorite film, *Casablanca*, because it was a romantic movie, and that was the way the date felt that night. He was still on his best behavior and didn't even think about doing anything, because he was a man of his word.

Toward the end of the film, she looked at him, smiled, and planted a big kiss on his lips. Since things were going so well, Michael figured, **What the hell?** and kissed her back, which led to more kissing and the bedroom. Michael knew that wasn't the plan, but overall, it had been a great first date, and she was so freaking gorgeous. Earlier, at the restaurant, he'd thought about what she would look like with no clothes on. He hadn't expected anything to happen that night but was pleasantly surprised by the eye candy. A nineteen-year-old gal with a nineteen-year-old body—what could be better?

They got up late the next day, and Michael asked her what her plans were for the day. She didn't have any but also didn't have a change of clothes, so she decided to go home, change, and come back. Michael was excited to spend the day with her, which was unusual, because he couldn't wait to get rid of his dates under most circumstances. Something was different about this gal. She was gorgeous and frank. She had no motive to screw things up; she just wanted to hang out and enjoy herself.

They spent the day together. They went to a park and played Frisbee, which Michael loved, and then went to buy a few things from the store. Michael suggested grilling some steaks, and Alicia quickly agreed to the plan. In the back of Michael's mind, he thought, *I'll bet my friends wonder where the hell I am; plus, the clubs are hurting from the lack of my business.* He laughed to himself. Since she was so young, Michael couldn't take her to a club, because the drinking age was twenty-one, so the next best thing was to party at his condo. She was down for that too, which was another big surprise, but what did one do before turning twenty-one?

They watched another movie and drank Michael's favorite wine from the Tuscany region of Italy. Alicia had never had wine before, especially high-end wine, but enjoyed it very much. She had class, Michael thought. Alicia was thankful to have tried high-end Italian wine and thanked him for turning her on to it with a long kiss. Michael was in shock because most women he went out with expected to be treated like royalty or at least wanted to be spoiled rotten regularly, and to his surprise, she was laid back. Alicia was a refreshing date. They could just hang out while enjoying each other's company and watching a movie over a bottle of wine.

Alicia stayed over on Saturday night too, so when Saturday turned into Sunday, Michael got up first and called Dave to cancel his usual golf game on Sunday. Dave questioned him at length about what the hell was going on.

"The truth of the matter is, this date started Friday and has continued until now. She is different from most of the women I've gone out with in the past. I can't explain now, but I'll come down to your condo later to explain it to you then."

"Okay, talk to you then."

Alicia heard Michael talking on the phone, and she got up and asked, "Who was that?"

Michael said, "I was canceling my golf game with a neighbor who lives a few condos down from me."

"If you have plans today, I can leave."

"No, please don't," Michael said quickly. "Don't go unless you want to."

She answered promptly, "No, my plan is to hang out here, if that's okay."

Michael thought, *This is like a dream come true, spending the entire weekend with Pam Ewing's twin.*

They spent most of the day together on Sunday and genuinely enjoyed each other's company. Alicia indicated she had dated her high school sweetheart for two years until he'd moved on a few months ago, and they'd broken up. Michael said he was sorry to hear that, but he'd enjoyed the weekend and hoped they would go out again. She agreed. It was getting late, and she had to get ready for work tomorrow. He walked her out to her vehicle, a shiny red Toyota. Just for a second, he thought maybe Deborah would be outside stalking him again, but the coast was clear. They kissed again and said good night.

He locked his door and then went down to Dave's condo and spilled the beans about the weekend. Dave was in shock. "You mean the younger Hugh Hefner spent the whole weekend with one lady?"

"It happened, and my report to Chuck for the contest hasn't happened either." They both laughed. "I'm shocked too," Michael said, "so stop looking at me with such disgust, you asshole. This one seems different, and you're getting married, fucker, so stop being so negative, Dave."

Dave laughed and asked, "So did you propose marriage to her?"

"No, the proposal was to see each other again next weekend. Are you happy?"

"Are you going to kick me out of the hot tub like we did to you recently?" They both laughed.

Michael said, "No, I'm going home. I can get this type of abuse anywhere, just not here. Talk soon."

Michael went back to his condo and thought about the weekend and how special it had been—another first for him, given the fact that he wanted to see her again.

Monday morning came around again, and Michael was in the office, talking with T. J. about the weekend. "You know, I am going to treat this one differently because she is different," Michael said to T. J. "Not only gorgeous but a real find among the sluts and road whores I usually go out with, so I'm going to give this a chance."

T. J. said, "Wow, seriously? Are you hanging out with one woman? That is hard to believe!"

"True, but I'm going to give it the old college try," Michael said.

Art came into the branch office, went to his office, and shut the door without saying a word. T. J. and Michael looked at Susan, and Michael said, "What the fuck is up with that attitude?"

She said, "The audit results came in, and he is reading through the report now."

"Did you read it?" Michael asked.

"Nope, sure didn't, and I'm hoping it is good news."

Ten minutes later, Art came out of his office and asked everyone to go into his office for a meeting. Art immediately said, "The audit results are in and final."

T. J. said, "What the fuck does the audit say?"

"There were a few findings."

Michael said, "Impossible. Shit, we combed through those files meticulously, so there has got to be some sort of bullshit going on!"

Art said, "Let me finish and rephrase my statement. There were a few *minor* findings but nothing that would classify as a terminating offense."

"Oh shit, you scared the shit out of us all," Michael said.

"So we passed?" T. J. asked.

"Yes, we did, damn it!"

A massive sigh of relief filled the room, and everyone gave each other a high five. "We dodged a bullet on that one," Michael said.

Art said, "Not only that, but also the fact that these audits don't happen very often, so we can all breathe easier because it won't happen for a good number of years."

T. J. added, "Very accurate! Hell, we will all be dead for the next audit or at least retired by that point."

Art agreed and asked everyone but Michael to stay in his office. "It's early, but let's plan to go to lunch today."

Michael agreed and left Art's office.

The usual lunch at the Hofbrau on Shepherd Drive ensued at about noon. It was always busy and packed, but since Art was a regular customer, he got a table more quickly than most patrons. There was a reason Art wanted to do lunch that day: to discuss the last two years, especially the previous month. After they ordered a couple of beers, Art started the conversation. "I have gone to bat for you many times with Davis. His management style is sink or swim, and you were in the deep end a few times, asking for help but not asking me for any help."

They both laughed, and Michael said, "I figured that was what you were doing, especially when you walked down to his office announcing the large accounts we wrote recently and the Valley game plan's success. Corpus and the Valley are increasing. Within a few years, these areas will be over twenty million dollars in premiums. I'm genuinely thankful for your faith in me."

Art continued. "I saw how hard you worked before and during the audit, and that spoke volumes about your trust in me and how much you didn't want to see me get into trouble with the chickenshit home office or the regional office."

Sternly, Michael said, "You got me out of that sentence I was doing at Commercial Standard, and my employment went from working for a shitty company to working for the Mercedes-Benz of companies. It was and is very much appreciated. I'm never one to forget a favor, and CIC is a great place to work. Plus, the sex is better at CIC and more often than at any other time in the past." They both laughed loudly and then ordered a big steak, the Hofbrau's specialty.

Michael added, "I'm not sure the relationship between Davis and me will ever improve, but if it stays like this, I'm not disappointed. You do my reviews, and even though Davis runs the branch overall, my course of action will be to keep you pleased with my performance, and fuck the rest."

"Yeah, right, but you need to worry about a few other things, such as the regional home office. They will be hot on you again in the future because of your performance during the audit. No one wants the analyst position in the region, which is a known fact throughout the company. The natural progression of things is to accept a promotion to the regional home office; learn from them for a few years; and then, once a sales manager position opens up, get the job."

"I'm aware of those facts. Still, my predecessor didn't go to the region, and neither did my friend Mike Grant in Atlanta, so why the fuck would sitting on my ass and listening to the maniacs in the region twenty-four-seven be even remotely interesting to me in the first place? Sounds like a job made in hell if you ask me," Michael said as the steaks arrived.

"Well, I know you have a good handle on that hierarchy of things. My plan of action was to make sure you were aware of some glaring facts, but we will hear from the region again soon."

"Okay, it's understood, and so business as usual then?"

"Yes."

"Great, and by the way, the parking garage record is up to six now because the new gal in the claims department helped me out a few weeks ago."

Art said, "You haven't said anything about the parking garage record recently. What the fuck is up with that?"

Michael said, "Davis is a pretty ego-driven guy and was getting pissed off with all the conquests I've had, so the plan was to lay low and not say anything about any new women, because it pisses him off."

"I thought, *Michael is probably in a dry spell*, but I should have known better."

"If it's of any consequence to you, I've recently met a new lady, and we had a great time together. She is drop-dead gorgeous too. We spent most of the weekend together, and I feel like I'm in high school again, with butterflies and all the shit going around in my stomach."

"That is usually the beginning of the l-word," Art said.

"As you know, Art, this is all new to me because I'm not big on the l-word, just the s-word." They both laughed.

Art said, "Let's get the hell out of here, and by the way, great job on the Valley game plan and keeping my ass out of home-office jail."

"No problem, Art. That is the main reason you hired me, right?"

"Yeah, Michael, so great job on the audit and entertaining the audit team, because it will pay dividends soon."

They finished their steaks and drove back to the branch office reasonably sober.

It was nice to hear Art appreciated all Michael's hard work over the last few years, plus all the extra work regarding the audit. Work was going well for Michael, and as the years went on, Art was so appreciative about the audit and the successful business writings that everything changed from that point on after the Hofbrau luncheon. Not only was Art thankful, but he trusted Michael almost like a son. Art had two sons around the same age as Michael, so the working relationship became sort of like a father-son relationship. They still liked raising hell together, but it was a great time for Michael professionally and personally. However, all good things must come to an end.

Over the next few months, everything went exceptionally well for Michael at CIC. The Valley and Corpus agents were producing loads of business, and his Houston agents were increasing business exponentially. Things were going so well that T. J. and Michael would sneak off to the beach to gawk at the bikini-clad women a couple of times a month, and no one ever said anything or even knew where they were on those days.

His relationship with Alicia turned from a mutual crush to something more serious because Michael decided not to go out with anyone else except for her. Who in his right mind would have gone out with anyone else anyway? Hell, even Bobby Ewing could never say no to Pam, and that was the same boat Michael was in. He didn't frequent the clubs much, because she wasn't twenty-one yet, but they always found other things to do that helped to make their relationship even closer.

A few months passed by, and Michael figured out Alicia was still living at home with her folks, which was the reason she came over to his condo for dates. Her financial situation improved considerably, and she was ready for a change of venue. Alicia wanted a place of her choosing and started looking around for an apartment. Her parents owned a rental house that was vacant, so Alicia contacted her best friend from high school, Laura, and asked if she wanted to share the town house with her, plus the monthly rent. Laura said she and her boyfriend were thinking about moving in together, so the arrangement would be perfect if Alicia didn't mind Laura's boyfriend living there. It was an excellent deal for them all because the rent would be split three ways, which made it affordable. Alicia spent most of her time at Michael's condo anyway, so it was no big deal.

After Alicia moved in with her friends, a few weeks later, Michael dropped by after work with a wine bottle to celebrate her new digs. Her condo was close to his office, and it seemed everything was going great in their relationship—until he met her roommate and her boyfriend. The boyfriend was okay, but her best friend, Laura, did not like Michael for some unknown reason. Alicia told him so the next weekend at his condo.

Michael told Alicia, "She is a nobody going nowhere, so who gives a flying fuck what she thinks of me?"

Alicia said, "You had a tie and suit on, and she hates authority figures."

"I'm fucking successful in business, and I'm not making an excuse for it, but keep in mind that this wasn't all handed to me. My work ethic is incredible, and I've worked my fucking ass off for everything and make no apologies to anyone." He was a bit harsh and raised his voice with her, and she teared up at the strong, louder-than-ordinary words.

Even though Michael was great with wining and dining the ladies, he wasn't very good at conflict or communicating his feelings well. He was not even twenty-six, so he had a lot to learn about the female psyche and how to express his feelings and understand a woman's feelings. It was a problem in the relationship, but things quickly blew over because love conquered all, and they had makeup sex for the rest of the weekend.

In the future, Michael ignored Laura if he ran into her at Alicia's condo and wouldn't even say hello or acknowledge her presence. Michael usually liked everyone unless the person gave him a reason not to, as Laura had. Michael did not have a big ego, but he just ignored people he didn't like. It always worked, and one day it would even work on Davis. However, it seemed Laura was another situation, as she was always talking shit and trash-talking behind Michael's back to Alicia. Alicia ignored that type of conversation because she was beginning to have feelings for Michael, and she knew he was on his way up the corporate ladder. Hooking on to that rising star would be a good thing, if not a great thing.

Another Monday arrived with more fucking meetings about nothing, but business was booming, and so was dating Alicia. Since the branch office had increased in size over the last few years, Davis instituted a branch-wide meeting for the entire office every quarter. Since things were going well, Davis opened up with corporate results and talking about how well the Houston branch was doing in the overall scheme. It was always a positive meeting because that was the way Davis wanted it to be. He always ended with the statement "We are looking for new employees, so talk to your friends, and have them apply for open positions."

One life insurance rep who worked for O'Rourke upstairs was always first to get to the free doughnuts. He looked like he was fifteen months pregnant, which didn't make him look any better when he took six doughnuts for himself. Michael always asked him, "How come six doughnuts and a Diet Coke? I don't understand that thinking; maybe you can help me out on that choice."

He said, "Well, I couldn't have had the sixth doughnut without the Diet Coke."

T. J and Michael always cracked up laughing, but they gave a bunch of shit to people, mostly guys who loaded up on the doughnuts and didn't need them.

A few hours later, T. J. and Michael were on their regular Monday lunch hour, talking about the usual weekend stuff and women. T. J. was surprised to hear Michael was still going out with Alicia. "It's been over two months, hasn't it?" T. J. asked.

"Yep, and I'm enjoying her and her company and all the other things that go with dating someone steadily."

"You mean you guys are going steady?"

Michael laughed. "Hell, I'm not sure, but we don't see other folks, so maybe we are in a relationship, and we just haven't made it official yet."

"Okay, how does it feel to fuck Pam Ewing?" T. J. asked.

Michael laughed again. "Feels pretty good, and glad you asked, because I'm still kind of surprised we have been dating this long. I'm under the impression sex stops after a few months of dating, but I'm unsure if that is true, because as you know, I'm not one who hangs around very long." They both laughed. "Do you know that producer in Harlingen for April and Associates? He has a condo on South Padre Island and offered it to me to use whenever the beach feeling hits, as long as it is not rented out to another party. I'm taking him up on that offer next month, and I'm taking Alicia—or Pam Ewing—with me." They both laughed again.

T. J. said, "That sounds like a great idea, and try not to get sand in your pants; it hurts when you try to bury your stinger on the beach." They laughed and left the restaurant to go back to work.

The month went by like wildfire, and Michael and Alicia left on a Thursday to go to South Padre Island. They spent the night in Corpus Christi because they had to pick up the key from Mark Trajan in Harlingen on Friday morning and proceed to the condo. It was beautiful that weekend, not Florida beautiful but close to it, and they found the condo, unpacked, and hit the beach.

They were inseparable all weekend, and since Michael knew the area well, he took Alicia to some restaurants he knew she would love and made it a great weekend. Restaurants didn't check IDs much in the Valley area, so they drank a lot of wine and beer at each restaurant and drank even more on the beach.

Unfortunately, the weekend was coming to an end. Since Michael had dated Alicia for nearly four months, he knew something was amiss with her on the drive home. The drive was around six hours, and Michael kept asking what was wrong, but she just kept saying nothing was wrong.

While driving, Michael thought, *I've been a gentleman, I took her on vacation and spent a shitload of money, and now something is wrong.* He reviewed the last few days, and nothing came to mind. Alicia loved the beach, and Michael loved the beach too, especially seeing her in her bikini.

Finally, when he dropped her off at her house, she got her luggage and slammed the door shut.

Well, shit, not even a kiss or even a "Fuck you," Michael thought. *Wow, who the hell was I just on vacation with anyway?* He thought he would not talk to her for a few days and would let her cool off because he didn't know what was wrong in the first place.

A few days went by with no calls from her, so he thought, *I'll call her and break the ice.*

She picked her phone up at the office, and he said, "Hi. How are you?"

She said, "Okay," but her voice was icy.

"We haven't talked in a few days, and this is probably the longest we have gone without talking in over four months, so what happened?"

"Nothing," she said.

"Well, whatever the situation is or isn't, please accept my apologies," Michael said. "Maybe things can go back to the way they were before we went on vacation."

"I'm going through a few things with my mom and my stepdad, and I don't feel like talking about it, okay?"

Michael had never seen this side of Alicia before and was in shock at her treatment of him since Sunday. He was never one to just roll the dice and hope for the best, so he came right out and asked, "Are we over?"

She said, "I just need some time to think."

"Does that mean yes? Just be honest with me. I've got feelings for you, Alicia, and I've been honest with you and treated you like a queen, so are we fucking over?"

"Let's not talk about it, and yes, we are done."

"It's your fucking friend Laura, isn't it?" Michael asked in disgust.

She promptly hung the phone up.

Michael knew Laura was behind the disastrous situation.

T. J., eavesdropping like always, heard the conversation and said it didn't sound good.

"Do you think?" Michael asked harshly. "The minute I'm nice to a gal, she blows me off and breaks my fucking heart. This truly sucks goat balls. This treatment was long overdue. I should have known the treatment I handed out to the gals in my past would come back and bite the shit out of my ass sooner or later." Michael turned to T. J. "You see why it is so difficult to treat these gals nice now?"

T. J. said, "Yeah, I understand now, but you did take advice from a guy who has been married since he was twenty." T. J. was trying to be funny, but it didn't work, because Michael was hurt over the breakup.

It had been a great four months, some of the happiest in his dating life; however, the next few months would be challenging. He was crazy about Alicia, but it was too late to do anything about it now or in the future.

The business was still growing, so at least that part of Michael's life was going great. Over the next few months, he tried to call Alicia to see if there was any way they could patch things up and continue the way it had been before. The calls went unanswered and were never returned. He talked to Clarissa to find out how Alicia was doing since she never returned any of his phone calls, but Clarissa had nothing to say other than "She is doing fine." She didn't know what the problem was with the relationship either.

Within a few days after the breakup, Michael decided to get back into his old lifestyle and hopefully find a way to forget Alicia. He knew it wasn't going to be easy, but he was up for the task, even though it was tough to forget about her. The thought crossed his mind to call Deborah, but after checking around, Michael heard from a friend that she'd gotten married after meeting a guy and dating him for less than two months. *Okay, that one is a no-go.* He laughed to himself. He figured he'd dodged a bullet with Deborah, because he knew a marriage to a psycho hose beast wouldn't last long. Michael knew she'd just wanted to get married, and it seemed it didn't matter which swinging dick she married, but he was glad it hadn't been him. Walking down the aisle with Deborah seemed like the Greg Kihn music video for the song "Jeopardy." It was a relief not to restart that relationship, especially with a psycho nutcase.

He thought about his past failed relationships, especially with Alicia. The thought of walking down the aisle was not as bad as he first had envisioned, but he was starting over at this point in his life alone. Except for a one-night-stand junior and senior prom date that hadn't worked out in high school and the married gal he'd met at a club in Corpus Christi, no lady had come close to breaking his heart. This situation was different because things had gone so well when he dated Alicia. Michael chose now to live as he used to, with a new woman every weekend, but deep inside, he knew it would take a long time to get over Alicia.

A few days later, he was back to the same old habits of partying, wine, women, and hell-raising. Everyone noticed the change in Michael, from friends to coworkers. He wasn't his happy-go-lucky self and wasn't telling jokes most of the time.

His high school friend Chuck had cooked dinner for Michael and Alicia one night while they were still dating, and they'd had a great time, so Chuck was concerned about his friend, because he noticed the change. Since Michael hadn't reported his weekend trysts to the competition in a good while, Chuck felt he was out of the game for good. Since they had been good friends for so long, Chuck would help his friend as best as he could, because this had never happened to Michael before, so it was uncharted territory. Chuck was a great guy and friend. If Chuck was sober enough, he would help a friend out during a tough time; however, he wasn't sober most of the time.

Things were settling back to the way they'd been before Alicia. The parking garage record wasn't safe, because Michael went all out to get over Alicia and have fun again at the expense of any single gal around. The parking garage record was now up to seven because Michael was hanging out at the Metropole in downtown Houston a lot, the ladies were gorgeous at the club, and it was a quick drive to the branch office off 610, near the Southwest Freeway. The usual excuse he used at the Metropole was "Oh shit, I forgot to accomplish something at my office" or "Do you want to see my workplace?" It usually worked.

About a month later, a call came into the office, and Michael picked the phone up. It was Alicia.

"Oh wow, Alicia, how are you doing?" Michael tried to hide his excitement and surprise that she had called his office.

"I'm okay, but I wanted to tell you a few things, Michael. Firstly, I've heard you are partying a lot like you did before we met, and it appears you are over me, which is good. I've run into some financial problems, and I'm going to be moving to Birmingham, Alabama, where my dad lives, at the end of the week."

Michael not only had missed the sound of her voice but also heard a woman in distress. However, he was so hurt inside that it was hard to show any emotion of any kind. Michael said, "I'm truly sorry to hear about that. Would you like to have lunch? I would like to say goodbye in person, if that is okay."

She said, "Sure, when?"

Michael said, "Tomorrow, Tuesday, at the first place we met: Houston's."

She agreed, and they hung up.

Michael turned to T. J. and said, "Did you have anything to do with that phone call?"

T. J. asked, "What phone call?"

Michael knew he had, because T. J. felt terrible about his bad advice, and he had talked to Clarissa, who'd indicated Alicia was leaving town soon. T. J. was just that kind of guy: if he screwed up one way, he would make it up in another.

"If you did have anything to do with that phone call, it's much appreciated, but this is probably the last hurrah, because I'm not optimistic about the outcome. But we will see tomorrow," Michael said.

The next day came around quickly, and so did lunchtime. Michael was at Houston's before eleven thirty, the time they'd agreed to the previous day, mostly to get a good table. When Alicia walked through the door, it was as if nothing had happened over the last few months, as if they were still dating. She looked stunning.

He hugged her as his heart skipped a beat, and they started with small talk that turned into a more serious conversation. "So what have you been doing the last few months?" he asked.

"Not much, but my roommates moved out, and the rent is unaffordable for me living alone. My stepdad has been treating me like shit. An idea came to me to move in with my real dad in Birmingham."

"I'm very sorry to hear about all of this bad news. The truth of the matter is, I've truly missed you, Alicia."

She said the same thing to Michael. They hugged and decided not to eat but to go back to her town house to enjoy the afternoon in bed. It was her next-to-last day at the agency, so she didn't bother calling in sick.

The afternoon went by quickly, as most perfect afternoons did, and the world felt perfect and in place to Michael, but he was unsure what to do next. Like a dumbass, he didn't express his feelings and just left, saying goodbye, because there were many thoughts going through his head at that moment, and he needed time to sort them all out.

On the way home, he stopped by a drugstore and bought two cards: one for good luck in the future for Alicia and one to ask her to move in with him. It was a tremendous step for Michael, but he'd figured out that day that he loved Alicia, and he finally was ready to make a giant leap toward the unknown.

He called Alicia and said, "Thanks for the afternoon; it was beautiful. But let me ask you a favor."

Alicia asked, "What favor?"

"You are leaving soon, but can we get together tomorrow for lunch, as there are a few things that need to be cleared up in person and not just to have sex again, okay?"

She agreed and asked, "Where tomorrow?"

Michael said, "The Black-Eyed Pea on Bellaire," which was near them both, and she decided to meet him again.

Michael showed up in the office the next morning as excited as a teenager on his first date and told T. J. he was going to ask Alicia to move in with him and not leave for Alabama.

T. J. was shocked. "You're going to ask her to move in with you?"

"Yes, I'm serious about her," Michael said, "and I'm meeting her for lunch today to see what she says."

"Wow, you are crazy about her, aren't you?"

Michael nodded.

Lunchtime came around, and he arrived at the restaurant early to read over what he'd written in the two cards. He also planned to explain how much he was in love with her and ask her to move in with him.

Eleven fifteen turned into eleven forty-five with no Alicia. He waited at the table by himself until twelve forty-five and then left, concerned something had happened to Alicia. He got back to the office and immediately called Alicia's office to find out where she was and spoke with Clarissa.

Clarissa said, "Michael, I'm so sorry, but she left for Alabama this morning, and she is already gone."

Michael's heart hit the floor with many emotions—sadness, emptiness, and anger. He'd missed his chance. She'd not even called or left a voice mail to cancel their meeting that day. He'd not received even a "Fuck you, asshole," just silence. Michael felt horrible, filled with emptiness and regret.

"Okay, thanks, Clarissa. I appreciate your help on everything." After Michael hung the phone up, he said out loud, "Fuck!" He looked around to make sure no one watched and put his hands over his face and started to question his life, feelings, and idiocy for not doing something sooner.

Nothing was happening in the office; Susan wasn't even at her desk, so Michael packed his shit and left the office. On the way home, he picked up a couple bottles of his favorite high-end Tuscan wine and decided to get drunk.

He got home, put on a movie, and began to drink heavily. He put on his favorite film, *Casablanca*, with the hope it might make the pain go away. As he watched the movie, it held a different meaning to him now. It had always been his favorite film, but the unrequited love and pain Rick felt made even more sense to Michael now after the last few days. He knew how Richard Blaine, played by Humphrey Bogart, felt when he was at the train station, waiting on Ilsa Lund to show up, which never happened. Michael thought Bogart was a great actor, showing his true feelings on the train station platform while waiting in the rain for the woman he thought might be his future wife. But as in Michael's case, she never showed.

The bottle of wine was three-quarters empty when Bogart read the letter from Ilsa, so there wasn't any more pain, just some introspection about the last four months. Bogart's acting was so good that Michael could see the pain in his eyes and feel every word written in Ilsa's letter to him and what might have been different in the future while the rain came down heavily. Michael thought about what he could have done differently during his time with Alicia, but like Bogart, he'd treated his girlfriend like a queen and wanted the best for her. No answer came. He felt what Bogart was feeling: loneliness and regret. He wanted to be Rick's friend on the train platform and to help him out during his challenging time, as his friend Sam did. As Sam led Rick onto the train bound for Casablanca, Rick was in a sad state of mind, and Michael felt the same way. The movie, after that week, held much more meaning because he drew so many comparisons to his own life.

Michael started on his second bottle of wine, but much like Rick in the movie, he passed out in his recliner after a few gulps of wine.

When Michael woke up the next morning, he thought, *Well, Rick got a second chance in the film*, but in the back of his mind, he knew two days ago had been the last time he would ever see Alicia.

7

Chapter

Fun, Golf, and Booze

*I*t had been a good year before Michael met Alicia. With business writings going so well, Davis met with the sales department and gave the same motivational speech annually, because the branch was tasked with an ambitious growth plan. Sometimes the goal was 7 percent growth, and other years, it was double-digit growth, but the branch office always exceeded any target given. The branch had all the right people in all the right places, which was the main ingredient for success. Davis met with the sales department every year and always said, "Blow your expense accounts out. Find out what your agents like to do, and do it with them, whether it be golf, bars, or topless joints." He smiled at Michael. "Whatever it is, just do it with them, and get them to commit to business increases. I will check on the results quarterly, and if we aren't on target, you will hear from me. If we are at or above the target, you won't hear from me."

This management style was not wrong and was more of the Wharton School way of doing business: "Don't overmanage your employees or be a kindergarten manager, and don't talk

176

about target percentage results daily. Give your sales department time enough to do their jobs, but if the business isn't increasing exponentially, then come down hard on the underachievers."

At the beginning of the year, there was always a kickoff meeting at a bar or restaurant with underwriting and sales, including each department's management. The idea was to get everyone motivated to write more business for the upcoming year. The events were fun times, except when the bill came; since Michael was the newest employee present from the sales department, he usually got stuck with the bill. The bill always went on Michael's expense account. Since he was the new employee, his spender code was unused and below target. It made sense to break in the new expense account holder.

The kickoff meetings were to motivate employees to write business and thank them for the prior year, and they usually worked. At one kickoff meeting in particular, the bill came in, and it was more than $750 with the tip. Michael was a bit concerned about hitting his credit limit on his credit card, but it went through.

Usually, during those types of meetings, one saw the office affairs in full swing—in other words, who was fucking whom. Even though the folks tried to hide it, it was undeniable when they were making advances or making goo-goo eyes at each other all night. T. J. and Michael would usually figure out a pairing and watch for more office antics between the two. It was always a fun time because so much information was passed on without anyone noticing.

At the kickoff party in 1988, Michael met a loss-control rep who seemed infatuated with him, and she was drop-dead gorgeous. When a commercial account came into the branch to be quoted by underwriting, if the account qualified, the loss-control reps would ascertain if the account was quotable after underwriting submitted a request to inspect the account. They would make appointments with the commercial business, review their safety programs, and give recommendations to make the account a safer place to work and prevent losses from occurring—an integral part of an insurance company. She was ahead of her time because she dressed and talked provocatively and was fun to talk to. She immediately asked what Michael thought of her boob job, which was fairly new. Since Michael was a bit shy in talking about women's breasts during a first conversation, he indicated they were nice and accentuated her outfit, without sounding too interested.

Michael said, "It must be a problem to go on a loss-control appointment on a job site with all the construction workers staring at you with their tongues hanging down to the ground."

She said, "It's no big deal because I go up to them, slap them on their back, and ask them how their day is going, and they can't find any words to say." She laughed.

She introduced herself as Maryann Merryman, and when she shook a person's hand, she stuck her tits out even farther to gain some attention. As the conversation continued, she indicated her distaste for human resources and the manager who ran the department, Gene Davenport. One of Maryann's favorite outfits was a black miniskirt with a handcuff belt. Her manager told her not to wear it in the office, but she did anyway. That type of outfit generated a letter from HR or Gene to her manager, Dave Laythem, to talk to her about regular office attire and the handcuff belt. Maryann said Gene was jealous of her figure because Gene was a fat pig, had horrible taste in fashion, and had no intention of changing her outfit or dressing in the office. Her manager, Dave, was an asshole too but treated her fairly well because he liked the sexy outfits she wore and hated HR too.

At the kickoff meeting, Maryann seemed to pay a lot of extra attention to Michael, which made him interested in her. Michael told Maryann about his run-in with human resources and told her he almost hadn't gone to work for CIC because of Gene's incompetence and the letter she had written to him before he started at the company. Michael asked the usual questions regarding how long Maryann had been with the company and where she had worked before, and when he got to the question of marriage, she indicated she had been married for about five years. When Michael heard that statement, he backed off a bit because his only affair with a married woman had been the one he met in Corpus Christi. He'd felt horrible about the situation when he found out she was married, so he figured this would be a short conversation; however, Maryann had other plans.

While he tried to end the conversation and move on to the next person, she kept going on about her life—and she was hot looking. Michael could not find a way to move on to someone else. He usually was an expert at ending a conversation, but she wouldn't stop asking questions about his life. She was making it clear she wanted to talk to him.

Art happened by and said hello and indicated he needed to talk to Michael about a business issue. Art knew Maryann was married and had seen the conversation from the other side of the bar.

Art and Michael walked away, and Michael said, "Thank you for getting me out of that conversation, because she was getting way too friendly."

Art said, "No problem, but don't get too close to her, because she is married."

"I've already figured that part out, so thanks again for walking up and getting me out of the conversation. Don't go anywhere yet; let's pretend we are talking about an account, so it

doesn't look too suspicious or end the conversation too quickly."
They both laughed.

The party ended with everyone leaving the bar, and of
course, Michael had to pay the bill. He paid and was about to
leave, but it was a long drive home, so he thought he'd go to the
bathroom before leaving.

On his way out of the men's room, he ran into Maryann
leaving the ladies' room. Michael thought to himself, *Ah, she
was just waiting in the bathroom for me to walk by and continue
the conversation.*

She said, "Oh, hi again. Are you leaving now?"

"Yes, I am. It will be a busy day tomorrow. It was nice to
meet you finally. I've seen you in the office before, but no one
introduced us before tonight."

"Yes, likewise, and don't forget to invite me to all the future
happy hours you put together. They sound like fun, or at least
I've heard they are fun."

Michael said, "No problem, and by the way, one is coming
up next week at Midnight Rodeo."

Maryann said, "Goodbye, and remember, the quarterly loss-
control inspection for company cars is next Monday, so don't
forget to wash your car and clean it out over the weekend."

"Ah, thanks for the reminder. My car needs a wash badly. It's
a huge mess, mostly because of allowing Davis in my company
vehicle." They laughed because everyone knew Davis was a big
drinker and regularly trashed everyone's car. Davis was a pig,
and his piggish ways were legendary; when he rode in a car,
it was usually filled with empty beer cans when he exited the
vehicle.

Maryann gave him a big hug goodbye, which Michael wasn't
expecting, and she also decided to rub her big fake tits all over
his chest during the hugging process to make a point, maybe to

garner some interest from Michael or maybe even to give him semiwood. Either way, it worked, and Michael was at a loss for words.

"Okay, good night, Michael," she said with a shy grin. She walked away in such a sexy way that it would have made any male around drool uncontrollably.

The next day in the office, the talk was about the party from the night before, including how much fun it had been and all the information gained about the office affairs. Davis came out of his office and immediately said to Michael, "Maryann in loss control is married. It doesn't matter to me who you fuck, but so you know, it probably wouldn't be a good idea for you to hit on that situation."

Michael said, "I'm not hitting on her. She was hitting on me, and I'm not into the married thing, so a very true statement."

Michael questioned how Davis knew about the night before with Maryann.

"Damn it, Michael," Davis said, "it was my party, even though you paid for it, and it was obvious you two were talking extralong about whatever, so my estimation was you two were talking about fucking last night."

One never had to guess what was on Davis's mind; he always talked about a subject, gave his two cents' worth, and walked away, sometimes laughing uncontrollably. Davis and Michael were still on speaking terms at that point, though Davis told everyone about Michael's escapades with all the women in and out of the office. Only about half the stories were right, and no one could have lived up to that much action, but Davis was trying to sabotage Michael's future dates. It didn't work. Michael wasn't interested in Maryann, but she was interested in him.

The next Monday reared its ugly head, and Michael forgot about the company vehicle loss-control inspection. He was running late and pulled into the company parking lot, where all the other company drivers were parked, awaiting an assessment. *Oh fuck, the inspection*, Michael thought. He saw Maryann inspecting vehicles with other loss-control reps. He thought, *Maybe she will check my car and possibly pass the examination, especially since she is interested in me.* Michael laughed because his vehicle was in severe disarray, with beer cans everywhere and trash in the backseat.

He drove up to get in line and saw the management team talking about each person's vehicle. Michael thought, *All of this because of Hal's past indiscretions with his company car. What an asshole.* He laughed again.

He was two cars back, when Maryann saw his vehicle. He saw her smile while talking to the management types and doing inspections of the other company vehicles. The smile gave him some hope for passing the assessment; he knew the smile was meant for him. He looked into his backseat and saw several to-go sacks from different restaurants and trash of all sorts littered in the seat and thought, *Well, at worst, I can just blame it on agents I took out recently.* Most of his agents were pigs too. However, he didn't count on what was underneath all the trash in his backseat: a shitload of empty beer cans. They were his empty beer cans and those of Davis and other folks who had ridden in his company vehicle recently.

Michael's car was next in line to get inspected, and as he exited his company vehicle, he greeted Maryann with an uplifting "Good morning!"

Maryann looked at him, said good morning, and started to look his company car over. Michael asked how her weekend had gone, but she looked at him and whispered, "Don't ask; management is watching me do my job. Act like we do not know each other."

Maryann asked when his last oil change had been, and Michael pointed to his front windshield, where the answer was located. It indicated there were two thousand miles left until the next oil change. She then looked into the backseat, inspected all the trash and beer cans located there, and said, "This is a wreck." She looked at Michael with a smile and said, "Nothing has changed since the weekend?"

"No, not really," Michael replied. He was proud of the mess he'd left in his backseat; it was almost a badge of honor.

Davis, who was standing near his company car, gave her a look that said, "Don't fuck with this car, because it is in the protective zone."

Maryann checked the oil level and other items under the engine, checked again in the backseat, grabbed several empty beer cans, and threw them away in a trash can near where the inspections were going on. She looked at Michael and said, "A driver cannot have this many empty beer cans in a company vehicle, okay?"

Michael said, "Yes, I understand, but what if they are from the branch manager?"

She looked at him again and tried not to let anyone see her laugh. She said, "Okay, this one is okay. Excellent job."

As the inspection ended, he breathed a sigh of relief. The chief offenders were brought to the attention of the service department, the branch office's gestapo in disguise. Unfortunately, the chief offenders were the management staff.

Art's oil was so black that loss control concluded he never had changed his oil since the car was new, and the loss-control manager, Dave Laythem, had no oil in his company vehicle. Everyone was surprised his engine had not blown up, and he was embarrassed about his failure to take care of his car. Management at the branch office were always circulating memos telling employees to take care of their company vehicles, but the chief offenders were usually those sending the memos. It was typical of the management staff at CIC.

T. J. said, "The managers at this company are a joke, and this inspection proves these fuckers are the biggest fuckups at CIC." T. J. took his company vehicle seriously and took great care of it, mostly since he drove it most of the time, and he indicated Michael should do the same thing. The only problem with Michael's company car was that it was dirty, with many beer cans and who knew what else hiding in it. He took care of the car because it was the right thing to do.

The next happy hour was in full swing on Thursday with a larger-than-usual attendance from the branch office. Maryann showed up for the party too. Michael had asked her earlier in the week to wear her leather miniskirt and handcuff belt to the office if she took requests. They both had laughed at the comment, but she looked gorgeous at the happy hour.

After talking with some of her friends at the happy hour, Michael commented on her outfit and said he was thankful she took requests. Maryann said it was an excellent double dip because she wanted to look good at the party and also piss off Gene in human resources. She accomplished both that day.

Everyone enjoyed the music and drinks. After the crowd cleared out, only Maryann and Michael were left. Michael excused himself to the bathroom, and again, when he walked out, she was waiting for him, except this time, she planted a long kiss on his lips. Michael hadn't expected that to happen and kissed her back immediately.

Michael said, "You are married, and I'm not into married ladies."

Maryann asked, "You have a conscience?"

"Well, sort of. It came from someone recently. She didn't tell me she was married. It was complicated, but my conscience got the best of me. Tell me about your marriage."

"Nothing to tell," Maryann said. "I'm just bored with it all and looking to find someone else."

That statement didn't give Michael the warm feeling he was looking for in the conversation.

Maryann continued. "Why don't we get a hotel room and talk more about this situation? You want me as bad as I want you. Agreed?"

"Yes," Michael said, "but it would be very wrong."

"Wrong, yes, but very pleasurable for us both. I've heard rumors in the office about you, and I'm curious if they are real."

Michael laughed. "What stories? Davis makes up so much shit; if everything he said was right, my knees would have bandages around them." They both laughed.

Maryann said, "I've heard you're above average in many different areas."

"That's true, but the fact remains: you're married."

"I'm past that, and don't you like what you see?" She grabbed her breasts and rubbed them in Michael's face. They smelled beautiful and aromatic, like a perfume he hadn't encountered before, and he was beginning to give in to her attention.

Michael sat down, feeling a bit overwhelmed, and as soon as he did, a guy walked up to Maryann.

"Hey, dear, sorry I'm late." It was Maryann's husband.

Michael breathed a sigh of relief and hoped her husband hadn't seen his face full of Maryann's tits. It appeared he hadn't, and he was reasonably drunk too. They exchanged pleasantries and decided to leave after one dance. Michael bid farewell to them both and left the party. He was thankful Maryann's husband had shown up at the club.

On the drive home, he decided to avoid her in the future because it wasn't his type of deal. Michael knew Davis would give him more shit about Maryann tomorrow, but he didn't care. His bed looked inviting but a bit cold because he was alone.

During that time and most of his tenure at CIC, Michael played an excessive amount of golf with his agents, sometimes three times a week. His golf game was close to being a scratch game; he was an excellent golfer. Golf went hand in hand with Davis's annual motivational speech of blowing out a rep's expense account and playing golf with agents or doing whatever each agency owner wanted to do for fun to increase business.

Michael set up a golf game with Davis, Art, and a new agent at his country club. Even though Michael lived on Sharpstown Golf Course, he was a member of a private club called Riverside Country Club in West Houston. There was a big difference between the clubs, because Sharpstown was a public course, and Riverside was a private club. The idea was to get everyone together for five to six hours of golf, enjoy the day outdoors, and just have fun, with a little competition thrown in for good measure. It also provided a better working relationship, whether in the CIC office or in the agent's office.

The game that day was just like any other golf game, but Davis was in a joking mood, which was unusual. Davis enjoyed playing at a golf club he had never played before, so his attitude was different because he was not at his home course.

They played wolf to add a little intrigue to the equation. It was an entertaining game played all day with positive results for everyone involved. Davis loved to play golf and bet money.

Whenever Michael appointed new agents for his territory, his second question was "Do you play golf?" which had been Art Hower's second question to him when he interviewed for the job at CIC. Michael felt that appointing more agents who played golf would increase his chance of more play during the workweek.

After he asked if the agent or anyone in the agency played golf, the next question was "Where do you play golf?" Michael made it a point to play at every course located in and around the Houston, Corpus Christi, and Valley areas. During his tenure at CIC, the only golf course he never had had the opportunity to play was the Houston Country Club because it was exclusive and costly to join, so it was difficult to find someone who was a member. Joining was almost as difficult as joining Augusta National, where the Masters Tournament was played every year, because it was that exclusive. Those memberships were handed down through wills after members' deaths, and the few new memberships available were $150,000. Not many people had that kind of money to spend on a membership. Michael had played at River Oaks Country Club twice with an agent. It was at about the same level as the Houston Country Club, but the latter proved to be an elusive trophy to obtain.

As the years went by at CIC, Michael either appointed agents or had current agents in his territory who were all members of different golf clubs in the Houston area, including Raveneaux Country Club, Northgate Country Club, and Champions Country Club. All the bases were covered when it came to playing the best courses in town.

All agents had producers who reported to them and also worked for them to produce business. Most of the producers were friends of Michael's too, because that generated more business; plus, most of them were golfers. The producers were more fun to play golf with and not as serious as the agency owners. In particular, at least once a week, Michael played with two producers who'd attended high school together in Houston: Wes Anderson and Danny Graite. They were producers for different agencies. Most producers, including Wes and Danny, were around Michael's age, so they had a lot in common and enjoyed each other's company. In addition to Michael's golf game on Sunday, he played from two to three other rounds in any given week. It appeared he was a golf addict.

A lot of the weekday golf included tournaments or scrambles, which usually had nice trophies and prizes for the top three teams. It was golfing at its finest. Michael, Wes, and Danny made it a moral imperative to play golf once a week because they all loved to play golf and hang out afterward at the nineteenth hole, where they would talk business, drink a lot, and talk about women. Wes was divorced and single, and Danny had been married for ten years to the same woman, so the mix was perfect between the guys. Playing golf with them was usually like playing with a comedy team, maybe Martin and Lewis or the Three Stooges minus Larry. Not only was it fun and competitive, but something always happened to make it even crazier than it already was on the links.

Michael usually won at golf, but he planned and managed his golf game well. The better golfer between Wes and Danny was Wes, and since Wes was single and dating a woman whom Michael knew well and conducted business with, Michael knew how to screw up Wes's golf game. Michael always called her up at her office before the game started and asked her to call Wes in a few hours, after they began to play, to cause havoc and get him to stop concentrating on golf. Cell phones had finally become popular in the business arena. Everyone was using them, especially in business, but at that time, no one had thought of it as a heckling tool to win at golf. If Wes got too far ahead on the scorecard, Michael would call Wes's girlfriend, Sandy, and ask her to call Wes. She always called him soon afterward to harass him, and it appeared she liked fucking with Wes as much as Michael did. She would raise hell with him about one thing or another, and it always ended up with Wes blowing the golf game. It was convenient.

On another golf outing, the threesome played at a public course in Houston called Deer Creek Golf Club. Michael had grown up playing on Deer Creek and knew the golf course well. Even though it was a public course, it was challenging to play, especially the Master's Course. They had three different skill-level courses, and the Master's was always a tough round of golf.

It was the summer of 1989. On a weekday, the golf course was usually empty, and that day was no exception. They all arrived earlier than usual, about one o'clock, and given all the tomfoolery that happened that day, they arrived at the nineteenth hole around four o'clock, which was unusually early for them to finish playing golf. Wes loved Crown Royal, and Danny and Michael loved Weller, all bourbons, and after a hot round of golf, it was the perfect way to finish the day.

Wes and Michael liked their bourbon with Coke, but Danny always drank it straight with a glass of water. The water never really got lower in the glass, but the Weller sure did.

After about five rounds of drinks, it was only six thirty, so Danny said, "Hell, there is plenty of light left; it won't get dark for a few hours. Let's get our drinks and play some more golf!" Everyone laughed—not because it was funny but because they were all drunk, and Wes and Michael knew how this round would turn out, if they made it past the first hole.

They rode up to the first hole, and Michael and Danny drove their balls into the fairway. Wes, however, was hitting a good twelve inches behind the ball and could barely stand up straight.

Danny and Michael started laughing uncontrollably, and so did Wes because he could not make contact with the ball. After three tries, he finally hit the ball, and it went screaming down the fairway.

Wes continually hit about a foot behind the ball as the laughter continued, so they agreed to drive their golf carts over to the eighteenth hole and finish out from there. While they were driving, Michael turned his golf cart into Danny's cart, hit it hard, and knocked off a bumper plastic section. They all laughed louder as they arrived at the last hole.

They played their second shots, but Wes decided to ride up to the green with Michael because Danny's attempt was short of the green. He hit up onto the green, and Michael drove on the cart path next to the green. Michael turned around and saw Danny coming at full speed toward them, and Michael yelled to Wes, "Incoming!" They both exited the golf cart quickly as Danny slammed into their cart at full speed.

The impact was loud and violent, and the parked golf cart was struck so hard it ended up on top of the concrete barrier that separated the cart path from the grass. The eighteenth hole was next to the clubhouse, so when Danny's golf cart hit Michael's with a thunderous banging noise, Michael yelled at Danny, "Really? Right next to the fucking clubhouse?"

The only thing louder was the threesome's laughter. Thankfully, no one was hurt. The resulting crash always played in Michael's head in slow motion, especially when he brought it up to the other two in the future, because of the insanity of it all and the great memory too.

They sheepishly walked off the green to go back to the bar, or the nineteenth hole, to drink more, looking around to make sure no one had seen the golf cart wreck. The threesome knew everyone in and out of the bar had heard it because of the loud crashing noise. There were no golf marshals at the clubhouse, so they dodged a bullet and a golf cart that day, but more tomfoolery was to come.

The threesome were at it again the next week, when there was an altercation that became a barroom brawl at Deer Creek. As they hit their second shot on a par five that landed next to the green, they were waiting for another foursome to get off the green. An errant ball came screaming up to them about that time and stopped about five feet from Wes. Since Wes and Danny were big guys around 230 pounds apiece, they looked back in anger and shouted out, "Don't fucking hit on us, asshole!"

The foursome drove up behind them to rush the threesome even more, and Wes took his time because he wanted to say something to them as they drove their golf carts closer. They were about thirty yards back, when Wes screamed out loudly, "Don't fucking hit on us again, damn it!"

One guy screamed out, "We didn't!"

The answer incited Wes even more, and he loudly said, "Yes, you did, you dickhead motherfucker!"

The foursome were quiet behind them, as Wes and Danny were big guys, and it appeared the guy screaming back cowered down a bit.

As Wes, Danny, and Michael left the green, Michael looked at Wes and said, "Dickhead motherfucker? I like that combo!"

For the rest of the day, Michael called Wes a dickhead motherfucker, or DHMF for short, and the acronym and nickname stuck. They called each other that for the rest of their friendship—in a friendly way, of course.

As they finished the round and retired to the nineteenth hole for some bourbon, something unexpected unfolded. The foursome behind them walked in, sat down right next to them, and started talking trash. The loudest one was the smallest one, which happened most of the time. Coincidentally, the smallest guy was the one Wes had called a dickhead motherfucker earlier in the day.

Wes, Michael, and Danny looked at each other because they all knew the situation would get bad soon when the little guy said, "I don't appreciate being called a motherfucker, and you are an asshole."

Wes looked up from his Crown and Coke and said, "Don't hit up on us anymore, dickhead motherfucker, and I won't say anything to your shrimp ass." There it was again: DHMF.

The foursome looked at each other and stood up as Michael's threesome did the same. It was about to get real. The little guy walked up to Wes and said, "You think you're big, but you're probably just a wimp, asshole, so let's see what you have, fatso."

At that, Wes pushed the little guy so hard he went flying across the room and hit a table. Chairs went flying, and punches were thrown. Luckily, most punches missed. It was like a wrestling cage match since the room was so small. Everyone was drunk.

The fight ended quickly, with only a few punches hitting their mark, so Michael and the bunch chugged their drinks and left before the police could arrive. The place was quite a mess, with chairs and tables broken and scattered everywhere. A lull in the action ensued, so Wes, Danny, and Michael decided to exit the nineteenth hold for greener pastures.

The next day, a conference call happened with the three golf buddies to review the goings-on from the previous day. Michael started the conversation with "Hey, guys, we can't go back to

Deer Creek for a while because of the mess we made, not only in the nineteenth hole but also with the golf carts."

"They probably have golf hit men looking for us as we speak," Wes said.

Danny said, "My hand still hurts from hitting that guy's face. He must have downed a lot of milk growing up." They all laughed.

Michael said, "All right, I'm a member of Riverside Country Club, but we can't tear the shit out of the place like we did at Dear Creek, okay, guys? It doesn't matter how drunk we get; all the members know me there, and we can't get away with all that shit we did on the public course, okay? I know how you guys treat golf carts, like a destruction derby, so no more head-on collisions. And, Wes, stop pissing on the back of your golf cart in the open; there are plenty of bathrooms on the course, and they're called trees. Most of the time, you guys end up running over my golf ball on purpose and parking your golf cart on top of my golf ball, and we can't do that at my private club, damn it! Plus, Danny, you can't scream out, 'Wet, hairy pussy!' every time you miss a putt either. The tomfoolery has to be at a minimum at my club, okay? If we can all agree to a few rules, we can play at my club, but we have to behave like gentlemen on my home course."

Wes and Danny kind of said yes under their breath, so Michael said, "I didn't catch that answer."

"Okay, okay, tomfoolery is at a minimum at your club, damn it." Wes ended the conversation by saying, "The private clubs sure do take a lot of fun out of playing golf, but I think it is a good idea to stay away from Deer Creek for a while because of all the damage we caused."

"Yeah, true," Michael said, "and we may be banned from the place anyway." The phone call ended as everyone laughed at the situation.

Michael also took out other agents and would invite other CIC employees so everyone could get better acquainted, and it was good for business. Michael invited the underwriting manager, Marco, to his home course once because he felt it might help business writings if an agent got to know the underwriting manager. Michael knew no one like Marco, but maybe he would act differently under fun circumstances, such as a golf outing, he thought. Michael had heard a few stories about Marco's shitty attitude on the golf course and his poor scorekeeping, but he wanted to see if it was true or not. *How can one play awfully all day and still beat everyone on the course?* Michael wondered. Everyone questioned the final scorecard, but since he had the power to make or break an agent, no one bitched, and they let him win.

At Michael's home course, he played with Marco and a new agent he'd appointed a year ago who was producing well. Michael thought maybe this would help business writings even more in the future.

The round of golf turned out well, until the seventh hole. Michael talked to the agent while Marco was about to putt. Marco wore all white and looked like an ice cream man. He had already messed his shirt up with all the food he'd eaten at lunch—typical Marco. As Marco leaned over to pick his ball up, it was undeniable he sharted his pants, because the stain went through his underwear and bled through to his white shorts. The back of his white shorts was now brown with a large skid mark down his ass.

Michael looked at the agent in disgust and said, "Did you just hear that car?"

The agent said, "No, I didn't."

Michael said, laughing, "It was the sound of a vehicle *skidding* its tires." Obviously, the joke was about the skid mark on the back of Marco's shorts. It took everything the agent had not to bust out laughing, especially at the look of disgust Michael had on his face.

The golf round concluded at the nineteenth hole with a few drinks, talk of business, and more food for Marco to spill on his shirt during the process. Michael was ready to go because no one could stand to be around Marco for long, so everyone left the course. As Michael had heard from management, Marco was a horrible golfer.

On the way back to their vehicles, Marco told Michael, "That agent will never be a good producer for the company, and what a wasted day it was," instead of thanking him for a great golf day out of the office.

Michael said, "Well, check out their production, Marco; the agency is already producing very well and will do better because they have committed a large book of business to us."

Marco not only was a dumbass with a shitty attitude and poor eating skills but also could not effectively wipe his ass. He was not a person to spend a lot of time with, and Michael never again took him out on a golf day. Michael always wondered what Marco's wife said when he came home with the big skid mark on the back of his shorts. After Michael filled everyone in on the skid mark situation from the previous day, most of the office agreed his wife must be a slave to Marco or maybe just a talented clothes washer. It didn't matter how much one took Marco out to play golf or out to lunch; his attitude was always the same, so why waste time? There was no way to get on his right side, and Michael mostly ignored him, as he did Davis. The approach proved one thing: if one ignored people, the person seemed to get their attention without trying hard, because no one liked to be ignored.

After the laughter died down in the office about Marco's golf day, which became known as "the brown shorts day," Michael usually played golf two or sometimes three times during a workweek. He played most of the time with Wes and Danny but other times with different agents in his sales territory. Some were scrambles or tournament play, and other times, he played to build camaraderie with an agent, so his golf game became outstanding. Living on a golf course did not hurt his game either, and being a member of a private club was icing on the cake.

While visiting with an underwriter about an account, he found out that underwriter, Tom Bailey, was a golfer. He was a member of a little-known course in West Houston called Dovetail Golf Course. Michael hadn't heard about the golf course and wanted to add it to his list of courses he'd played. Tom invited him out after work one day when it was convenient sometime soon, because Tom lived within a mile of the golf course.

A week later, Michael asked Tom about golf the next afternoon, and they agreed to meet at the course at about two o'clock. The underwriting staff at CIC included about fourteen underwriters, so no one would notice if one was missing. Tom indicated to his supervisor he was playing golf with an agent that day, to ensure he wouldn't be missed. Tom was an approachable underwriter, unlike most underwriters, but amusingly, he looked and talked like Vincent Price, the horror movie actor, though a better-looking Vincent Price. Tom was, in fact, a Vietnam veteran who'd been assigned to an artillery unit and seen his share of horror and all the crazy shit in Vietnam.

It didn't seem to affect him much, and he came out of the war unscathed, unlike some of his Vietnam-era war buddies.

Michael spoke to Tom about meeting some buddies out that night, so unless something crazy happened, which it usually did, he would be at the course around two o'clock after making sales calls on agents in the morning.

As luck had it, Michael met a lady that night at a club called Studebaker's, a.k.a. Stud Broker's, which usually attracted an older crowd, but there were also younger ones to choose from too. The gal Michael met was a good eight to ten years older than he was, but he didn't give a shit; he was still trying to get over Alicia and couldn't have cared less whom he met or their ages. It turned out the lady, Jackie, was in sales too. Michael invited her to the golf outing the next day and gave her some crappy directions to the golf course—not on purpose, but he was having a good time slamming bourbon shots. Michael didn't believe she would show, but she was a short-haired blonde with a killer body, his target market, so if she made it, great, and if not, no big deal.

The golf day was a perfect day. The course was old, outdated, and not what Michael used to, but it was fun. After the seventeenth hole, Jackie pulled up in her car, exasperated. She said, "I finally found this damn course. Really shitty directions, Michael!"

Michael apologized and gave her a beer to shut her up. He introduced her to Tom, and they went to the nineteenth hole to chat for a bit. After all the pleasantries were over, Tom excused himself to go home to his wife but said Michael should show Jackie the course because it wouldn't be dark for another hour or so, and the golf cart was parked next to the bar, or the nineteenth hole.

Michael obliged and showed her the course, but around the fifteenth hole, Jackie indicated she had to pee badly after all the driving around and the beers they'd drunk. They were right next to a large, bushy tree, and after pulling up her dress to relieve herself, she came back to the cart with her silk hose in her hand. Since Michael was no slouch in the female department, he knew what that meant: she was ready for some action.

The sun was getting low in the western sky, and they started to kiss in the golf cart. Her dress was strapless. After a few minutes of making out, he pulled down the top part of her dress to expose her tits, which he happily enjoyed for about ten minutes. The thought of the parking garage record crossed his mind, but he decided he would work on that with her in the future.

He went down south for a bit until she made a loud but pleasing noise, but he raised his head when he heard a car approaching. They acted as if they were just enjoying the view from the golf cart. After the car passed, it was her turn, and she did a great job and had things finished up within about fifteen minutes.

As they drove back to their vehicles, they agreed to meet for dinner off Westheimer, near Dairy Ashford, to get to know each other better. Since they had worked up an appetite on the golf course, they were hungry. They already had exchanged business cards the night before, so they kissed goodbye until the next meeting after they ate dinner.

The next day, Friday, Michael was in the office, gearing up for the weekend, and he thought about thanking Tom for the golf outing. When he went over to the underwriting department, Tom hung his phone up and said, "Hey!"

Michael opened up with how much fun the game had been and thanked him for a great afternoon of golf.

Tom was curious about how things had gone with Jackie.

"I showed her the course," Michael said, "and then we went to have dinner afterward."

Tom asked, "Did you see anyone else out on the course?"

Michael immediately went into damage control, because someone must have seen him getting a blow job on the course or worse. "Yeah, there were a couple of other folks out there, from what I remember."

"Ah, okay," Tom said. "The golf pro called me this morning and said he saw a couple out on the course in a golf cart, getting very friendly."

"Hmm," Michael said, "wonder how that could have happened and why people would do anything like that on a golf course."

Tom looked at Michael sheepishly, as if he knew he was not being truthful, much like Vincent Price would have done in a movie, and it took everything Michael had in his body and soul not to start laughing out loud. Michael knew he was caught, but he was smart enough not to admit any wrongdoing on a golf course. His philosophy was "Always deny everything, unless someone produces a picture, and then keep on denying." It would be challenging to explain to anyone why he'd gotten a blow job or gone down on a gal in a golf cart on a golf course, so he would just play dumb about the situation.

Michael thanked Tom and excused himself, claiming he had a meeting, which was bullshit; he was just trying to get out of digging the hole deeper. Plus, he could not hold in his laughter any longer.

He went back to the sales department and told the story to T. J., and T. J. could not stop laughing during and after the story. "Do you always get a blow job on a golf course?" T. J. asked. "Maybe I should take golf up as a hobby too."

Michael laughed and said it couldn't hurt. "We both had a rib eye steak afterward, and my strength finally came back after all of that nonsense."

They both laughed uncontrollably, and Art came out of his office to figure out what all the laughter was about in the sales department. "What the hell is going on out here?" Art asked.

T. J. explained the situation. "Michael got a blow job at Tom Bailey's golf course yesterday."

Art laughed and said, "You got a blow job from Tom yesterday?"

T. J. roared with laughter, and Michael said, "No, a new lady met us at the golf course, and one thing led to the next."

Art asked if Tom had watched while it was going on.

Michael said, "No! He'd already left the course."

Art loved ribbing people, especially his sales reps, because he got a charge out of it. As long as it wasn't Monday, Art was always ready for a good story or a good joke. That day was no exception, but Michael grew tired of all the bullshit he was getting from Art and walked outside for a breath of fresh air and had a smoke.

Unfortunately, someone saw him smoking a cigarette from her office window. It was Sheila, one of the parking-garage-record victims. Sheila was not like Deborah. She wasn't crazy or jealous but was someone nice to shoot the shit with and talk about anything under the sun with.

She asked how things were going, since they hadn't talked in a while. Michael apologized and said things were crazier than ever, trying to make an excuse for why he hadn't called her recently. She asked if anyone had brought up the parking garage incident or asked why they had been in the parking garage, doing whatever. She smiled from ear to ear while asking the question, which Michael picked up on quickly. She was ready for round two, Michael thought.

Michael answered, "Not a word from anyone about anything." They both laughed. "Things have slowed down some upstairs, and we passed the audit recently, so the pressure is off for a bit. Maybe we could have a drink sometime soon." Michael could see her mind was hard at work, trying to form an answer or maybe an excuse.

Sheila said, "Yeah, sure, how about tonight? It is Friday."

Michael said, "Great. Do you want to come over to my condo or meet somewhere?"

She said, "Let's go out after work today and figure it all out from there."

Michael agreed and indicated he would come down to her office after five o'clock. She had on a beautiful white dress, and as she walked back to her office, he watched her walk into the building. Michael thought, *Wow, she is a hottie.* The only problem was, he'd just met Jackie, and he wasn't over Alicia yet, so he knew it was not going to turn out well for either one of these two hotties. He decided he was going to play the field until he figured everything out in his head.

Five o'clock hit, and Michael was in the elevator, heading to the first floor and Sheila's office. He walked in and asked, "Where to, gorgeous?"

She indicated there was an icehouse down the street. Before she could finish her sentence, Michael said, "The icehouse at 610 and 59? Yep, I'm familiar with it because we often have sales meetings at that location." They both laughed and left the building.

Michael grabbed a few beers at the bar, and they sat down at an empty table. It was Friday and a gorgeous day. It was difficult to find a good table, but Michael was a regular customer, and they found a nice table. Sheila asked about the audit and if everything had turned out okay. Michael answered, "Yeah, it turned out very well for all of us, and we still have our jobs." They both laughed.

About that time, Davis and Art pulled up in their cars and decided to join the party. Michael introduced everyone, and immediately, Davis began to talk to Sheila. He clearly was hitting on Sheila, but Michael wasn't worried because she ignored Davis to talk with Art and Michael. Sheila told Michael later she thought Davis was a gross person with a caveman's personality.

The conversation centered on the audit, Art's hiring of Michael a few years ago, and how well things were going for the branch office and Michael too. Art knew the discussion would burn the shit out of Davis. After all, Art knew Sheila was not interested in him in the least.

After about six rounds of beer, Sheila excused herself to go to the ladies' room. Davis looked at Michael and asked, "Are you banging her tonight?"

Michael nodded with a smile, and Davis got up and left the table. Michael looked at Art and said, "I hate poor losers." They both laughed, when Sheila arrived back at the table.

She asked, "What's so funny?"

"Davis got pissed off and left the icehouse."

Sheila said, "That's a good thing," and Art and Michael laughed again.

Art left soon afterward, and Michael said, "We could finish the day off at my condo if you're interested."

She didn't say a word; she just grabbed his hand and followed him to his condo.

It was a late night, and Michael was concerned with all the noise he was creating, because his walls were thin, but he didn't care; he was celebrating two nights in a row. Maybe he was on his way back from the debacle with Alicia.

After a few hours of action, Sheila was ready to leave, so they kissed after he walked her to the door. She indicated that was the most fun she'd had in a good while. Michael said they would do it again soon.

Jackie was a hottie, but she'd met Michael at the wrong time in his life. Alicia had just broken up with him, so Michael had decided to utilize the Hammer Protocol to get over Alicia. The Hammer Protocol had been Michael's invention to help his friends out when a gal broke up with them. It worked for him too, especially after the two nights in a row with Jackie and Sheila, because he started to feel better after the breakup with Alicia. Michael felt like the best unlicensed psychologist on the street, because everyone came to him for advice on women, and at that juncture in his life, the biggest problems his friends had always involved women. The Hammer was an easy fix to get guys through the tough weeks after a breakup.

Michael counseled his brokenhearted friends to listen to his help using the Hammer Protocol, saying, "Listen, it's over with your girlfriend, so pick yourself up, and utilize the Hammer Protocol." Everyone usually questioned what the Hammer Protocol was, so Michael indicated a person needed to party a lot and sleep with every willing female out there until the ex-girlfriend in question was out of his mind. The Hammer worked 100 percent of the time, and within a few weeks, everything returned to normal for his friends, and they were thankful for the advice and the Hammer Protocol.

While Michael was utilizing the Hammer, Jackie invited Michael over for dinner the next Saturday night, but he had plans with his friend Chuck. She said, "Ask him too!"

"Are you sure? One never really wants to feed the wild animals, you know."

Jackie laughed and said, "Be here at seven thirty."

Michael agreed and showed up with Chuck at the appointed time with an Italian valpolicella since she was cooking spaghetti. Michael thought, *The blow job was pretty good on the golf course recently, so what the hell? Maybe it will be round two.* He gave Chuck directions, and they met at her apartment complex. When they showed up at her apartment, she had another friend with her, her next-door neighbor. Chuck wasn't impressed by the gal, so he wanted to eat and get the hell out of her apartment to find more entertainment elsewhere, but that was Chuck.

The spaghetti was pretty good, the wine was too, and the conversation was cordial. They all sat down to watch a movie on Jackie's VCR, and about halfway through, Chuck indicated he needed to leave, and so did her girlfriend. With all the garlic in the spaghetti, everyone kept getting up to fake going to the bathroom, but everyone was busy farting uncontrollably. Garlic did that to everyone. The next day, Michael would find out that Chuck didn't make it to the exit gate of Jackie's apartment complex without blowing out five to ten farts. Michael saw him drive off and wondered why his car windows were down. It wasn't that hot out, but they laughed about it a bunch the next day during a phone conversation.

It was time for round two after everyone left the apartment, and it was one for the books too, especially with the blow job. Michael felt a bit melancholy, thinking about Alicia, so after he finished, he got up, kissed her goodbye, and left. He wasn't sure if it was how he felt or the number of farts escaping his body, but he didn't feel right with this new gal. Michael wasn't sure if he wasn't over Alicia, but there was a hint of gas in the air that made the evening a little less pleasant.

The next Monday was like any other; everything was empty, including Michael's energy level. The usual phone calls from friends on Monday to talk about who'd gotten laid the most over the weekend and who was the winner of the contest were the day's talk. Everything was back to normal. Utilizing the Hammer Protocol left Michael feeling empty, even though most of his body was empty too. He thought, *There is no way I'm ever going to meet anyone worth a shit by acting like this, so maybe I should try out something new in the future, such as a relationship. Well, probably not.*

It was lunchtime, and the regular report to T. J. about the weekend goings-on was on tap at their favorite Mexican restaurant. Usually, T. J. drove, but since it had rained that day, Michael offered to drive, as there were puddles of water everywhere, and he thought it was time to catch up on the contest.

They had lunch at their favorite Mexican restaurant and talked about business and monkey business, with a joke or two thrown in for fun. As they left, Michael perused several laborers standing about two blocks away. He counted seven and knew this would put him into the lead in the tomfoolery contest.

T. J. was oblivious to his plan, so they walked to Michael's company car and got in. The setup was perfect, with puddles everywhere and laborers waiting near a bus stop, and the lead in the contest was awaiting a new champion. Michael took a different exit out of the parking lot, and T. J. said, "This is a new way out of here. Where are we going?"

Michael didn't say a word. He gunned the gas to gain some speed, and the reality of what was about to happen garnered T. J.'s attention.

"Oh shit!" T. J. saw the upcoming water puddle and the laborers standing there oblivious to the speeding car coming their way.

As Michael's vehicle hit the standing water, he saw the laborers' faces, which looked like faces of disgust and anger, but some were laughing too. The tidal wave hit the intended targets as the laborers used hand gestures and four-letter words to let Michael know they were not happy about getting soaked.

The car hit the puddle with such force that no one escaped getting soaked, and soon afterward, loud noises of laughter sounded in the company car. Michael almost lost control of the vehicle because he was laughing so hard. T. J. couldn't stop laughing either.

When Michael and T. J. regained composure, Michael said, "The total is now seven, and I'm in the lead."

T. J. said, "Oh fuck, you're right."

They arrived at the branch unscathed and in a cheerful mood because of the lunchtime antics. They reported back to Susan Taggert, the new leader in the unholy contest. Susan's hair was usually immaculate but was messed up a bit as she asked about the happenings at lunch. T. J. knew right away she'd had lunch with her boyfriend and asked how lunch had gone, plus the dessert portion. Susan said, "Fuck you, T. J." He laughed because he knew she had blown the guy at lunch and because her hair was messed up. It was just another Monday at the branch office.

In two weeks was the annual insurance agents' convention, and this year, it was in Corpus Christi. Davis called a meeting after lunch in the big conference room. T. J. and Michael knew it was essential to attend to see what was going on in the branch office.

The big conference room meeting included Davis, Art, Michael, Susan, and T. J., and Michael started the meeting with "What's up?"

Davis said, "A good question. The annual independent agents' convention is in two weeks at the Hershey Hotel in Corpus Christi."

Michael interrupted and said, "Yes, I'm familiar with that hotel. It overlooks the bay in Corpus. I usually stay there when I'm working the area. And to top it off, there was a murder in the Hershey Hotel, and I'm sure charges will be filed against me because my DNA is in just about every hotel room."

The whole room broke up with laughter; even Susan laughed, because she knew Michael spent a lot of time in Corpus, and she'd heard many stories from T. J. about his liaisons in the hotel.

After the laughter died down, Davis continued with his speech. "I will be on vacation in two weeks, and Art's wife is having surgery, so I'm putting Michael and T. J. in charge of this convention and the hospitality room."

Susan spoke up. "Isn't that like putting a fox in charge of the henhouse?"

Everyone laughed again, but Davis said, "T. J. and Michael have done this before. I'm convinced the hospitality room will be a success, so blow your expense accounts out, and get some fucking business in the process, okay? There is also a golf tournament, and I assume, Michael, you will want to play in this tourney?"

"Oh, hell yeah, because my team usually wins the damn thing every year. I'll put together a great team within two weeks."

T. J. had to make a joke and bring up the past, but that was T. J. He asked if he could play tennis at the convention, joking about the time Davis's balls had been hanging out of his tennis shorts.

Susan cried out, "Please stop, T. J.!"

Davis was oblivious to the conversation, even though T. J. was talking about him. In Davis's mind, that was long forgotten.

Everyone asked about Art's wife and her upcoming procedure. It was a minor surgery, and everyone was relieved to hear the news.

After the meeting adjourned, T. J. and Michael were already coming up with plans to make it a convention to remember.

"Well, what do you think, T. J.?"

"Hmm, I'm thinking we will have a shitload of fun, and that is about it, but let's have a planning meeting about it and fuck off for a bit. I'm kind of tired today."

"Okay, I'm kind of tired too," Michael said. "It was a busy weekend." Any planning meeting with T. J. included a nap to get motivated, especially if it was just the two of them. "Let's go up to the life department and use their small conference room to plan for the convention and get some rest." They both laughed.

They laughed most of the way to the conference room on the fourth floor. They rested their feet on a few chairs and took a thirty-minute nap since both of them were fatigued from the weekend. T. J. had polka-danced with his wife all weekend, and Michael had been partying late every night and having sex all weekend. They joked that they were both happy to be back at work to get some rest.

A knock on the conference room door woke them both up. It was Ted O'Rourke, the life insurance manager. "I know you guys asked for permission to use the conference room, but all I've heard is a lot of snoring. Either that or prehistoric T. rex noises." All three laughed. "What the hell are you guys doing here?"

"Oh, sorry," Michael said. "We are planning for the convention in two weeks in Corpus, but we are both beat up from the weekend, so we figured a power nap was in order. It's kind of like a motivating thing for both of us."

Ted laughed so hard he sat down in the conference room to gain his composure. Ted didn't give a shit because he depended on the property-casualty reps, such as T. J. and Michael, to help obtain life insurance business from their agency force and always welcomed them to use his conference room. The relationship T. J. and Michael had built up with their agency force always helped Ted meet his targets, and he was grateful for the help. Ted had a great sense of humor and was always current with CIC's latest corporate information and was an invaluable asset to have as a friend. He always knew about corporate changes or CIC employee changes before anyone else, and the relationship was a good one and valuable too.

Ted continued. "So where is the convention going to be this year?"

Michael said, "In Corpus Christi, and we are planning all the convention's ins and outs after a motivating nap."

Ted laughed and said, "Understandable, so I'll let you guys get back to work then. By the way, did you hear CIC is looking to expand through corporate buyouts of competing companies?"

"No, we didn't hear that," T. J. said, "but we are growing by leaps and bounds, and it's very doubtful this will affect us much."

"Okay, I just wanted you guys to know this fact."

"Thanks, Ted," they both said.

"Back to the grind of planning the convention," Michael said. After Ted left the room, Michael asked T. J., "How do we handle the booze and all that stuff?"

T. J. said, "The hotels charge an arm and a leg for alcohol, so we will run by the liquor store before checking in, buy a shitload, and smuggle it into the hotel. Then all we have to do is buy a fifth or two of bourbon from the hotel and save the company money. Of course, there is a fudge factor involved." T. J. laughed.

"What's the fudge factor?" Michael asked.

"Well, you know rum is my favorite, and you like bourbon, right?"

"Yes, of course, and beer too."

"Well, we buy a bunch of alcohol and take some for our usage, but we can't get too greedy, okay?"

"Not a problem," Michael said. "So who is going to handle making the reservations and all that nonsense?"

T. J. said, "We will get Susan to do it," and they both laughed. "She's in a good mood today since she got laid at lunch, and it will be easier to ask; plus, she is used to doing this sort of thing. She gets to go to the convention too, and it won't be a problem. All good news because one never wants to piss Susan off, because she has gotten sales managers fired in the past."

"All sounds good, so the meeting is adjourned?"

As they left the conference room, they thanked Ted for the use of the room. Ted said, "That was a brief meeting!"

"Oh yeah, the longest part was the nap," Michael said, and they all laughed.

On the elevator ride down, T. J. said, "With management not in attendance, this will be the best convention ever, and we will have a crazy weekend and hospitality room."

"Agreed. I'm not bringing a date," Michael said. "There are a few customer service reps I've been working on, and they are playing hard to get."

"Okay, we will plan to leave on Wednesday, or a week and a half from today, so start getting ready for a crazy-ass weekend."

"I'm looking forward to it, especially the part about management not being involved." They both laughed.

The week and a half flew by, and Michael, T. J., and Susan met at the Hershey Hotel in Corpus Christi on Wednesday. They took T. J.'s vehicle to the liquor store. Michael was familiar with the store because he had bought alcohol there many times in the past.

"Hmm, let's start with the fudge-factor end of things," T. J. said. "Get a few bottles of your favorite, and I'll get mine and a few cases of beer that we can put in our company cars for later on." They both laughed and went through the store, picking out their favorites, plus other different kinds of alcohol, including vodka, bourbon, rum, and tequila. They also rented a margarita machine. The bill was around $850, and they paid with Michael's credit card.

"Wow, that's a lot of booze!" Michael said.

They went back to the hotel and unloaded the boxes of alcohol, which T. J. had labeled as "Visual presentations." It was a way of throwing off the hotel management, because they usually got angry if outside alcohol was brought into the hotel, which meant they couldn't overcharge for drinks.

"So you're going to order the food for the hospitality room from the hotel, right?" asked Michael.

"Oh yeah, but let's look at the menu together and figure out what we want first." They both laughed loudly.

After that was finished, Michael said he had to make a few phone calls about the golf tournament tomorrow and see who was playing. Since that was Michael's territory, he knew who the best golfers were in any given city, and it was better to win than not win, so he figured he would try to get the best team in place for the tournament.

An agent who represented CIC, Mark Williamson, indicated the best golfer in Corpus was a guy named Steve Paine, a producer for an agent who did not represent CIC.

"Ah," Michael said, "are you friends with him?"

"Hell yes, and he teaches golf when he is not selling commercial insurance, damn it."

"See if you can get him on the team, and tell him you're playing with CIC's sales guy who handles and appoints agents in the Corpus Christi area."

Mark said, "I don't want you to do business with him, because many of my business clients are with CIC, and I don't need any more competition from other agents, okay?"

"Don't worry about that; I just want to win tomorrow, so find out if he wants to play on our team."

"Okay, I'll see what the game plan is, and I'll see you on the links tomorrow." They hung up.

T. J., Michael, and Susan were getting the hospitality room in order on Wednesday night because it opened the next night, and Michael would be at the golf tournament all day the next day. As they went through the boxes they unloaded from the company cars, they inspected the spoils, or the fudge-factor booze, first and got the margarita machine in working order.

"Ah, my fudge factor has gotten bigger," Michael said, because he had two fifths of bourbon, a fifth of tequila, and a case of beer.

T. J. said, "Wow, one hell of a party when you get home," and they both laughed. T. J. got his three bottles of high-end rum out of the box.

Everything was set up for a fun weekend, and they adjourned to downtown Corpus to enjoin some delicious seafood. Corpus Christi had many seafood restaurants in the downtown area, and the seafood was always excellent. An argument broke out about who would pay the bill between T. J. and Michael. They flipped a coin, and T. J. lost.

"I'll order another drink before the bill comes," Michael said. T. J. was not happy about his loss but paid the bill anyway without Michael ordering another drink. "It's okay, T. J. I'll need to be reasonably sober at the golf tourney tomorrow. If the urge hits me, I'll just open up one of my bottles in my room." They laughed.

T. J. said, "No date tonight?"

"Nope, I'm saving myself for the hospitality room and the rest of the weekend. I am getting older, you know," Michael joked.

"Ah yes, things start to fall off when you get older, and hair grows where it shouldn't, like in your nose and ears. Too bad doctors haven't figured out how to transplant nose and ear hair to your head yet, damn it," T. J. said. His hair was falling out, and he was almost bald.

"Let's get some rest; it's a big day tomorrow. I'm sure you two are going to your rooms to get some sleep, so see you both tomorrow afternoon." Michael left the table and walked back to the Hershey Hotel, which was only two blocks away. When he got to his room, he opened one of his bottles, took a bourbon shot, and was out fast.

The next day, Michael showed up at the golf tournament at Blue Hills Golf Club and hit some balls to get warmed up and ready for the tournament. He walked up to Mark Williamson and asked, "Mission accomplished?" Mark just nodded.

Mark and Michael rode together in the cart with the other two players behind them. They listened to the golf marshal's instructions and, soon afterward, were off to their first hole: hole number eight, a par five. Everyone introduced himself, but obviously, Mark and Michael knew each other and had conducted business together.

After the introductions, they talked about who was the longest off the tee box. Michael always felt, and had proven, he was the longest, because he could drive the ball well over three hundred yards consistently. Mark knew that and suggested Michael be the fourth person in the foursome to tee off. The kid or Randy would lead it off because he wasn't that good of a golfer. Steve would go next because he was so accurate with his shots, followed by Mark and then Michael to clean up if the balls were in good shape. Then Michael could hit it as hard as he could to get a better distance, because this was a scramble golf tournament, or best ball, meaning the team figured out the best shot, moved their ball to the best shot, and kept going until the hole was played out.

Mark's and Steve's shots were in great shape in the fairway, so Michael took out his driver—or the mallet, as he called it—and swung hard. The ball ended up about 320 yards out, which left about 220 yards to the green.

Steve commented on the drive. "Wow, what a drive! Can you do that all the time?"

"Hell yes, just ask Mark."

Mark said, "Yep, Michael is long off the tee box."

They moved their golf balls to where Michael's ball was located and thought about their second shot. "Hmm, well, what is everyone hitting?" Michael said.

Everyone except Steve was hitting a five iron. Steve was hitting a six iron. Mark and Randy shanked their shots, but Michael's shot was about twelve feet from the cup. Steve walked up and hit a gorgeous shot about six feet from the pin. If there had been a crowd present, they would have been screaming and hollering like on the PGA tour, and everyone in the foursome screamed and hollered like a big crowd. They drove up to the green and were in awe of the shot.

"Do we need to get out of the cart?" Randy asked.

"Well, let's at least take a few shots at the putt," Mark said. "I mean, one of us will make it without even trying."

Mark sank the putt for an eagle on the first hole—what a way to start the day off.

After a few holes of the same type of play, Steve got up enough guts to ask if CIC was looking for any new agents, because CIC was a sought-after company in the insurance world.

Michael replied, "Of course we are, but it's a pretty stiff commitment for the first couple of years production-wise. Most agents have to commit to around two million in business the first two years, and not a lot of agents can pull that off."

Steve asked, "So I'm speaking to the right person, right? You're not in the life department but work in the property-casualty end of things, correct?"

"Yep, that would be me."

"Oh hell, why didn't you say so? I'll pull out my best game now and show you how this shit is done!"

"You mean this hasn't been your best game so far? We are six under par after five holes!"

"Hell no, we should go in at about seventeen under par, so hold on to your golf socks; we are going to rock now," Steve said. "Do you know I teach golf as a hobby?"

"No fucking way," Michael replied. "I didn't."

"You've got a hell of a swing," Steve said. "You just need a few refinements, and with a little help from me, free of charge, your golf game will improve tremendously."

Michael laughed. "Let's keep playing, because I'm going to need a beer after the next few holes, especially if we keep playing like this. By the way, here is my card."

Mark was not excited about this turn of events, but nothing had happened except an exchange of business cards and great golf. Michael thought, *Wow, free golf lessons and a new appointment! Hmm, this is a perfect day.*

The tournament ended just how it had started, and Michael's team finished at seventeen under par for the day. The closest team was fifteen under par. Michael's team took first place and received a big trophy and a fat gift card to use in the pro shop for golf shirts, golf balls, and other golf items. Usually, the winning team received a $300 gift card for the pro shop, but the prize had gone up to $400 apiece for the winning team since the tournament was full. There were also side games, such as closest to the hole on all par threes and longest drive on the par-five holes. As the other golfers finished and came in to report their scores, Michael's team were curious to see the winners of the tournament and if their closest-to-the-pin and long drives stood up against the competition. As it turned out, it was a banner day for the team because Michael and Mark won the longest-drive competition, and Steve won the closest to the hole on the par threes. The other teams were pissed that no one won a damn thing except for Michael's team. There were some giveaways after the trophies were presented, but they were mostly trash. Everyone was disappointed not to win a damn thing that day, except for Michael's team, who were ecstatic.

Just about all the agents Michael had appointed in the Corpus Christi area were present that day and were not happy to see him playing and winning with another agent. But Michael thought, *Hell, they didn't invite me, so fuck them.*

A few of the agents came up to Michael after the trophies were presented and said, "I didn't know you were playing today, Michael."

Michael thought to himself, *Yeah right, you fucker.* Michael's mind wandered off for a bit. *Hmm, let's see. I've fucked your customer service rep. I've fucked two of your service reps, and*

I'm glad they don't talk to each other. He laughed to himself. Michael said aloud, "It was a last-minute thing," as his mind stopped wandering about fucking all the customer service reps.

Michael went to talk with one agent in particular because he had a hot red-haired gal as one of his customer service reps, and Michael wanted to get to know her better. Michael asked the agent, "Are you coming to the hospitality room tonight?"

"I didn't know CIC had one, but I'll be there!"

"Make sure you invite your entire agency because we are blowing the thing out tonight!"

"Okay, no problem," the agent said as Michael wandered off to get a beer.

Michael had to leave soon afterward because the hospitality room opened at eight, and it was already five thirty. He bid everyone goodbye and invited them all to the hospitality room later in the evening. It would be a night for the record books and a hospitality room that no one would ever forget.

Michael took a quick shower and went to the hospitality room an hour and a half before it opened at eight. The other CIC employees were already in attendance. Susan had brought her husband and talked him into being the bartender for the night. He mostly served margaritas and tequila shots that night, and for his trouble, his payment was free alcohol all night, so he wasn't bitching. It was probably the most work he had done over the last few years.

The food arrived at seven forty-five, and everyone was busy getting set up for the party. T. J. looked at Michael and said, "At least Davis isn't here to screw up the evening."

"Why is that?" Michael asked.

"Kind of like the convention in 1986, when he played tennis that day, and his balls were hanging out of his shorts the whole time. Davis left a chair soaking wet with sweat, and someone sat in it a few minutes later and screamed out loud." They both laughed, and T. J. made sure Susan heard the conversation.

Susan begged, "T. J., please don't bring that memory up anymore," because the visual was too much to handle before the big party, and she was in an excellent mood.

"Okay, not a problem," T. J. said, and Michael laughed again. "So your team won the golf tournament today, eh?"

"Hell yes, we did, and we have a shitload of new golf apparel to prove it!"

"Congrats then, and were there any female players on the course?"

"Yeah, they were just riding around handing out free shit, like koozies and free golf balls, but no one to mention. At least the usual suspects, or my regular golf partners, were not present today, which meant tomfoolery was at a minimum and mostly just some damn good golf."

"Okay, good," T. J. said. "Maybe I should take that shitty habit up one day. Seems you have a lot of luck on the golf course."

"You should because what place can provide a salesperson with undivided attention for five hours straight except a golf course?"

"Maybe a topless bar," T. J. said with a laugh.

Michael laughed and said, "Well, that is too expensive, right?"

"True. Perhaps you can teach me one day," T. J. said.

"Okay, agreed, and everything looks fantastic here in the hospitality room. Let's get ready to open up the room."

The doors opened up promptly at eight with no one showing up, so the group decided to start drinking without any agents in attendance yet. Since there was so much alcohol, everyone drank doubles, and T. J. drank triples in a big glass.

The first agents showed up at eight fifteen, a mixture of T. J.'s agents and Michael's agents. Since CIC was such a well-thought-of company, everyone in attendance at the convention made a stop by the suite. Within a few minutes, the place was packed with agents, customer service reps, and more. By far, it was the busiest room in the hotel, not only because CIC was the company to represent but also because the agents who didn't represent CIC wanted a contract. The room was full of people enjoying themselves and drinking heavily. Everyone in attendance commented on how good the food was, and the drinks were wonderful.

The alcohol kicked in at about nine o'clock, and the laughter and loud talk were deafening because the room was so busy. Susan's husband was the bartender and the margarita machine captain, and everyone was feeling buzzed big-time. Michael looked at T. J. and walked over to him with a smile, indicating that things were going well and that management would be pleased with the results.

"Hell yes," T. J. said. "A nuclear bomb could go off right now in Corpus Christi, and I wouldn't even give a shit because I'm fucking up already." They both laughed.

While they were talking, a breathtaking redhead walked into the suite with a few friends. Michael immediately recognized her as Tiffany, a customer service rep who worked for one of his Corpus agents. He hadn't had the opportunity to bang this gorgeous gal yet, but she was on Michael's radar.

Tiffany immediately walked up to Michael, gave him a big hug, and said loudly, "Hi, Michael. Nice party!"

"Oh, hi, Tiffany. You look great, and maybe you could introduce me to your friends, please?"

After Tiffany introduced everyone, she whispered into Michael's ear, "There will be an after-party when this closes down, if you're interested."

"Yes, I'm very interested. It depends on whether or not I'm still standing upright after the hospitality room closes," Michael said. They both laughed, and Michael offered Tiffany and her friends a drink and walked them to the bar. They all ordered different drinks, but the ladies were more interested in doing some tequila shots to start. "Ah, good choice, and we have excellent tequila too. Don Jose is the smoothest tequila ever invented, and we spared no expense for our agents, especially the prettiest ones," Michael said.

Tiffany turned away from the compliment as Michael ordered the tequila shots. She whispered something into her friend's ear, and they all laughed. She wasn't feeling a lot of pain at that point, and she thought she whispered, but her voice was loud as she said, "I'm going to blow this guy tonight."

Even Susan's husband heard the comment and looked at Michael with a grin as he served the tequila. He poured the tequila into small cups because they didn't have any shot glasses and whispered to Michael, "What I wouldn't give to be in your shoes right now, you lucky fucker."

Michael looked at him and said, "It's not luck, just the chase that gets me going. The chase is great, but I lose interest quickly because it's not thrilling after the kill."

He turned back to the ladies present and offered a toast. "Thanks for coming to the hospitality room, and cheers!" They drank the shots quickly and requested another round. "Okay, no problem. It is smooth tequila!"

Michael looked at Tiffany's ass as he turned and ordered four more shots. The ass was way too nice, and his thoughts turned toward the rest of the evening after the hospitality room closed. "Tiffany, what about the after-party you spoke of earlier?"

She said, "There is a band playing right down the street, and we are all going there after the hospitality rooms close."

"Okay, get me before you all leave, please."

"Great. We will, or more so, I'll get you." She grinned from ear to ear. She hugged him and said, "We will be back!"

As they left, Michael walked over to T. J. and said, "Good news. I've got a date after the hospitality room closes with that gorgeous redhead."

T. J. said, "Really? Try not to make too much noise, or you might get kicked out of the hotel like last time." They both laughed as the hotel manager walked into the room and asked for T. J. and Michael.

"Yeah, what's up?" they both asked.

"There is too much noise coming out of this room, and we have already received complaints from people staying in the hotel."

They both said almost simultaneously, "Well, fuck them," and they both laughed loudly.

Michael said, "It's only ten o'clock, and we have another hour before we close, so you take care of it, because we prepaid for this room, damn it, and everyone is having a great time. We've spent a bunch of fucking money too at this hotel, so take care of the early bird motherfuckers, okay?"

The manager left in a huff as T. J. and Michael looked at each other and laughed loudly. The food was almost gone because it was delicious, and the booze was running low. There were only thirty minutes left, and every agent in the hospitality room indicated it was the best room he or she had attended in years and maybe ever. The hospitality room was in the books as the best by far, as everyone was drunk off his or her ass, and the food and company were great.

Michael said to T. J., "Okay, the hospitality room is closed, and now it's time for the real business to happen." Tiffany had just stopped by the room and said to meet her friends in the bar on the first floor when everything was finished.

Within ten minutes, Michael was in the bar, mixing it up with Tiffany and her friends and having a great time. They soon left the bar and went outside to the bar down the street, where the live band was playing. After waiting in line for a few minutes, they entered the bar and picked up where they had left off earlier by doing more tequila shots. The band sucked ass, and everyone took turns going to the bathroom before the long drive home. While her friends were in the bathroom, Tiffany gave Michael a big kiss and said, "There's more where that came from if you're interested."

Michael responded, "Oh hell yeah, so do you want to go back to my hotel room?"

"No, you're going to take me home to my house because my friends called a cab, but I would much rather ride with you."

They proceeded back to the hotel parking garage, got Michael's company car, and drove off into the night. "Where to?" he asked.

"Just keep going down Shoreline Drive, and I'll give you directions."

Michael felt no pain whatsoever and was going slower than normal, hoping not to attract any unwanted attention. At that point, Tiffany decided to add some fun to the mix, and she unzipped his zipper and went to town. The only time she stopped was to give him directions, but it was hard to concentrate while being so drunk and getting a blow job simultaneously. After several twists and turns, they finally arrived at her house.

The clothing did not stay on long because Michael was interested in finding out if the curtains matched the drapes. Within a short period, he found she was, in fact, a true redhead while returning the favor. Michael had never encountered a true redhead before but was attentive to make sure she never would forget him or that night. The liaison went on for a couple of hours until they both fell asleep.

Since it was Saturday and nothing was going on at the convention till the big dinner that night, no one was interested in getting up early. Michael woke up first and began to get dressed. He hoped to exit the house before she woke up, but he failed miserably. He was not a quiet dresser, because he lived alone, so there was no reason to be quiet.

She woke up and asked, "Leaving already?"

"Yeah, I need to get back to the hospitality room to help clean up, but that was a fun, crazy-ass night."

Tiffany agreed and said, "Until next time?"

"Oh yeah, for sure," he said as he exited the house.

His drive back to the hotel should have been twenty minutes, and Michael knew Corpus Christi well, but since he had a hangover, he didn't remember the drive to Tiffany's house the night before. It took close to an hour to get back to the hotel. He went to his room to change clothes and went to the hospitality room to help with any leftover cleanup.

After Michael knocked, T. J. opened the door and said, "Wow, you look like shit."

"Thanks, dude. My head feels like shit too."

"You also have that freshly fucked look, so did you get lucky last night?"

"Yep, that too. Do you need any help with the room?"

"Nope, the maid has already been here, and everything looks great."

Michael was relieved to hear the news. "It seems like everyone had a good time last night."

"Yep," T. J. said with a grin, "the best in these conventions' history!"

"Okay, good then," Michael said. "I'm going back to Houston today because I hate these big dinners with the rubbery chicken and hard-ass bread rolls." He used the excuse that he was still feeling bad about the Alicia situation and wanted to have a party at his house back in Houston to drink all the fudge-factor alcohol he had stashed in his car.

T. J. said, "Whatever you want to do, because it is all covered for one more night, and then I'm out of here."

"Okay, see you on Monday, and I'll have some updates for you at our usual Mexican spot." They both laughed.

The drive from Corpus Christi to Houston was a dull trip because there was not much to see on the highway, just a lot of trees and bushes, along with a few small towns, such as Refugio, Victoria, El Campo, and Wharton, Texas, all around Highway 59 going toward Houston. On the boring drive, Michael was thankful his company car had a cassette player, and he'd recorded all his favorite songs on cassette tapes to keep from getting bored on the road.

His mind wandered back to the wedding of one of his high school buddies, Mark Huff, and the trek he'd made with his high school buddy Chuck to Laredo, where the wedding was located. Whenever Michael was on Highway 59, he always thought about that crazy weekend in Laredo.

Three years ago, when he was still working at Commercial Standard, he took that Friday off. Chuck was the designated driver for the trip in his big-ass Bronco because he'd promised his father he would not drink that weekend. They left Friday afternoon in mid-April 1986 and started the long drive to Laredo from Houston, usually a six-hour drive. After they hit the Houston city limits, they stopped for gas, and Michael picked up some chips and a six-pack of tallboys for the trip. Chuck said, sounding like a dad on a long journey, "We are not stopping any more till we arrive at our destination!"

They had already picked up their tuxedos for the wedding and now just had to make it to the rehearsal dinner. Two other high school buddies were on their way too: Louis Ferrantelle and Bill Mullikin. The five friends had graduated high school together in Houston and hung out with each other during and after high school. The party had broken up when Bill and Louis decided to get married to their respective spouses and tried to act like normal human beings. That had put an end to all the hell-raising they were used to having, but they still kept in touch. Bill and Louis were in the wedding party as well. Chuck and Michael were still single. Now that their friend Mark had decided to take the plunge too, it seemed all of Michael's friends were dropping like flies.

The speed limit at the time on Highway 59 was fifty-five miles per hour, but with a 315-mile trip ahead of them, they planned to exceed the speed limit whenever possible. Chuck should have had numerous traffic violations on his motor vehicle report. He avoided many because he employed an outstanding attorney and had the money to get things taken care of in the entire state of Texas.

As they approached the halfway point, San Antonio, a few things happened. Michael had finished three tallboys and needed to go to the restroom, and he told Chuck about his problem. Chuck was pissed off and said, "Why didn't you go before we left?"

Michael said, "I did go, but it's three tallboys later, and it's almost an emergency."

Chuck said, "I'm not stopping, so just hang out the Bronco's back, and I'll roll the window down."

Chuck was doing seventy miles an hour, and since Michael was a tall individual, five foot eleven, he could barely get out the window and stand to relieve himself. Chuck saw piss coming out of his Bronco's back and figured some tomfoolery was in order. He slowed down a bit and shook the car from left to right, which made Michael lose his balance and fall into the moving vehicle's back. It was tough enough to take a piss while standing halfway out of the Bronco, but piss went everywhere when he fell back into the car.

Michael was a pretty laid-back guy, but he was pissed off—and pissed on—big-time. "You motherfucker! Damn it, pull over, because now I have to change pants and finish what I started, you asshole."

Chuck laughed and obliged because he knew Michael was angry and would retaliate whenever he figured out an opportunity. Chuck pulled over, and Michael retrieved another pair of pants from his suitcase and finished pissing by the road's side.

"All right, fucker, let's go!" Michael screamed out.

They pulled out of the far right-hand lane, and as usual, Chuck punched the gas and got up to eighty miles an hour in no time. Unfortunately, a state trooper was parked on the side of the road about a mile after Michael relieved himself by the side of the road, and naturally, the trooper pulled Chuck over to see why he was in such a hurry.

"Nice day, Officer," Chuck said. "What's the problem, Officer?"

The trooper said, "You realize I clocked you at seventy-eight miles an hour, or twenty-three miles over the speed limit? Why are you in such a hurry, sir?"

"We have to be at a wedding rehearsal dinner in Laredo, and we are late," Chuck said.

The officer asked to see his license and proof of insurance. The trooper returned after a license check to see if there were any outstanding warrants and said, "I'm citing you for speeding, sir." As he opened up his ticket register, the officer shouted, "Fuck!"

Chuck looked at the officer and asked what the problem was, and the officer said, "This is your lucky day, Charles!"

"Okay, call me Chuck, but why is it my lucky day?"

"I just ran out of tickets on my last stop, and unfortunately, you are free to go, but slow down, damn it!"

"Yes, Officer," Chuck replied with a smile.

As they entered the freeway again, they both started laughing uncontrollably, and Michael said, "This kind of shit would only happen to you, Chuck! That officer would have written me three tickets, but you get away without getting a single one, you asshole!" They continued to laugh uncontrollably.

The rest of the trip was uneventful, mostly because Chuck slowed down a bit. They showed up at the rehearsal dinner. They'd missed the wedding rehearsal ceremony, but both of them had their tuxedo jackets on with warm-up pants—not the most attractive outfits, but they wanted to show respect for the wedding party.

After eating some fajitas, Chuck went missing for about an hour and then showed back up at the rehearsal dinner with a movie camera he'd rented from a video store in downtown Laredo.

"Oh shit," Michael said, "so we now have evidence of this crazy weekend?"

"Yep," Chuck said, "and I'll be filming all the shit, so don't be an asshole."

"An asshole like you always are?" Michael asked.

"Yeah," said Chuck, "and by the way, fuck you too!"

They proceeded to check into their hotel rooms after the party broke up and enjoy a few libations. The party was just beginning. The women went into their rooms, and the men went into another hotel room, where the alcohol flowed like a river, mostly straight bourbon and straight tequila. The party raged until hotel management came to the door to ask them to hold the noise down around five in the morning. The party slowed to a crawl, and everyone decided it was time to go to bed a few minutes later. Chuck and Michael passed out on a couch, and Mark passed out on the bed.

A few hours later, around eight, Michael woke up to the sound of a bong hit that Chuck and Mark were inhaling. The television was on, showing Bugs Bunny—it was Saturday morning, so Saturday morning cartoons. It was not a good thing to wake up to, bong hits and cartoons, and Michael rolled over on the couch and said, "Seriously? You guys didn't party enough last night, and you're now doing bong hits and watching cartoons?"

"Hell yes!" they both roared.

"All right then. One only gets married once, or twice, so yeah, but understand we probably slept three hours last night or today or whatever," Michael said.

"Yeah, but you haven't heard the funny part yet," Chuck said. "We are going to Mexico, to Nuevo Laredo, in about thirty minutes, so get your ass up!"

"Okay, okay."

There was a knock at the door. It was Louis's wife, Melanie, shouting, "Good morning! Are you guys ready to go to Mexico? Oh wow, what's that smell in here?"

Michael said, "It's either the cartoons or the weed Mark and Chuck were smoking." He laughed loudly. "Anyway, we will be ready." Michael said to Chuck, "Smoke all the weed you want because I promised your dad not to let you drink any alcohol this weekend. After all, he called me last week again! He is worried that you drink too much and wants to enlist my help to stop you from drinking so much."

"Oh, fuck that noise. I haven't had anything to drink in a few weeks. I've just been smoking weed."

"Okay, okay, the agreement was made to make sure you would not drink anything this weekend, and so far, you haven't."

"True, so let's get ready to cross the border!"

They spent the day in Nuevo Laredo and ate some delicious Mexican food and drank many cervezas, except Chuck. They all bought assorted trinkets to take home in memory of the wedding weekend, and Michael bought a stiletto knife and smuggled it back with no problems. They got back with plenty of time to get ready for the wedding, and Chuck broke out his rented VHS movie camera and started filming the video. As the hours clicked away, many more tequila shots were consumed before the wedding. Chuck and Mark hit the weed with a vengeance until they could barely stand up. Mark couldn't find his dress socks, so he wore a pair of white tube socks with a hole in the top, but his white tuxedo pants covered the bulk of the hole that showed. They drew straws to see who would be the best man, and Michael drew the largest stick to be the best man. They all loaded up into their cars and drove to the church. It was a Catholic wedding, so everyone had to look somewhat sober.

Chuck filmed near the church's front as everyone filed into the pews for a Catholic wedding and mass. As Mark and his soon-to-be wife, Mary, knelt near the church's front, a cat without a tail decided to crash the wedding and stepped on Mary's wedding dress. Mark turned around and threw a pen at the cat, and it ran off screeching because the pen hit the cat on the head. The whole church cracked up.

The wedding was almost finished, and when the deed was done, everyone exited the church and went to the reception. All in all, it was a beautiful wedding. Champagne and beer flowed at the reception, and as the VHS tape would prove, a lot of tomfoolery happened at the reception.

When it came time for the garter toss, one of the ladies in the wedding party grabbed Michael's arm and escorted him to catch the bride's leg garter. It hit Michael right in the face, and he watched it drop to the ground. Another guy picked it up. Everyone laughed.

After the reception, everyone went back to the hotel, except Mark and his bride, where the old high school buddies continued the evening in their hotel rooms, drinking and talking loudly. Many farts were heard during the wedding documentary filming, especially since everyone in the wedding party had consumed a lot of fajitas and beans.

Chuck looked at Michael and said, "Let's drive home tonight. This hotel sucks, and I'm not staying in this shithole hotel another night."

Michael said, "Seriously? We've only had three hours of sleep the entire weekend, and now you want to drive home for nearly six hours?"

"Hell yes. I'll have Louis take the movie camera back tomorrow, and we can load up and leave."

"All right then, let's get moving because it's almost eleven o'clock," Michael said.

Everyone said goodbye, and Chuck and Michael hit the road with virtually no sleep. Chuck stopped to get gas before they left Laredo, and Michael still had three tallboys leftover but felt it was smart to buy one more tallboy just in case. Chuck bought some Coca-Cola for the ride home.

When they entered the Bronco, Michael looked at Chuck and said, "Hey, I'm real proud of you for not drinking, especially with alcohol flowing everywhere all weekend."

Chuck looked up from the driver's seat and said, "Oh yeah, no problem," with a big grin on his face. He was grinning because he was pouring some Coke into a glass and mysteriously produced a fifth of Bacardi rum.

Michael laughed and asked, "When did you have time to buy a fifth of rum?"

"Oh, I got it when we were in Mexico, because it was so much cheaper there, so I smuggled it back with my trinkets I bought for my nephew."

"Oh shit, your dad is going to shit egg rolls if he finds out!"

"Don't worry about it. Just sit back, relax, and enjoy your beer because I'm going to enjoy the shit out of this Bacardi right now."

They pulled out of the gas station with the radio blaring '80s rock and roll as both of them chugged their drinks of choice. After about an hour and a half, Chuck ran out of Coke, so he pulled over after passing San Antonio and searched his car for something to add to the Bacardi. He found Gatorade, which was not smart to mix with any alcoholic drink, as it hit your system faster.

For the next two hours, Michael pounded his beers, and Chuck pounded his Bacardi as they joked about all the crazy shit they had done and gotten away with in high school, especially the incident on the infamous hill next to their school.

Michael noticed Chuck had run out of Gatorade and was drinking straight Bacardi and suggested he might drive, because there were only a few sips left in the bottle.

"No way. Don't worry about it. I'm okay, so take a nap if you want to; it's already three o'clock."

Michael knew better than to let Chuck continue driving after consuming almost a whole fifth of Bacardi, but he fell asleep for about twenty minutes.

He awoke to Chuck exclaiming, "Hey, buddy, we are home!" Chuck had exited the freeway, but the freeway exit was for El Campo—still another hour and a half from home. Chuck could barely keep the Bronco on the road and kept hitting the rock shoulder on the feeder road.

Michael yelled, "We aren't home, you drunk fuck! Where are all the big-ass buildings in Houston?"

Chuck looked around, saw nothing but trees, and said, "Hmm, where the fuck are we anyway?"

Michael laughed and said, "You just took the El Campo exit, dumbass."

"Oh shit," Chuck said, "maybe you should drive the rest of the way because I am fucked up."

Michael thankfully agreed, and they did a Chinese fire drill, and Michael was back on the road in no time, heading to Houston. They had only about an hour and a half left on the trek, but it was early Sunday morning, and with only three hours of sleep for the weekend, they both were tired. Chuck passed out immediately, and Michael turned up the radio so he could stay awake. He listened to Ozzy talk about one of his recent hit songs, and after that went off, he turned off the radio because it was playing only talk shows with people bitching about everything imaginable.

Since Michael was so tired after virtually no sleep, he began to hallucinate that the radio was still on and was talking to him as he drove. He had a nice conversation with the radio about when it had been born and who had installed it in the vehicle; plus, Michael asked if it liked Chuck and his crazy driving and lifestyle. The radio was not pleased with anything and bitched about Chuck's shitty driving habits and how much the radio hated rap music. With about twenty minutes left on the trip, Michael turned the radio off again and made it home to watch the sun come up. He offered to let Chuck sleep on his couch, but Chuck wanted to sleep in his bed, and he left for his house.

Michael drifted back from his memories into the current situation: driving back from the convention on Highway 59 from Corpus Christi. He was still thinking about yesterday's conquest and about Alicia too, but there was much more fun to be had soon. Michael wondered again how they had made it home from Laredo without much sleep and how they had drunk so much alcohol in two days, but he was thankful everyone had made it home safely.

As soon as he got home and started to unpack, he called his friends to tell them about the fudge-factor booze and said to get over as soon as they could before he drank it all. A gorgeous blonde named Vanessa lived a few units down—she was also the sister of the manager who ran the day-to-day operations of the condo complex—and of course, she was one of the first people Michael called, because he had met her a few weeks ago at the swimming pool and been awestruck at seeing her at the pool with her bikini and great figure. The fact that she was gorgeous did not hurt matters either.

Vanessa had indicated she was getting divorced and had a seven-year-old daughter when they'd first met at the pool a few weeks ago. Michael had gotten her phone number while at the pool, and he called her after he arrived home and said, "Get your sister, and come over. I'm having a party with a shitload of booze!"

She agreed and was at his condo for the first drink. Vanessa loved tequila and started on that with a beer chaser. As he poured two more shots into shot glasses, he wondered if he should not have invited so many people to come over, because the two-person party was working well.

Vanessa's sister showed up for one shot and then left, and a few other folks showed up and left quickly because they already had plans for Saturday night. It looked like it would be a two-person party after all. Michael filled in Vanessa on the fudge factor and the free alcohol. "So no reason to be shy about drinking all night."

Vanessa said, "Get the bottle, and let's go back to my place because my daughter is with my sister at my condo, and she probably wants to go home."

They went to her condo and wished her sister a good night, and things began to get kind of funky. Vanessa was not an ordinary gal; she did some modeling and was almost as tall as Michael at about five foot ten, and her long, beautiful blonde hair was captivating. She talked about how her husband could not satisfy her in bed and was an asshole, among other descriptors she used; plus, he had a little dick.

Michael had heard about guys being bad in bed about ten thousand times and wondered, *What in the hell is wrong with guys these days?* Michael always thought premature ejaculation had gone out of style with the old western stars from years past.

The Hammer Protocol was on tap for the night. Michael was not entirely over Alicia, but he figured Vanessa might be the gal to get over her with and move on with his life.

Unfortunately, the tequila caught up with them, and they both passed out on her couch before anything could get started.

Michael woke up first the next morning and thought, *Oh shit, I left my condo door unlocked all fucking night!* He woke up Vanessa and said he should go before her daughter woke up, but they agreed to see each other again soon and maybe go out dancing the next weekend.

Michael got home, and luckily, everything was okay. He was surprised nothing had happened, not only to his condo but to him as well. *That damn tequila*, he thought. *Tequila is a double-edged sword that can either make or break a night. Unfortunately, it broke the night.* At least he'd gotten laid on Friday at the convention. *There is always next weekend or next week.*

Michael and Vanessa talked a few times during the workweek and made plans to go out dancing the next weekend on Saturday night. She had never country-western danced before, so he decided to take her to the Midnight Rodeo because it was always a lot of fun. The regular haunt of Michael's was not too far away from their condo, in case they drank too much.

They danced and drank a ton of beer up until closing. When they danced together, they stared into each other's eyes, so Michael knew she was ready to make up for last weekend. She had boots on, so she was as tall as he was, and it seemed the entire club was watching them, because they were a strikingly gorgeous couple.

The drive back to the condo was uneventful, and Michael parked his car in his usual spot and invited her in for a nightcap. He poured two shots of tequila—or "to kill ya," as Vanessa called it—and they drank them. They found themselves in Michael's bedroom in no time, with all their clothes off in a long, warm embrace.

After some loud, screaming oral sex, it was time for the real stuff to happen. When things progressed to the point of actually having sex, Michael immediately thought, *Oh my, where is my two-by-four to attach to my freaking ass?* Michael was way above average in the girth department, but this gal was incredibly large. He thought, *Oh wow, even a nuclear submarine is small in the Grand Canyon.* He was genuinely disappointed and knew she would never be happy, because it would have taken a well-endowed male porn star to fix the problem.

They awoke the next morning and said goodbye and how much fun they both had had, but the search was still on for a compatible girlfriend. It was Sunday, his golf day with Dave.

Dave asked the first question. "How was the date last night?"

"It was good, bad, and ugly," Michael said, and they both laughed on the golf course. "We had fun dancing and drinking, but I had to call 911 for some assistance when we got back to my condo."

Dave laughed and asked, "What for? Was there trouble?"

"My bottom torso was removed from her twat." They both laughed loudly.

"You mean ..."

"Yep, she has an ultralarge yanger." They both laughed hysterically.

Dave was in shock and said he would never look at her the same way again.

"Do you have thoughts on ending the relationship? Because it was like screwing the sheets, you know?"

"Yeah, I know," Dave said, "but she is so freaking gorgeous!"

"Do you have a two-by-four to nail to my ass then so the police won't come out again?" Michael asked. They both laughed and continued their play.

As was usual in late summer in Houston, it was a sweltering but beautiful day. As it turned out, Vanessa had recently contacted a high school boyfriend, and she moved to Virginia within two weeks, so there was no need to end things in a bad way, which was especially good since she lived in the same condo complex as Michael. Sometimes good luck happened when one least expected it to happen. Michael had thought Vanessa might help him get over Alicia, but like most of the ladies he'd met over the last few months, she'd been just another one-night fling.

It was another workday and another round of golf with the usual suspects. Wes and Danny called and invited themselves to play at Michael's club and wanted a friend to join. Michael said, "Make sure he knows the rules, damn it. No tomfoolery at my home course, okay?"

"No problem at all. We will have fun, as always!"

The next day, they met up on the links, and Wes and Danny introduced Charlie Heimer to Michael. Michael said, "Nice to meet you, and I must say, you keep some pretty seedy company, Charlie." They all laughed and teed off the first hole.

After about five holes of play with some minor tomfoolery, such as throwing a tee at someone's feet while he was teeing off from the tee box or running over a golf ball in the middle of the fairway, Michael decided to relieve himself at one of the many bathrooms located on the golf course, or a tree. During his process of relieving himself, Charlie pulled up in his golf cart, saw what was happening, and said, "Hey, nice dick, dude!"

The foursome all cracked up. The joke was from a show on TV Charlie recently had seen, except the person on the show had had a small appendage.

After regaining composure, the foursome teed off on the next hole. Michael's golf club was surrounded by homes, as most country clubs were, so a person had to be careful not to hit near them. Charlie sliced his ball into a homeowner's backyard and had to jump a fence to retrieve his ball. When he climbed the fence and jumped down to get his ball, he came face-to-face with a growling rottweiler. Charlie slowly moved back as the dog barked and growled. Many other golfers had hit into that person's backyard, and the homeowner was tired of people invading his yard.

Charlie threw his golf club over the fence and jumped onto the fence but caught his shirt on the fence's top. His shirt tore as he fell to the ground on his ass.

Michael went over to check on his well-being because he hadn't gotten up yet. Everyone surrounded Charlie and asked how he was feeling. Charlie said, "My shirt is ruined, but my balls are cut, and they may be on the fence."

"Seriously?" asked Michael.

"Yeah, either I've pissed myself from the damn dog, or I cut my balls jumping the fence."

They helped Charlie up slowly, and he proceeded to go to the nearest bathroom, or tree, to inspect the damage. He found a mixture of piss and blood, but it was just a minor cut, and everyone was relieved to hear the good news.

"Never a dull moment playing with you guys," Michael said, and everyone laughed.

"Nope, it's never a dull moment, so let's finish this round and hit the nineteenth hole. Maybe that will kill some of the pain," Wes said to Charlie.

They adjourned to the nineteenth hole, and the usual bullshit ensued about who the best golfer was, plus bets about going back out to the course to prove it, but by that time, everyone was already drunk on bourbon. Michael bid them goodbye as the night crept up, as he had work tomorrow, but the weekend was creeping up too.

The next day in the office, Davis called a meeting to talk about business and a few other items of interest, because he had just gotten off a conference call with the bigwigs in the home office. By that time, things had changed a lot between Davis and Michael because the Valley game plan had been successful, and Art had indicated to Davis all the help and hard work Michael had put into the audit, which made him sound like a team player interested in more than just getting laid all the time. Davis even had stopped spreading rumors about Michael's female exploits around the office, because he was interested in keeping him around now; plus, Michael had gotten Davis laid at a few happy hours recently with a few customer service reps who worked for his agency force, so the past was forgiven. The bottom line was, business was way up, everyone was happily getting laid, and the sales department had passed their audit recently.

Davis started the meeting and indicated the CEO of CIC would be visiting the Houston branch office in the next month. "With all the increases in business over the last few years, the CEO wants to come down to personally congratulate all the employees at a branch-wide meeting."

"Oh great," Michael said. "That sounds like a lot of fun because he will give a speech and then ask for questions during a Q-and-A session, right?"

"Ah, you have been through this before?" Davis asked with a laugh.

"Yep, and you guys will want me to ask the first question because no one else has the guts to say anything, so yes, I've been through this before."

"Okay, then the meeting is adjourned," Davis said with a laugh. "Just kidding, but just an FYI to everyone: business is up to ten percent, and the home office is pleased with the results. If those fuckers are happy, then I'm delighted. Also, Christmas is coming up, and we need to have a great Christmas party. Since I'm the fattest one, I'll be Santa Claus again this year."

T. J. spoke up. "We have invites to a shitload of Christmas parties this year, and Michael and I will be crashing some of the biggest parties we weren't invited to anyway. Does anyone else want to go?"

Art said no because he had other plans with his wife, but Davis said, "Yeah, I'll go have a few with you guys. I assume you're going too, Michael?"

"Of course, Davis. It will be a target-rich environment with many single gals in attendance—who wouldn't want to go? Steven S. Jacobs throws the biggest and best party, usually held at the Junior League, which is an uppity-type place. The food is nice; plus, the owner, Steven, has been friends with my uncle for many years," Michael said. "Plus, it's by invitation only. The best food, the best-looking gals, and free booze—what more could a person want?"

Davis was convinced by the talk of good-looking gals attending the event. "First things first, we all are invited to the independent agents' installation dinner, where they install new officers, so I'll ask that everyone try not to get too drunk, because it's a professional engagement, and anyone who's anyone will be in attendance."

Art said, "Isn't that like saying not to go over the speed limit at the Indy 500?"

"True," Davis said, "but let's keep it to a minimum." The meeting adjourned.

T. J. and Michael spoke afterward about the meeting. T. J. said, "Coming from a guy who drinks two beers at a time, his telling *us* not to get drunk is the pot calling the kettle black."

"Yeah, I know, but he is older and leaves earlier than us, so it should be no biggie. This year, it's at the Houston Country Club, so it should be very nice. Howard Hughes grew up playing this course, and I've always wanted to see this course at least and drink some of their booze, because no one could afford the hundred-thousand-dollar initiation fee." Howard Hughes was a hero to Michael, and he wanted to see some of the things Howard had seen and done in his youth while growing up in Houston. "Maybe the alcohol tastes better," Michael said with a laugh. "And by the way, I'm still ahead on the tomfoolery contest, so you'd better catch up, asshole."

T. J. said, "I've not forgotten, but it hasn't been raining much recently. There is no expiration date on this contest, and never count an older guy out of any competition."

A week later, the installation dinner was upon everyone, and the branch office was without Davis, Art, T. J., and Michael because it took all day for everyone to sober up and get ready for the event. That was total bullshit, but everyone felt it was a great excuse not to work that day and probably not the next day either, because they needed recovery time from all the alcohol. It was an open bar, and the folks in CIC's attendance were never too far from the bar—or bars, as it turned out. There was a happy hour before the dinner, and then the boring speeches ensued before the new officers were installed, so it made sense to get as tanked up as possible before the boring stuff happened.

Everyone was sitting in different places with different agents who represented CIC. Davis was seated with CIC's largest agent with Art and his wife, and T. J. and Michael were seated with some of the other larger agents. T. J. and Michael were always looking out for Davis and Art to make sure nothing happened, since they both were huge drinkers. It made sense to get tanked up at these things but not so tanked up that one could not look out for fellow employees, especially if they fell down and needed help.

Halfway through the speech of the newly installed president of the association, T. J. and Michael watched as Davis got up to go to the bathroom. He had already had about thirty beers, but that was not his limit. His limit was usually around forty to fifty, and he seemed okay when he left the room.

As it turned out, Davis went to the bathroom not just to take a piss but also to take a shit. While he sat on what looked like a gold-encrusted toilet seat, the speech ended, and some other guests ventured into the bathroom. Davis enjoyed his time alone on the gold toilet, smelling the place up, when he overheard two men talking while taking a piss at the urinals. Even though the smell was a bit overwhelming, the two folks did not know it was Davis in the stall and started talking shit about CIC and Davis himself. They had not seen him leave to go to the bathroom while the shitty speeches were happening. As it turned out, the two guys at the urinals were the owners of the two largest Jewish agencies in Houston.

One said to the other, "Did you see that fat Davis Bryant? What a fucking pig, and you know the reason why neither one of us has a CIC contract, right?"

"Yeah, because he is anti-Semitic, and he is a first-class piece of shit. I'm going to call that fucker on Monday to see if he will give me a contract, because I have lost enough business to CIC, and I'm sick of that shit. I'll put on my best act for that fat asshole."

As they left the bathroom, they both commented on the overwhelmingly bad smell in the bathroom, but neither man knew it was Davis taking a shit in the stall. Davis immediately started laughing because the smell was so bad and because neither of them had known it was him.

After the dinner was over, as everyone was leaving, Davis asked his employees to go to the Marriott near the Houston Country Club to continue the evening. The Marriott was off 610, near Westheimer, and it was way too nice for Davis's taste, but everyone was dressed well, and he felt it was appropriate.

They all sat down on the hotel's oversized chairs, and Davis began to speak. "While we were at the Houston Country Club, I was in the gold stalls in the bathroom, which were not only nice but also one of the best places to take a shit in Houston." Everyone laughed, and Davis continued. He said the names of the guys who'd been taking a piss and started to talk shit about him and CIC. "You all know these guys, but truly, I'm not interested in whether someone is Jewish, Hispanic, Asian, or otherwise; if they can get us business, we will do business with them. Hell, one of our largest agents is Hispanic, and he is a good friend of mine. These guys did not know who was in the stall and weren't aware of anyone else in the restroom when they started to talk shit about me. My shit was going well in the gold bathroom, when those fuckers walked in and started spitting out trash talk. The shit that pisses me off is when someone comes up with the crap of 'He hates Jews' or 'He hates Hispanic people.' I'm not sure if I've ever talked to these guys in the past even. Has either of you talked to them?" he asked, pointing toward Michael and T. J.

Both chimed in at the same time. "Not to my knowledge."

"Okay then. One indicated he was going to call on Monday, so be ready, but I'll be damned if we appoint these fuckers to do business with us, because of all the shit they talked about me."

The drinks were beginning to hit everyone because everyone had been drinking for many hours that night. Davis said, "The last business thing I'll mention is the fact that the CEO is going to be here sooner than originally planned; he will be here next Wednesday."

Everyone said at the same time, "Oh fuck."

"He is staying at the Wyndham and is having dinner with a few of our largest Houston agents and the suboffice agents in Austin, and the Austin branch manager will be here too."

Everyone said, "Oh shit."

"Not Larry Arnum. What an asshole," Michael said with a grimace. "His mouth is as big as his ego, and no one can stand to be around that guy for more than ten minutes."

"Correct, but we will get through this like we always do; besides, it's a great experience to meet the CEO of a large company. Plus, you get to know all the shit these fuckers put me through daily," Davis said with a laugh.

The days came and went, and the CEO, Ed Daniel, flew into town and greeted everyone in the hotel lobby. It was great to meet the man who'd brought CIC from near bankruptcy in the 1970s to the Mercedes-Benz of companies in the '80s—a brief period to conduct such a change in the entire operation.

Larry Arnum was the first to run up to shake Ed's hand and offer anything available for his comfort in Houston. Larry was not only an asshole but also a colossal suck-up to higher management. Even Davis knew it, so he looked at everyone with his eyes in the air. Later on, Davis would comment, "The gall of this asshole to jump ahead in line to suck up a bit."

Everyone met Ed and was impressed with the man and his flawless, high-end Gucci suit.

Michael introduced himself and wondered how one person could make such a massive change in a company so quickly and was impressed with Ed. They ventured upstairs to a group of tables to talk business with agents when they started to arrive about ten minutes later. There were only about twenty. Ed liked these informal meetings and did them nationwide to spur more business writings and check on each branch office.

T. J., Michael, and Susan were downstairs, directing agents to walk up the stairs to meet the company's CEO and have a drink or two on the company. Larry Arnum would look down from the upstairs dining area and scream at Susan with his obnoxiously loud voice to check with the front desk to see if he had any messages. Susan would look at T. J. and Michael with a frown and say, "What an asshole," before yelling back up after checking with the front desk, "No messages!" This action went on three to four times with Larry screaming down to see if he had any messages. She complied but was getting tired of his crap.

Finally, the dinner and meeting started, so Michael, T. J., and Susan went to the bar to enjoy a few drinks on their own and relax because they were finished for the evening. Everyone ordered his or her favorite beverage: a rum and Coke for T. J., bourbon for Michael, and a White Russian for Susan. As they sat in the oversized chairs, they discussed Ed Daniel and what a great guy he was, plus Davis and Art and how glad they all were that things were going well for the Houston branch office.

After about four rounds of drinks, everyone decided to go home, but first, the bill arrived. T. J. said, "Oh fuck, did we drink that much booze?" The bar bill was close to $100.

"Wow," they all said.

T. J. said immediately, "I've got an idea. Larry Arnum is such an asshole that maybe we should do something to put him in his place. We should put this on Larry Arnum's room." They all had heard his room number when he was yelling down to Susan to check his messages.

They all laughed, and Michael said, "What a dickhead Larry is, and he deserves to buy us all a few drinks because he is such an asshole." Susan and T. J. agreed.

When the waitress returned, Michael said, "Put this bill on my room, room four zero four." He signed the bill with the name Larry Arnum and put his room number on the check with a nice tip. They all laughed hysterically after the waitress took the bill away, and they couldn't get out of their chairs for about ten minutes, because they knew Larry would be pissed off big-time.

As they left the Wyndham Hotel, everyone agreed to fake ignorance if anyone brought up the incident in the future, so no one would get into trouble, but they all continued to laugh as they got to their vehicles and drove off into the night.

The next day, Ed Daniel was in the branch office, giving his speech to all the employees, who totaled more than 250 due to all the increased growth. Davis had instructed Michael to ask the first question to get everyone loosened up to ask more questions. After the speech, Ed looked around the room and asked for any questions, saying, "Don't make me pick someone," and the whole room laughed. Michael raised his hand, and Ed said, "Yes, you, and introduce yourself, please."

"Hello, Mr. Daniel, and welcome to Texas! My name is Michael Deforest, and I'm in the sales department under Davis Bryant and Art Hower."

"Yes, Michael, what's your question?"

"With all the growth we have experienced over the last three years, is there a plan for CIC to become one of the largest commercial underwriting insurance companies in the United States, or is it just a by-product of an aggressive game plan? In other words, are we planning to be in the top three commercial insurance companies in the United States?"

Ed replied, "Good question, Michael," as Davis said something to Art quietly. "Yes, we have been aggressive in our underwriting approach and many of the association business writings during the last few years. This plan of action will continue in the foreseeable future because we are making large profits in our business writings. Our parent company is very pleased with the results, especially since they own ninety-two percent of the outstanding stock. In my last meeting with their board of directors, they wanted me to get out of the office more often and thank every branch responsible for this tremendous growth, especially the Houston and Austin offices. This office was only second to the Chicago branch office, and I want to thank each of you for your hard work and determination. Please continue doing a wonderful job in the future.

"My conversations with our agents last night at dinner indicated the largest company in their office was CIC, and they plan to continue premium increases in the future. That was a testimony to all the people here in the Houston branch office and all the hard work that goes on here. So to answer your question, it doesn't make a difference to me or the board of directors if we end up being the largest commercial insurance company, just the fact that we are making money, so if the by-product, as you put it so eloquently, increases the number to three or to being the largest commercial insurance company, it doesn't matter. We are interested in turning a profit for the company and being partners with our agency force. Thanks for the question, Michael."

Michael looked over at Davis and Art to see their reactions without their noticing. Michael could see they were beaming with pride at all the good things Ed had said about the branch and the tremendous growth the office had incurred.

Many more questions were asked until the meeting adjourned. After Ed left the branch, everyone was in Art's office, asking how the dinner the night before and the branch-wide meeting had gone.

"Ed was pleased with the dinner last night and the branch-wide meeting today," Art said, grinning from ear to ear at all the good news. "Good job, Michael. That was a great question to get things started, and Davis wants us to eat dinner at the Hofbrau for a celebration. I'll be surprised if we eat anything, though," Art said, laughing. "Everything is going great, so we might as well celebrate after work."

After work, at the Hofbrau, everyone was in a festive mood, and the drinks flowed. Davis, as usual, ordered his beers two at a time, and Art ordered Jack Daniel's shots chased by beer. Michael excused himself to add another date on the bathroom wall and to see if anyone else had commented on his writings on the bathroom wall.

"Hmm," Michael said. No one had commented on his writing about Lisa. Lisa had taken it there big-time without any grease, which he'd written a few months ago. He laughed to himself because he'd thought someone would know Lisa. What a shame because Lisa was another gorgeous blonde who liked it everywhere and anywhere. That had been a few weeks ago and another in the long list of conquests Michael had had that year. He was still trying to get over Alicia and was shocked that he was still thinking about her, but maybe he would hear from her one day, or maybe not.

Everyone was drinking heavily as Michael exited the bathroom and sat next to T. J. "It looks like you picked the right time to join this company," T. J. said.

Michael agreed and said, "True, but I'm still ahead on the tomfoolery contest." They both laughed loudly.

T. J. said, "It's close to the weekend too, so we might order a bigger steak than usual to get our strength up."

"Good idea," Michael said, "and hopefully no ladies from the past will show up, because it's going to be a big weekend for me with a few new gals ready for some action."

"How do you find these gals anyway?" T. J. asked.

"It's mostly like a friend-of-a-friend introduction or at nightclubs in Houston. It's like shooting fish in a barrel, but one has to have the attitude and the balls to go up to some of these gals, because some are high maintenance and stuck up. When I'm done with them, they are brought back to earth, so I'm trying to help out my fellow brethren by getting them off their high horse, you know?"

"Yeah, I see what you mean now."

The party was almost over with, and Michael was chosen to follow Davis home to ensure he didn't total another car while driving home. Davis's house was on the way to his condo anyway, and he didn't have to get out of his car; he just had to make sure Davis made it home okay.

Davis had consumed nearly forty beers in about three hours, so he felt no pain at all. No one expected him to be in the branch the next day, because he would have a badass hangover, and everyone was getting used to Davis's standard of living. Davis would drink dozens of beers in a night, and then no one would see him for a few days. It was pretty comical but typical of Davis. The branch office was doing great production-wise, and Davis would disappear sometimes for days at a time and then reappear just as quickly to drink a bunch more with his staff or at least get some work done in the office. He wasn't always as forthcoming about his dating habits but did occasionally talk about his latest conquests.

Everyone was pleased with the week's happenings, and everyone bid the others good night until tomorrow.

A few days later, Art was in his office with the door closed, which usually meant a bad conversation, or someone was in trouble. Michael was at T. J.'s desk, talking about what he had on tap for the weekend. T. J. enjoyed hearing about the weekend plans because they made great fodder for their next Monday luncheon, when Michael caught him up to speed.

"So just another weekend of your usual sex and booze then, huh?"

"Yep," Michael replied, "just another fun weekend on tap."

Just then, Davis walked out of Art's office with a sheepish grin on his face and went down to his corner office. Michael looked at T. J. and said, "Wonder what that was about, especially with Davis."

Art looked out of his office and said, "Michael, could you come into my office for a bit?"

Michael looked at T. J. and said, "Fuck. I've not done anything recently to get into trouble—except, well, maybe that customer service rep I banged the other day in her office."

T. J. laughed and said, "Good luck then."

Art said, "Shut the door behind you before you sit down."

"Damn, Art, this sounds serious."

"Yeah, it is," replied Art. "I just got off the phone with Larry Arnum in Austin, and he was pissed off beyond words and bitched on the phone for thirty minutes. I'm only going to ask you this once: Did you, or do you know who, put a bar tab on Larry Arnum's room at the Wyndham two days ago?"

Michael laughed.

Art said, "Listen, this is a serious matter and not funny, because Larry is a reformed alcoholic, and his wife found the bill and bitched him out about drinking again. He is pissed off, and he thinks someone here in the branch did it, and I want to know too."

"Okay, Art, my apologies, and I won't lie to you. No, I have no idea who put a bar tab on his room. Hell, it could have been an honest mistake by the bar staff anyway, but again, no, I don't know who did that. I've always wondered why shitty things happen to first-class pricks like Larry."

"Are you sure, Michael?"

"Of course I'm sure. We had a few drinks at a restaurant after we left the Wyndham and didn't drink there."

"I'm just checking because I didn't think you would do that, but maybe T. J. would."

"I wouldn't put it past him either, but again, we all went to Pappadeaux's afterward, and we had a few drinks there, but that was on my expense account, so just check it out." Michael had invited his latest conquest to meet him after the Wyndham meeting to cover his tracks without anyone's knowledge. They'd drunken heavily and eaten like three people to make it look realistic. It had turned out well because the gal, Christy, had been easy pickings after all the booze. The thought had crossed Michael's mind to go back to the branch and increase his parking garage record, but he had been too drunk to drive back to the office, so they'd just gone to his condo. Plus, he was still worried about getting caught in the parking garage with his pants down again, and his condo was an excellent place to end a night in seclusion. The record stood at eight at this point, and Michael knew no one would even get close to his record, but it was always a good thing to increase your records so no one could catch up. Michael always thought a few steps ahead because it kept him ahead of the game.

The Larry Arnum bar tab problem went away quickly like a fart in the breeze, so it was back to business as usual. The next Monday, at his regular Mexican luncheon with T. J., Michael brought up the debacle with the Larry Arnum bar tab. They both laughed hysterically about the situation for a few minutes and then ordered lunch. They were amused especially by the fact that no one knew he was a reformed alcoholic.

T. J. said, "No wonder he is such an asshole. Maybe we should offer to buy him a drink the next time we see him." They both laughed again.

During Michael's tenure with CIC, of which he was in his third year, things were going swimmingly; business writings were going through the ceiling, management and upper management were pleased, and everyone was getting laid and drunk. "How could it get any better?" Michael asked T. J.

The Fair-Haired Boy

*D*uring Michael's third year at CIC, a strange thing took shape. At that point, Michael was no longer on the outside looking in but was an insider whom everyone could trust to do just about anything he was tasked to accomplish. The audit, plus many other things Michael had helped to achieve, had not gone unnoticed by management in the Houston branch office. Davis and Art had taken note of his ascendency and were delighted with his progress in a short period. It also had gotten around the industry that a younger rep for CIC could go to and obtain a contract with CIC.

CIC had become the Cadillac of companies during the last five years because they were not a duck-and-run type of company and stood by the agents who represented the company. Other companies would see problems in the marketplace and just stop writing any problematic line of business. CIC never did that; they stuck by their agents through thick and thin, so most, if not all, agents wanted a contract with the company. Unfortunately, only a handful of new appointments were to be had every year, which the sales department were tasked with appointing for the company during any given year, so a good sales rep was always looking for the best bang for his buck. In other words, agents who could grow the fastest in any given year and agents who employed the best-looking customer service reps were paid more attention. That was always a prerequisite for Michael's agents, and they had to be members of a professional golf country club. A larger agency with the best-looking employees was the method to utilize. These prerequisites were not in any company manual but were located in Michael's manual for a new appointment.

Since everyone wanted to represent the company, calls came in frequently for an agency appointment, and Michael and T. J. would mail out a twenty-page form for the agent to complete so they could later schedule a visit with the agency and figure out if they qualified for an agency contract. Of course, if the agency employed gorgeous employees, that always helped with the appointment process. There were other corporate minimums an agency had to meet to be considered for an appointment, but Michael knew his job well and knew how to beat the system.

One prospective appointment in particular that employed good-looking employees and could grow exponentially and where the partners all played golf was the Dargon Agency. It was a triple threat in Michael's mind and an excellent prospect. This design was Michael's plan of action because it worked on many different business and personal levels.

While he was at the prospective agent's office near downtown Houston, in the conference room with the two agency principals, or owners, a customer service rep walked by with a miniskirt and matching jacket, all in white. Miniskirts were Michael's kryptonite, so while he was midsentence and the representative walked by the conference room and then walked back into her office a few minutes later, Michael was stunned by the sight. He was halfway through a sales presentation, when he lost his train of thought, and there was a hush in the conference room. He asked the partners, "Who was that person?"

"Oh, that is Ginger Jarvis, my customer service rep," Dan Dargon said with a grin on his face.

"Is she married?"

"No, she is divorced."

"Maybe we should have a meeting with her after we are done," Michael said. They all laughed.

Dan called her on the inner office speakerphone and said, "Ginger, could you walk by the conference room again, please?" They all laughed.

Of course, she said yes quickly and proceeded to walk by the conference room with a big smile. *Blonde too*, Michael thought. *Wow, a killer body to go with all of that other stuff.* In a joking manner, Michael thundered, "All righty then, you guys just got an agency contract!"

Both partners laughed so loudly that the other employees looked around the office to see what the commotion was in the conference room.

"I'm just joking about the contract, but the prospect for you guys obtaining a contract is looking good. Maybe Ginger could look over some new accounts with me, if that would be possible," Michael said, laughing.

Everyone laughed again, and Dan said, "Not a problem." He used the phone again and asked her to come to the conference room. She obliged quickly and introduced herself, and they shook hands.

Michael was delighted that even closer, she was a knockout with all the accouterments he liked. "Very nice to meet you,

Ginger," Michael said. "Next time I visit the agency, maybe we could review a few accounts and prepare them for me to review."

Ginger said, "Yes, I'll have them ready. Tell me when."

"Here is a listing of accounts we are interested in writing for your agency." Michael gave her a listing of businesses on a sheet of paper. He always left sales materials with agents because most people were visual learners, and it helped to see what the company's appetite for business was currently. "Do you have a card?" Michael asked.

"Yes, of course." Ginger left the conference room, probably so Michael could get an eyeful of the gorgeous blonde again as she went to get a business card. She came back, and they exchanged business cards.

"I'll be in touch, but very nice to meet you, Ginger."

"Likewise, Michael!"

The meeting ended, and Dan invited Michael to play golf at the River Oaks Country Club sometime during the next few days.

"You're a member of River Oaks?" Michael asked.

Dan said, "Oh yes, my father has been a member for forty years." River Oaks was the most expensive real estate in Houston, Texas, and the country club was exclusive and costly. The initiation fee alone was $250,000, if any memberships were available, and monthly dues were outlandishly expensive. There was a lot of old money in River Oaks and the club, and Michael was looking forward to running into a few local celebrities.

Michael shook their hands, thanked them for an exciting morning, and said he looked forward to playing golf at River Oaks.

Michael went back to the office and sat down at his desk, looking flustered. T. J. had just walked in too and said, "It looks like you just got laid. Why are you so tired?"

"I'm not tired," Michael said. "I just met a breathtaking blonde at this prospect's office. Wow, she was so freaking hot."

"You say that about all your new dates, you asshole," T. J. said, laughing. "Was it the agency owner or a customer service rep?"

"A customer service rep, and I'm going to call next week to make another appointment," Michael said with a grin. "I've got a busy weekend ahead, as one might imagine."

"It's almost lunchtime, and the weather has cleared, so why don't we get something to eat?" T. J. asked.

"Good idea," Michael said. "Then I'll fill you in on the rest of the story while we are eating."

Michael wasn't paying attention to what T. J. said, especially with Ginger rattling in his head. It had rained earlier in the day, but the tomfoolery contest had slipped his mind. T. J. said, "I'll drive if that is okay."

"Oh yeah, no problem."

They got into T. J.'s company vehicle and sped off into the soggy day. T. J. always had a coupon for lunch, and before they left the office, he said, "There is a place near Shepherd, off Highway 59, we should try because I have a coupon."

"That sounds great," Michael said.

Secretly, earlier in the day, off Shepherd Drive, T. J. had spotted a bunch of standing water and a lot of laborers standing around waiting to get hired. T. J. had planned out the attack perfectly from beginning to end.

As they turned left onto Shepherd Drive and approached West Alabama Street, there was a huge puddle of standing water, with ten laborers standing right next to it, near a bus stop. They'd left a bit earlier than usual because T. J. knew there would be a lot of traffic at lunchtime, and if the streets were not as busy as they normally were, he could get his speed up enough to rinse off all the people standing around waiting.

T. J. was normally a safe driver, but he wanted to get enough of the laborers wet to take a commanding lead since he was way behind on the contest.

When he approached the bus stop and the ten laborers, T. J. picked up speed up, and Michael said, "T. J., why are you in such a hurry, dude?" The speed limit was thirty-five on Shepherd Drive. Suddenly, Michael recognized what was going on and shouted, "Oh shit!"

The laborers were not aware of the standing water or the oncoming car, and none of them had umbrellas, as past victims had had in their possession.

T. J. hit the standing water with much force at forty-five miles an hour, and Michael could see the laborers' faces as the water rushed over them. All ten were soaked. One had a look of disgust on his face, another started laughing, another had his mouth wide open, and another had an angry look on his face and started cursing loudly. Laughter immediately erupted in the vehicle as T. J. tried his best to keep the car under control, because driving through standing water made a car hard to control, and hydroplaning at forty-five miles an hour was like hitting a barrier of sorts. The laughter went on for about ten minutes before they regained their composure.

Michael realized he'd just gotten bested by T. J. in the tomfoolery contest. "You son of a bitch! Nice, T. J. You planned this whole shit out in advance, didn't you?"

"Well, a good sales rep always plans." They both laughed.

"All right then, guess you have the lead in the contest, but the future possibilities are endless because you just taught me a great lesson about planning."

"Yes, that is what I'm here for." They both laughed again.

After the laughter died down a bit, Michael looked up and noticed a woman on the side of the road as they approached the restaurant. He said, "I think that is a hooker, so slow down." As they approached the alleged lady of the night, Michael rolled down his window to ask her a question. "Howdy, ma'am. How you doing?"

"I'm fine, honey. What can I do for you, good looking?"

"I have a question for you: How much for a hand job?"

"For you, twenty-five dollars."

"Not bad," Michael said.

She asked, "Well, do you want one?"

"No, not really. I'm curious how much money I've saved every time I beat off." Michael and T. J. erupted with loud laughter, and even the hooker laughed as they pulled into the restaurant parking area as Michael rolled his window up. They had to sit in the car for a while to regain their composure before exiting the vehicle. They had tears of laughter coming down their cheeks.

"Can you believe I just soaked ten laborers in one fell swoop?" asked T. J.

"I know! Quit gloating, or I'm not going to hit on any more hookers in front of you in the future." They both laughed, but Michael said, "Let's try to get our shit together before we go into this restaurant, because we will probably get some kind of bad fajitas in this Mexican restaurant if we keep joking around like this."

"Okay, you're right, and no more hooker jokes," T. J. added as they exited the vehicle.

The rest of the afternoon was uneventful, although Michael did make an appointment with Ginger to review some accounts with her early next week. The plan was to get to know her better and take her to lunch. The weekend was fast approaching, and Michael already had a few dates lined up, but the old contest with Chuck and his friends was over because no one could keep up with Michael's contest results on Sunday. They all stopped reporting their results, and Michael was declared the winner.

A few days later, Dan Dargon called about the golf outing at the River Oaks Country Club, and Michael picked up his phone immediately and asked how Dan was doing.

"The golf day is next Tuesday if it fits your schedule," Dan said.

"Oh hell yes, it does," Michael replied excitedly.

The day came quickly, and Michael was ready for the challenge. As he found out, River Oaks was a long and difficult course. The day was gorgeous, and Michael played well. Years ago, Dan had tried to qualify for the PGA Tour but failed miserably on the Nike Tour, but he was still an excellent golfer. He won hands down, but there were no bets that day, just beer and golf.

Afterward, in the men's locker room, they ran across a humorous sight. Many of the golfers were showering in the locker room, and most were older, seemingly ancient, men. Unfortunately, as Michael found out, they walked around in the men's room naked, which made Michael feel uncomfortable and disgusted. Seeing all the naked old-fart bodies walking around with their tiny penises hanging out for everyone to see was frightening.

Afterward, at the nineteenth hole, Dan commented on how gross it was, and Michael drew closer to say, "Most rich guys' dicks are miniature, but their balls are huge."

Dan laughed and said, "Look behind you; your friend is back."

Michael looked over his shoulder, and the same old naked guy was standing behind the sofa he was sitting on. Michael let out a groan of displeasure, but everyone else on the sofa laughed. Michael couldn't stand any more of it, so he thanked them for the golf outing and indicated he was working on their appointment and wanted to come look at a few accounts soon with Ginger. They all laughed, shook hands, and left.

The next morning, Michael was on the phone, making an appointment with Ginger. She indicated it was a slow day, and both the partners were still out, so she figured the golf day before had been a busy one, meaning everyone was probably drunk still or recovering. Michael said he'd left them at the River Oaks bar but didn't know what had happened after that.

Ginger said, "Come by this afternoon."

Michael said, "I've got a better idea. I'll take you to lunch, and then we will look over some accounts."

"Sounds great," she said.

"See you at eleven thirty then?"

"Agreed." They hung up.

Michael looked at T. J. and said, "I've got a lunch date with the hottie at Dargon."

T. J. said, "So you probably won't be back the rest of the afternoon then?"

"Probably not, so if anyone asks, I'm at the Dargon agency."

"Wishing you good luck would be a waste of time," T. J. said, "so enjoy your day." They both laughed.

Michael went by the agency, picked Ginger up, and asked where she wanted to eat.

"There is a Chinese food place very close that is highly rated called Chang's."

"Okay, sounds good. My coworker T. J. always wants Mexican food, and I'm kind of tired of the same ole thing. There is a Chinese food restaurant near my condo called Peking, and they have the best sweet-and-sour chicken in Houston, and their dumplings are fabulous. As a matter of fact, I'm thinking of moving soon because the lease on my condo is coming up, and buying one makes more sense. Peking would be closer to the new condo's location too, so I'm probably going to buy it very soon."

"That sounds neat. Where is the new condo?" Ginger asked.

"Westheimer at Woodland Park, a few blocks past Wilcrest. I'm not looking forward to moving but am looking forward to owning my place. I'll miss my condo on the Sharpstown Golf Course, though."

"So how was golf yesterday at River Oaks?"

"It was fun and challenging. I'm currently working on the agency appointment. To get this appointment approved, the appointment process requires a write-up on the agency and accounts you and the agency plan to submit the first year of being appointed, plus all the agency numbers from other companies the agency represents. I'm working with Dan on that exercise, but I'm sure you will get assigned that shit job." They both laughed.

They arrived at the restaurant and were seated quickly. Michael talked to the waitress and ordered tea, and he asked what Ginger would like to drink. She looked at the waitress and ordered a tea too. Michael paid close attention to her mannerisms to see if there was an interest. His senses were so strong with women that he knew right away whether a woman was interested in him. Mostly, he paid attention to the face and whether she was smiling or not, as a smile was a dead giveaway of enjoying someone's company, along with how relaxed she was.

Ginger was relaxed and already enjoying herself and enjoying the conversation. She was gorgeous too, with a great small-framed body and the obligatory blonde hair. She had nice tits too, which Michael stared at while Ginger ordered some noodles when she wasn't looking at him. So far, Michael was impressed with her professionalism and her damn good looks. He always knew most of the answers to the questions he planned to ask but wanted to see how she responded to each question, which always gave away the individual's true feelings. Michael always threw in a joke or two to see if the person had a sense of humor, just for good measure.

Everything seemed okay at that point, and he started asking a few questions he knew the answers to, beginning with "Are you married?"

She said, "No, I'm divorced."

"Okay. No boyfriend either?"

"No, I had one, but he was a piece of shit and mistreated me."

Michael had heard that many times in the past; he was waiting for her to say, "He had a small dick too." She didn't say that, but Michael was always sympathetic to women with shitty boyfriends. It seemed most boyfriends were a piece of shit, or at least most of the ones he met. Michael always treated women like queens, and the women loved it, but they never seemed to return the treatment. They treated him like a pauper. They never seemed to understand that fact, but he wasn't going to explain it to them; he'd let them figure it out independently. In the '80s, a person just stopped calling back to end a relationship, especially if messages were left on the answering machine. After a woman fucked up in one way or another, Michael would just delete the message and go on to the next one.

Ginger seemed different—almost as different as Alicia, just not as young. She had his attention at that point, and he figured it was time to go back to talking business.

"So did you review the types of accounts CIC likes to write and start to list those accounts the agency will submit to us?"

Ginger said, "Yes, but I'd rather talk about what we were just talking about," and she changed the subject back to the questions about boyfriends.

"Okay then." Michael laughed. "What would you like to know?"

She was straightforward and to the point about what she wanted to know and what she knew. She started by saying, "Your reputation proceeds you in the industry, and your reputation as a real womanizer is well known."

Michael interrupted and said, "You can't believe everything you hear, especially gossip."

She laughed and said, "I've talked to some of your past girlfriends, or flings, and the relationship always started hot but cooled off quickly."

Michael thought, *Wow, beauty and brains.* She was really on top of her game, but she also didn't know whom she was talking to or how he would answer that question or, more so, accusation.

Ginger continued. "At industry functions, there is a lot of talk about CIC and how everyone wants to represent the company. A lot of talk about you; your partner in crime, T. J.; and the people you report to, Davis and Art. It's almost like you guys are running some sort of rogue branch office with a whorehouse attached to the back of the building."

Michael's ears went up like those of a hound dog as he laughed to himself, but he smiled at her because he hoped she hadn't heard about the parking garage record, which was up to nine ladies currently. In his mind, Michael felt he should get an award for that record and dreamed about Davis presenting the award to him at a branch-wide meeting with doughnuts, but he quickly came back to the current concerns. Michael thought quickly because Ginger was smart and current on gossip in the industry. It actually wasn't gossip but was the truth; he just wondered how it had gotten all around the industry that he was such a womanizer or, as Davis said, a whoremonger—another convenient nickname by Davis, the nickname master.

Michael immediately thought to utilize the deflection method and said, "Listen, I'm single, and yes, I've dated a lot, but this industry loves to gossip, and so when there is gossip, it gets blown way out of proportion, you know? I'm fairly sure a lot of this talk has been started by competing companies that are jealous of CIC's explosive growth over the last few years. Most of those competitor employees are old fat guys who probably haven't kissed a woman in ten years." They both laughed. Deflecting a subject by trying to add some humor never had failed him in the past. It didn't fail him now either. Ginger was brilliant and direct, but she started laughing at his comment as the food arrived in the nick of time.

Michael changed the subject to how good the food smelled and said he wanted to try her dumplings, which was another joke he utilized to further distance himself from the whoremonger talk. When the waiter set her plate down, Michael commented on how her dumplings looked firm and smelled fabulous. She tried to fight the urge to laugh but couldn't stop herself, and she laughed for a minute or two and asked Michael to pass the Chinese mustard. Michael said, "Gladly, but be careful with Chinese mustard. If a person spills that stuff on the floor, a hazmat crew must arrive quickly to clean it up."

Ginger laughed again, except this time, she asked Michael to stop joking around, because her mouth was full of rice, and she almost spit it all over the table.

Michael thought, *Okay, mission accomplished. The subject has finally changed.*

They finished eating. Again, Ginger was no idiot, and she said, "I will have the list ready soon, but back to another subject we talked about earlier."

Michael thought, *We already talked about this, damn it, but let's see where she leads.*

Ginger said, "I know you are thinking about asking me out, but you will have to let me think about it for a bit. I'm still not over my last boyfriend, but I do like you, and you are so much fun."

"Thanks, Ginger, and yes, the thought crossed my mind to ask you out on a date, but it's difficult going through a breakup, so just let me know when things get better." Michael thought to himself that she hadn't asked about the parking garage statistics. He wanted to say, "I'm a fifth-degree black belt in tongue kwon do," but he thought it was too soon for that sort of sales approach. "Whether you would have said yes or no about going out, it won't affect the appointment process for the company or an agency contract, okay?"

She indicated she understood his comment and also the appointment process and what was needed to be considered. Michael thought to himself, *Maybe this will work out six months from now, and I'll just continue with the current list of ladies I'm dating and save her for a rainy day.* He drove her back to her office, and they bid each other a great day.

During Michael's tenure at CIC, business writings were way up, the ladies were everywhere, and weekends were legendary. Business was so good at the company that Davis showed up for a meeting or two during the workweek but then disappeared for weeks.

Art called a meeting in his office with T. J. and Michael and had a few announcements. Art indicated business was up. "Thus the reason we never see Davis much anymore in the office." Everyone laughed. "Plus, he has a steady girlfriend, and they spend a lot of time together."

Everyone was shocked. T. J. and Michael both said simultaneously, "Seriously?"

"Yeah, so just an FYI: I'm sure you both know the branch manager has a code he or she can use to override underwriting if he or she wants to use as an accommodation on an account."

"Yes, I've heard of the ZB code but didn't know it existed," T. J. said.

Art continued. "It exists, and since Davis is gone most of the time, he has given me his authority to use this code if we get in a bind with underwriting."

Michael said, "Seriously? Wow, that is good news, so all we have to do is come in with a fifth of Jack Daniel's, and we can write outstanding accounts without underwriting's bullshit?"

"Well, yes, especially with the Jack Daniel's added in for good measure," Art said with a laugh. "Seriously, though, if one of your agents received a declination on a new piece of business because we didn't have time to send out loss control, for example, come to me with all the information, and I'll decide on each account. Don't come to me with a small account but more like the one-hundred-thousand to half-a-million premium accounts, okay? We all know how much Davis likes the big accounts, right?"

"No problem," T. J. and Michael said almost in unison.

"Secondly, the home office has announced a sales contest for sales reps working for the company. It's a trip to Hawaii with all the higher-up assholes in the company." They all laughed. "The CEO and upper management will be in attendance, so it truly is a big deal for the company, and they are planning to make this a permanent contest for the future."

"What are the contest rules and regulations for qualifying for this trip to Hawaii?" T. J. asked.

"Year-to-date percentage to target results, loss ratio, and so on, so I'm under the impression you two would be tops on the list because we are all kicking so much ass this year, and the branch loss ratio is holding steady at fifty-eight percent. They will start updating me monthly, and I'll update you two afterward."

T. J. and Michael left Art's office in wonderment. Michael said, "Damn, I was under the impression that things couldn't get much better, but they have! Maybe I've got semiwood." They both laughed. He continued. "We don't even see Davis but a couple of times a month, and now all we have to do is keep Art plowed up with Jack Daniel's and keep getting laid on company and personal time, and the world will be our oyster." They both laughed again.

"True," T. J. said. "Things are looking up for us both. It's almost like you are a good-luck charm since you joined the company—even though you are behind on the tomfoolery contest."

Michael looked at T. J. as if he had two heads and said, "Thanks, asshole."

After a couple of months, the contest results came out, which was standard operating procedure for any home office: they wet a person's whistle with great news and then waited a few months to announce the leader board as everyone waited with bated breath. Unsurprisingly, T. J. and Michael were number one and number two on the leaderboard with only a few months left. T. J. said, "We are going to Hawaii. What are your thoughts on the subject?"

"Agreed," Michael said, "so I'd better find a date, because the contest is an entire week in Kauai, Hawaii. I'm not sure if being around one of my dates for a whole week is a good thing, or even a day or two, because they are so fucked up. Maybe hiring a hooker for the week or a topless dancer from the Colorado Club would work, and then I'd have no worries about the relationship at the end of the deal. The big shots in the home office won't know she's a dancer or otherwise, so maybe I'll hold some tryouts at the Colorado Club to see where that goes."

T. J. laughed and said, "Seriously?"

"Hell yeah, who would know except you?" Michael said, laughing.

"You'd better get to work on that, because the trip is coming up, and besides, no dancer can take a whole week off from work."

"I'm sure they get vacation time and some sort of benefits, but a good question. Guess I'll have to find out the answers. I'll have to pose that question tonight." They both laughed.

Within a few months, the contest winners were announced, and Michael and T. J. finished in the top two, so they began preparations for the trip scheduled to happen in a few weeks. Michael had checked out the Colorado Club without a positive result, because most of the dancers had kids or couldn't leave for an entire week without a serious problem with work or home life, so it was back to the drawing board.

Michael was with a few friends at the Midnight Rodeo, and he spied a gorgeous blonde walk into the club with a beautiful brunette. It was an easy choice because Michael was partial to blondes, so he planned his attack about fifty yards away from the beauties. He watched as they entered the club, ordered drinks, and sat down. Michael did not immediately go up to ladies right after they sat down; one had to wait a bit after a drink or two until they got comfortable in the surroundings.

After a few drinks, Michael moved in and asked the blonde to dance. She agreed. Michael's standard operating procedure was always to ask a potential date's name while they were dancing. She said, "I'm Nicole."

After he spun her around a few times, Michael introduced himself, just as any person from Texas who knew how to dance in a honky-tonk would have. They danced to another song and then left the dance floor, and Michael followed her back to her seat. "So what do you do for a living?" he asked.

She had a nylon jacket on her chair with the words *Rick's Club* on the back, and she pointed to her jacket.

"Ah, you work for Rick's, eh?"

Nicole smiled and said, "Sure do, and I'm the best-looking dancer at Rick's."

Michael was taken aback by the comment because she was gorgeous, with a hot body, but so was every gal he went out with regularly, so his mind began to construct a plan. Still, he needed more information before going forward with the program. They danced more during the night, and the shots flowed freely. The conversation became more intimate as the alcohol took effect.

Michael asked all the essential questions, such as if she was married and had kids. The answers were all excellent, so he asked if she had ever been to Hawaii in the past. Nicole said no, but it was on her bucket list. She felt she would never go because it was hard to find someone to spend an entire week with who wasn't married or fucked up in one way or another. Michael agreed wholeheartedly and told her about his predicament with the upcoming trip to Kauai and how he did not have a steady girlfriend but didn't want any complications on the trip because the big shots from the home office would be in attendance in Hawaii. He just needed someone to go who looked gorgeous and knew how to be quiet at the right times and be pleasant to visit with at other times.

The conversation moved to a Champ's restaurant off the Katy Freeway, near Gessner. Michael utilized his best and worst lines to see what kind of reaction she would have to both. She seemed to be unfazed; she was, after all, a dancer and had heard most of the bullshit at Rick's. Michael questioned her sharply because he wanted to see her reactions, and the idiots in the home office would have the same questions. Once the big shots got an eyeful and earful in Hawaii, she had to act more like a homemaker or girlfriend than a topless dancer. *So far so good*, he thought, and she could drink too, which was the primary reason for those types of trips anyway. The night ended at Michael's condo with all the activities Michael liked, but he also made sure she was satisfied when they passed out in his bedroom.

The next morning was uneventful, so after Michael handed out some aspirin for their hangovers, he asked her to go to Hawaii with him because she seemed like a perfect fit for the trip and a perfect fit personality-wise. She agreed to go, and Michael said, "This is what I need you to do for me. I've come up with a story if the big shots or other people on the trip ask about you and me, because people are curious about folks they do not know and are usually busybodies about other people's lives. The story is that you graduated from the University of Houston a few years ago, which isn't too far from the truth because you attend college there. Your major was psychology, with a minor in sociology, because I'm sure you listen to everyone's problems at work. You work for an entertainment company in Houston, a radio station selling ads, which, again, is not too far from the truth." They both laughed loudly. "And lastly, we have been dating for six months, which is a lie, but this will cover any questions inquiring minds want to know. How far are you from graduating from the University of Houston anyway?"

Nicole said, "About a year because I'm a senior."

Michael said, "Okay, no one will conduct a background check on you while you are on the trip, so the reason for all the bullshit is that it's close to what you do for a living, and it will be easy to remember. I will call the home office on Monday to add you to the list of attendees as my date, and plan to spend the night at my house the day before we fly out, so we won't be late. The flight departs in two weeks, and I'm sure you have a lot to accomplish, but let me know if you need any assistance."

Nicole ended the morning with a big kiss as she left the condo. *Hopefully*, Michael thought, *this will work out for the best, and who knows? Maybe she will hang around for a bit. Doubtful, though, because she is a dancer.*

Monday reared its ugly head again with the usual meetings and lunch with T. J. at their favorite Mexican restaurant near the office. Michael started with the standard reports about the weekend conquests; however, he added the part about Nicole and the Hawaii trip.

"Seriously, you are bringing a topless dancer on the trip with you?" T. J. asked.

"Yes, why not?" Michael asked. "Is there some rule in one of our chickenshit manuals that says a person can't bring a topless dancer on a home office trip?"

"Probably not, but just don't go advertising that fact, because one never knows what the hell home office pukes will do or why."

"I'm familiar with that fact; plus, do you think I'm going to stand up in a meeting in Hawaii and announce my girlfriend is a topless dancer?" They both laughed, and Michael continued. "If anyone asks, we already have a good story put together about her past and about her selling ads on the radio for a living. So I think we are good to go."

"Sounds good, but do you think she will show up and go with you on this trip?"

"I'm hoping everything goes as planned. We will see. It's only a few weeks away."

Michael took out Nicole the next weekend to test the waters on their relationship and check on her progress toward going to Hawaii. He took her out to dinner, and everything seemed fine while they were out, so it seemed like everything was on for the Hawaii trip and their relationship. Nicole wasn't the type of girl one could take home to meet one's parents but was a nice gal to hang out with, even though she was a dancer. Another bonus was that she had an insatiable appetite for sex and was very affectionate, probably due to her business's nature, because it was so professionally cold. She was young, a few years younger than Michael, so it was natural that they spent a lot of time in bed, and of course, she was drop-dead gorgeous.

They went to a restaurant in downtown Houston at the Hyatt Regency called the Spindletop, one of Michael's favorite restaurants because it was located at the top of the Hyatt and spun slowly to show Houston's skyline and many landmarks in the Houston area. It was also a romantic place for dinner, and Michael called it the Sure Thing because anytime he brought a date to the Spindletop, he always got laid.

Everyone at the restaurant knew Michael. He never brought the same date twice and was always greeted warmly by the maître d', as if they were old friends. That night, while Michael went to the bathroom, he ran into the maître d', who immediately asked Michael two questions: "Firstly, where do you meet these gorgeous women, and secondly, how come there is a new one every time you come to this restaurant?"

"All good questions, sir," Michael replied, "and by the way, I'm so appreciative of the hospitality when I visit the restaurant, but to answer your second question, it is luck and being in the right place at the right time. The new one tonight is from last weekend. We met at a club on the west side of Houston, and now we are going to Hawaii soon. And the other ones I've met out at different nightclubs, so the bottom line is just getting yourself out there and talking to them, because most guys are intimidated by their looks, but I'm not. If they don't want to talk to me, I just walk away and go to the next.

"Make sure the women see you talking to someone else just as good looking as they are, so they know what they've missed. They are always looking, especially when another gal I'm talking to is just as good looking as them and sometimes better looking. It's kind of a game, but I know how to play it because unfortunately, nice guys finish last. So keep your chin up, and keep asking the best-looking ladies in the bar to dance. That is how I roll and always will because when you are dancing with the best-looking lady in the bar, everyone notices it immediately. Any questions?"

"No, sir, and thanks for the education!"

The dinner was excellent, and after Michael returned to the table, Nicole was ready to leave. After a great bottle of Italian red wine, she was prepared to go to Michael's house for some fun before bed. Every eye in the restaurant followed them to the glass elevator as they left. Michael looked at the aquarium in the center of the restaurant, and it almost looked as if the fish stopped swimming to have a look too. He laughed at the thought.

As they finished the evening up, Nicole had a few questions, mostly concerns about the trip and not questions about their relationship. After they arrived at Michael's condo and took care of business, she finished with the items she'd started earlier. "What happens if someone recognizes me as a dancer?" she asked.

"They won't," Michael said, "because no one from Houston will be on the trip except one coworker, and he already knows about our relationship, so just relax. We are going to have a lot of fun and eat like a king and queen for a week and stay tanked up most of the time too. Just stick with the stories we went over, and everything will go very well. Plus, we get to hang out in Hawaii for a week!" It seemed like a good answer to placate Nicole, so they went to sleep as they thought about the trip, which was just a few days away.

The days went by quickly, and Nicole and Michael made it to the airport with plenty of time left for a drink or two at one of the many airport bars strategically located everywhere in every terminal. T. J. showed up with his wife, whom Michael knew well from different industry functions they'd attended over the years. "Hey, Joyce, how are you?" Michael asked.

"Hi, Michael," she said, and she asked to be introduced to Michael's date.

"Oh, no problem. She is in the ladies' room currently. Go figure!"

T. J. and Joyce pulled up some chairs, and they talked about how excited they were for the trip and made more small talk. About that time, Nicole returned to the table. Joyce looked up and was taken aback by her gorgeous looks and figure. Everyone knew women wanted to be the best-looking one at any event and even more so at the airport, but no one was better looking than Nicole at any event; she was just that gorgeous. Joyce said it was nice to meet her, but Michael and T. J. both could see the seething hatred emitting from Joyce's eyes. Some women could not hide their emotions well, and Joyce was one of them. Michael felt it was a good time to change the subject toward business and not Nicole and monkey business.

"T. J., I just heard we are about to break the two-hundred-million mark for the branch. Crazy growth, huh?"

T. J. knew what Michael was doing, so he quickly agreed. "Oh yeah, so it's only right for the best sales reps in the nation to be rewarded with a trip to Hawaii, and we are staying at the Hyatt Regency in Kauai. What more could we have asked?" They both laughed. It was a cautious laugh since the ladies were looking at each other with suspicion and apprehension. Michael and T. J. knew they would have to keep them separated for most of the trip because it appeared they had taken an instant disliking to each other. Luckily, they were seated on opposite sides of the plane.

As everyone boarded the plane bound for Hawaii, Michael and Nicole sat down next to each other. Nicole said, "Oh my gosh, what crawled up that bitch's ass and died?"

Michael laughed. "You didn't notice the jealousy in her eyes? You were the best-looking lady at the airport."

Nicole smiled, thanked him with a kiss, and said, "Well, I'm sure that was it, but she could have been nicer."

"Yeah, true, but keep in mind they have been married their entire lives since they were twenty, and I'm glad this happened here in Houston."

"Why?" Nicole asked.

"Because it's going to happen a lot more when we get to Hawaii. Many folks attending this trip have been married for an extended period, and it was good practice to get used to some of the other stuck-up bitches who will be in attendance." They both laughed. "And anyway," Michael said, "T. J. will have it all fixed up by the time we land in Kauai, because he knows the true story and will make up some kind of horseshit story between now and then. So just sit back, relax, and enjoy your flight."

At that moment, a passenger arrived with a baby and sat right in front of his seat. Michael looked at Nicole and mouthed, "Fuck." He whispered to her, "Oh, please don't let me sit behind a screaming baby for the next ten fucking hours. Please!"

Almost immediately, even before they left the terminal, the baby started to cry. Michael ran his hands through his hair and quietly said, "Fuck," again a few times. Nicole laughed a little, but they both knew it wouldn't be a good flight. They formulated a game plan for numerous drinks to order when the flight attendant came by.

After the plane took off, they both hit the pager button for the flight attendant and politely asked about headphones for the movie, which they both watched twice, and ordered several beverages to ease the pain.

A few naps and many drinks later, the plane made its final approach to Kauai. The baby had cried most of the way, but they both agreed it had been no big deal with the headphones and drinks. Since Michael was still trying to get to know Nicole, he hadn't known how she would take the crying baby, but it appeared it was no big deal. After the plane landed, it was a mad dash to get off the plane before the mom and baby tried to exit. They knew the baby would start crying again.

They met T. J. and Joyce in the luggage area and quickly found their shuttle to the Hyatt Regency. The Hyatt in Kauai was an outdoor hotel, and when guests walked up the stairs to check-in, they were greeted by a beautiful view of the Pacific Ocean. Since it was so windy in Kauai, the only air-conditioning was in the rooms; everywhere else was air-conditioned by Mother Nature. The view of the bay was spectacular. Michael and Nicole hiked the stairs to check in, and Michael enjoyed the view and pointed out to Nicole two or three whales in the bay.

She asked Michael, "How do you know they are whales?"

"Wait for just a second."

Like clockwork, two spouts of water came out from the ocean. The whales were using their blowholes, much like geysers at Yosemite Park, and it was a spectacular sight to witness. She had never seen a whale before and ran to look at the majestic creatures in the bay. Michael thought to himself, *What an entrance, and what luck to check in while two whales swim nearby!* He felt it was a good-luck sign for the week.

T. J. and Joyce were in semishock. With T. J.'s sick mind, he blurted out, "That would be a great head job," and he and Michael laughed.

Michael answered quickly, "That portion is already taken care of for the week, and I'm hoping we can pull this off with all these home-office assholes around."

T. J. said, "Don't worry. Things will go great, and if not, I'm fairly sure there isn't a rule in the company manual that says a person cannot bring a dancer on a trip."

They again laughed as Joyce and Nicole returned to check in, and it seemed the whale sighting had made them a bit less acidic toward each other. *Another welcome sight*, Michael thought.

The first dinner was not until the next evening, and everyone was on his own for the first night. T. J. and Michael decided to have dinner at a nice restaurant nearby called Ruth's Chris Steak House. Coincidentally, it was also Davis's favorite restaurant in Houston. The ladies were anxious to eat there because they had heard so much about the restaurant. After a quick cab ride, they were at the entrance. T. J. held the door for everyone as they entered the restaurant, and he looked at Michael with his eyes in the air and his tongue sticking out because Nicole looked stunningly beautiful. Michael grabbed his crotch so T. J. could see he was pleased with the way Nicole looked.

Unfortunately, the maître d' saw this too, and he asked them, "How many in the party?" with a big smile on his face because he too was admiring Nicole's looks and figure. The maître d' pulled out Nicole's chair and then went to Joyce's chair.

Joyce was pissed about being second and said, "I sure hope the steaks are better than the service."

The maître d' smiled and walked away but had to get one more look at Nicole because she was a sight to see in a gorgeous blue dress with a figure to match. The maître d' disappeared into the restaurant's back.

T. J. and Joyce had their backs to the kitchen where the food was being prepared. In short order, everyone from the kitchen and all the waitstaff came by to welcome the party to the steak house. In reality, they were getting a closer look at Nicole, which pissed the living hell out of Joyce because she was attractive but a good twenty years older than Nicole.

Michael said, "People are friendly here in Hawaii."

T. J. nodded, but Joyce continued to look at her menu and fume. When their waiter came by, Joyce let out another insult: "It's about time someone took our drink order."

"Yes, ma'am, what can I get you?"

"I want the most expensive wine you have in the house."

T. J. was in shock. "Wait a minute, Joyce; let's look at the wine listing and then decide. I mean, the most expensive wine is about eight hundred dollars. Give us just a few minutes to decide what we will have to drink," he said with a shaky voice.

While that was going on, Nicole rubbed Michael's leg underneath the table with her foot. She had taken her high heel off to mess with Michael. She was oblivious to the waiters' observation and to the attention she was getting from everyone in the restaurant. She was used to being the center of attention, but the attention never went to her head, as it did for most women. She focused all her attention on Michael, which he was used to but not with someone who was drop-dead gorgeous like Nicole. Women that gorgeous tended to be stuck up, cold, and into themselves. Nicole was close to being someone a person could take home to meet the folks, except she was a dancer with some baggage. She looked up from her menu and gave him a look with a smile that said, "When we get back to the hotel, I'm going to fuck the shit out of you." Michael knew what the look was all about and what would happen when they got back to the Hyatt, because Nicole was thrilled to be in Hawaii.

She had a sense of humor too. Michael found that most women he went out with didn't enjoy a good joke or bullshit or his shtick. Nicole laughed at his shtick, and he didn't have to explain a joke or a punch line at all, which was refreshing.

After T. J. ordered some wine for the table, Joyce went to the ladies' room, and T. J. looked up from his menu and said, "It's probably not going to be a good night for me with all the attention your date is getting."

Nicole and Michael laughed loudly. "I can't help it; she is drop-dead gorgeous," Michael said. He immediately regretted saying it, because he never complimented a woman's looks, because it showed interest. Once a woman knew you were interested, she lost interest.

Nicole looked up from her menu, set it on the table, reached over, and gave him a big kiss. Michael thought, *Well, maybe I'm wrong.*

The entire restaurant was watching, and it became almost morgue quiet during the kiss. Michael looked around to see what had happened. As he looked around, he saw every woman either kick her husband under the table or give her husband a foul look of disgust, because they all wished they were doing the kissing. Michael looked at T. J., and they both started laughing loudly as Joyce returned to the table.

Joyce asked, "What the hell is so funny?"

"Oh, nothing, Joyce. I just told a joke," Michael said.

Right after Joyce came back to the table, the waiter arrived with the ordered wine and started pouring. Joyce said, "It's about damn time," speaking in a hateful manner.

T. J. said, "Listen, Joyce, we are in Hawaii, and it's all free, so lighten up."

"Fine," Joyce said, and then she directed her attention to Nicole. "So what do you do for a living, Nicole?"

"I'm in advertising and sell ads for a radio station."

Joyce asked, "How long have you had that job?"

"It was the first job offer I received after I graduated from college, and I've been there for a year."

Michael thought, *Great. She studied her homework, and it's a good test for all the home-office idiots we will see tomorrow.* Nicole was a natural and probably could have been in sales, but being a dancer paid much better.

Nicole thought, *I'd better start making friends with Joyce because she might be the only friend here*, and she started asking the normal questions about how many kids she had and how long she and T. J. had been married. The questions broke the ice in a short period, and the relationship began to thaw. By the end of the night, Joyce and Nicole had created a nice friendship.

T. J. and Michael were in shock over the development. Nicole excused herself to the ladies' room, and when she was out of earshot, Joyce quickly said to Michael, "That is truly a sweet and gorgeous woman. Don't treat her like shit, like you normally treat your dates or conquests or whatever you call them."

Michael looked at T. J. with a surprised look and said, "Yes, ma'am, I like her too."

Joyce excused herself too and went to the ladies' room. Michael looked at T. J. and said, "You can't tell everyone about my dating history; it's like I'm here with fucking Davis and his bullshit lies."

T. J. laughed and said, "My memory isn't what it used to be, but I don't tell her everything, just some highlights."

"All right, you fucker, but I'm sure they are in the ladies' room talking about me and what a catch or a piece of shit I am. Hopefully it's not the latter, because I'm ready to get laid tonight, and you will get laid too if you order another bottle of wine."

T. J. waved at the waiter and ordered another bottle of wine. Michael looked at T. J. and said, "You might get lucky tonight if you play your cards correctly," trying to sound gay.

T. J. said, "Yeah, in your dreams, fucker." They both laughed loudly, but it had gotten so late the restaurant was empty.

Nicole and Joyce returned to the table, and Nicole said, "Maybe we should order another bottle of wine." About two seconds later, the waiter arrived with a fresh bottle.

"Anything you want, gorgeous!" Michael said. The whole table laughed. *Good timing on the waiter's part*, Michael thought.

They enjoyed some dessert, and there was a lot of conversation about Kauai. Michael thought about the last few years and how much fun he'd had and how thankful he was that things were going so well. His last thought before they left the restaurant was *All this, and I'm only twenty-six!*

They arrived back at the hotel full and drunk. They went to their rooms and bid each other a good night. Nicole came out of the bathroom with no clothes on, so Michael knew what was next on the list. After an hour and a half of activity and loud noises, they both fell asleep.

There was a meeting the next afternoon so CIC could write the whole trip off. There were two days of meetings, but they were bullshit meetings to go over company results. One of the home office vice presidents, Tim Musachia, took a liking to Nicole and introduced himself to her during one of the breaks. Tim had not been with the company long, and Nicole mentioned that she had not been in her job long either, so they had something in common. He seemed innocuous enough, without actually hitting on her, and it appeared they enjoyed each other's company during the break. Michael listened intently to the conversation, and nothing seemed unusual. Tim asked if Michael and Nicole would join him for dinner that night. At his table were the CEO of CIC and some other higher-up assholes. Michael accepted the invitation and indicated that it would be great but noted the seating was usually prearranged. Tim said, "Let me handle that end of things." Tim thanked them, said he looked forward to dinner that evening, and then excused himself and went to talk with other folks in the room.

The meeting finished in short order, and everyone adjourned to get ready for dinner that night. As soon as the door shut in their hotel room, Michael and Nicole embraced and kissed for what seemed like thirty minutes but was more like five. Michael said, "We have about two and a half hours, so maybe we should work up an appetite before dinner."

Nicole said, "Good idea!"

The couple adjourned to the bed for about an hour to gain a better outlook on dinner that night, and it was an attitude adjustment after the meeting. They took a shower together and got ready quickly because showering together saved a lot of time. They soon were on the third floor of the Hyatt. It wasn't a large hotel, with only six floors total, unlike some Hyatt hotels with thirty stories.

At those types of meetings, everyone had to wear a badge with his or her name and location—probably because if someone got out of line or got drunk, the home office knew whom to call after the trip. No one got out of line on the company trips, because they were exciting and because everyone, including the home office executives, were also drunk. Everyone was drunk, but no one got out of line. If individuals got close to the CEO or other higher-up executives, they would just sober up quickly, talk a bit, and then leave quickly. It was a game everyone played.

Michael and Nicole showed up in the hotel ballroom well dressed. Nicole could have worn a pair of shorts if she'd wanted to, because she looked great in everything she wore, but she'd dressed in a gown that showed her figure but not too much skin. It was almost as if they were Prince Charming and Cinderella. Everyone came up and introduced him- or herself, so Nicole felt right at home and welcome. They didn't see Tim but found T. J. and Joyce talking to some other reps who worked for the company and figured they would sit with them.

The soup was served while they were speaking to T. J. and Joyce, when a man walked up to their table and asked if they were Michael and Nicole. "Yes, we are," Michael said.

"Can you join us, please, at the table up front?"

Michael looked at T. J. and said, "Are you behind this?"

T. J. said no.

Michael looked at the man's badge, saw he was a vice president, and apologized and said, "Yes, lead the way, sir!"

They were led up to the front table, where Tim was waiting with Ed Daniel, the CEO of CIC, and many other folks were talking and enjoying their soup.

Michael apologized for being late, and Ed Daniel said, "Glad you could make it, and you two are the best-looking couple here." Nicole and Michael thanked him for his compliment.

All the men were with their wives except for Tim, so Michael immediately thought Tim would start to move in on Nicole, but he did not. The conversation was pleasant and unassuming and fun too. Tim was a regular vice president of sorts. He was a bit effeminate and was not with anyone, but Michael wasn't planning on questioning him about which side of the street he walked on. Michael would let Nicole figure out what to say, because so far, she had done everything correctly.

Dinner finished quickly, and everyone at the table stood up and started to talk about business. Ed Daniel walked over to introduce himself, and Michael was ready for this type of attack. Michael shook hands with Ed and indicated they had met twice before, once in the Houston office and at the dinner he'd attended in Houston. Ed said he remembered meeting Michael, but his memory wasn't what it used to be, and they both laughed. Ed indicated he was impressed with the Houston office's growth and asked what the secret was to all the success in Houston. Michael was not a suck-up or brown-nose type and attributed the branch's success to hard work and the management of the branch by Davis and Art. Ed was familiar with them both and spoke highly of Davis. He also indicated he had tried on many occasions to get Davis to take a promotion to the home office, but Davis had indicated he was delighted in running the branch.

Classic Davis, Michael thought. The truth was that Davis liked fucking, drinking constantly, and showing up at the office a few days out of the week, and a promotion to the home office would have forced him to start working again and wake up at a decent hour in the morning. The Houston branch office was on autopilot, and Davis only needed to grace the office with his presence for a short period, because things were going so well.

Ed ended the conversation by thanking Michael for his hard work and determination to succeed with the company. Michael said that he was delighted to be working for the company and that the direction he was given helped to make it a success, again placing the success at the feet of the Houston branch management. Michael never took credit for his success because he knew that meeting Ed Daniel wasn't going to happen often. The people to impress were Houston's management, especially since they did his reviews every year.

Michael introduced Nicole to Ed before Ed wandered off to get drunker than he already was, but he was impressed with the couple. As they all shook hands and stepped away, Michael snuck a peek over his shoulder to see Ed watch them walk away and say quietly, "Motherfucker," as he looked at Nicole's ass. Michael tried his best not to laugh out loud. Ed did not see him look back, so everything was still good in Hawaii. Ed looked toward the ground in disbelief at Nicole's ass. He was married but not dead yet, so Michael knew it would make great gossip and talk when all the executives got back to the home office's safety. The trips always provided good gossip for the home-office idiots. The executives also could notice upcoming talent from the branch offices and hold an impromptu job interview. No one knew it was a job interview except the home office executives. It was like stalking, when a couple went on a long, romantic walk in the park but only one of them knew about it.

Michael was happily finished with the exercise with the home-office idiots; it was time to find some familiar ground. Michael found T. J. and Joyce doing a few shots near a bar in the back of the ballroom, and since it was an open bar, Nicole and Michael joined in happily. T. J., who was not the type to be jealous about other people's success, asked, "How did it go with all the corporate-cancer types in the front?"

"It was okay," Michael said, "but I need some sanity and the company of some friendlies."

Nicole and Joyce excused themselves to go to the ladies' room, as women always did. T. J. asked again how it had gone, since the women were not around, because he wanted to hear the truth from the horse's mouth.

"It went great, but I'm sure we will have a meeting when we get back to Houston to discuss this trip with Davis and Art, so they can find out if anything negative happened, but I did see the CEO checking out Nicole's ass, so he enjoyed our company and Nicole's ass." They both chuckled and drank another shot of bourbon and rum.

"When you and Nicole went to the front to have dinner, do you know the whole place watched you two walk up there?" T. J. asked.

"Nope, didn't notice, because not shitting my pants was first and foremost on my mind. If the bottom line is that bringing a dancer on a trip provides this much positive attention, the future will be to bring another one or write a book about it." They both laughed, and Michael said, "She is entertaining, and the sex is insanely good. There might be a future with this gal; plus, she has a sense of humor. What more could a successful single guy ask for?"

T. J. said, "Well, she's a hottie too, and most of those types have many secrets and usually are fucked up one way or another, so don't get too attached. As well, you don't want another Alicia on your hands, do you?"

"No, probably not, but I'm about over that situation, and that bitch hurt me, so don't bring that name up anymore."

They agreed as the women returned from the ladies' room. Michael gave Nicole a big hug and whispered in her ear, "Thanks for being here, and great job with the home-office assholes."

She smiled back and whispered in his ear how great a trip it had been so far. "Let's keep the momentum going."

"Time for another shot!" T. J. said.

"Good idea," Michael said, "but this might be my limit for the night."

The shots were gone quickly, and they went to their rooms for the night.

There was a meeting the next morning at nine o'clock sharp, so Michael and Nicole got up early to get. Michael's internal alarm clock, which he'd warned Nicole about on the flight, went off at six in the morning. During the flight to Hawaii, Michael had apologized in advance about the alarm clock. He'd received a few complaints about it in the past. Nicole had asked, "What kind of alarm clock would garner so much attention?"

"The truth of the matter is that every morning at six, the alarm goes off whether I want it to or not, which is three very loud farts."

She'd been taking a sip of her drink while Michael explained the alarm clock situation, and she'd spit part of it out onto the airplane floor because she was laughing so hard. It had taken a while for her to regain her composure and ask, "Are they that loud?"

"Yes, they are, and sometimes not very pleasant to be around. I'm just warning you. Especially if we are cuddling and the alarm clock goes off on your leg, please accept my apologies now."

Nicole had laughed and said, "There are worse problems to have. It seems advantageous to have a built-in alarm clock. One will never be late for work, right?" They both had laughed, and Michael had agreed.

The alarm went off right on schedule the next morning at six, and they both woke up laughing at the situation. Nicole said,

"Like clockwork. You didn't fart on my leg, but unfortunately, that last one was pretty rank."

"Sorry," Michael said. "It's all of this rich food and the altitude, because we are located on a mountain, which makes it much worse." Michael hadn't slept well, because his farts had been incredibly nasty throughout the night.

While they were in bed, visiting about the upcoming day's festivities, Nicole indicated she'd had a horrible nightmare last night. Michael was concerned about it and asked, "What about, Nicole?"

She said, "I dreamed I drank skunk juice, and it tasted awful!"

It took everything Michael had not to burst out laughing, because he knew Nicole had smelled his farts during the night and subliminally dreamed about the smell.

Nicole laughed and said, "Let's hit the shower and maybe wash off the scent; it's awful."

They couldn't stop laughing, even in the shower, but they did find a way to finish up and get dressed. Michael told her a story about a meeting in Scottsdale, Arizona, with his previous company. "The altitude was much higher than Houston, and the results were worse because everyone at that meeting had a roommate. My roommate was Ken Ashley, the Dallas rep. We knew each other pretty well, and he was a tall, stately looking person, kind of like he looked like a US congressmen, and in his late fifties. That was the reason we always called him the Senator—because he looked like one. He had a crazy sense of humor too and was fun to be around, but he had a secret weapon. He could fart on command and utilize that as an exclamation point when he wanted to make a strong point about an exciting subject. We would go toe to toe on who could fart the loudest and longest and how bad it smelled. Many subtle levels of farting to choose from, but I couldn't do it on command like Ken did, which was regrettable.

"We were alone in an elevator in Scottsdale, going to breakfast, and Ken bent over twice and released the loudest fart I ever heard. Of course, we both started laughing hysterically. Ken looked in the air and laughingly gave a half-assed apology, but we both knew he wasn't sorry but was rather proud of that loud fart. So my experience in the farting world is very diverse and very well practiced. Laughing hysterically at someone who farts makes it worse because of all the pressure it puts on the lower intestine. Those sales meetings were challenging because everyone had the squeeze on during the sessions." That day would be no different.

Nicole and Michael put on their badges to attend the breakfast meeting and exited the hotel room, and Michael hit the button on the elevator. The elevator opened on their floor, the third floor, and no one else was in the elevator. Michael wanted to test Nicole's sense of humor and test her resolve. He also wanted to continue the humor momentum, and a plan came to mind. As the elevator door shut, he felt the need to let one go in the elevator, just as the Senator had a few years ago. Unfortunately, it was silent, but the smell was a ten on the fart scale. It was like a three-day-old dead-fish smell. Coincidentally, Michael had had fish for dinner the night before.

Nicole moved to the other side of the elevator and said, "You son of a bitch, that smells awful! Probably the worst I have ever smelled," but she said it in a laughing way.

Michael laughed hysterically. A thought occurred to him: *Fuck, hopefully this is the express elevator!* He looked back at Nicole, who held her fingers over her nose, and said, "Oh shit, please do not stop on the second floor!" He repeated the statement to himself and hoped Ed Daniel or any other executive from CIC would not enter the elevator on the second floor if it stopped.

The elevator slowed, and Michael's blood pressure went up because he didn't know who was about to enter the smelly elevator. A million things went through his head to come up with an excuse to save face or blame it on another passenger or maybe a random CIC employee who'd gotten on the elevator, farted, and gotten off on another floor. It was an emergency situation. He started waving his hands in the air to disperse the smell around the elevator, but that fart was one for the record books.

Nicole laughed as the elevator stopped on the second floor. The doors opened, and Michael held his breath. He thought, *Please don't be Ed Daniel or a high-up executive. Please!*

A couple from California entered the elevator. Michael was relieved because if it had been a vice president or the CEO, he would have been reported to the branch or reprimanded for such a bad fart. Michael thought, *Okay, now to save face with this couple.*

He introduced himself and Nicole and reached to shake the woman's hand, and she looked at her husband in disgust because she thought he had let the fart go in the elevator. Her nose and lips were pressed together tightly, and the look she gave him was comical. Michael tried his best not to start laughing and held it, unlike the horrific fart from a few moments ago. After pleasantries were exchanged, small talk ensued.

"What part of California are you from?" Michael asked.

"The northern part," the lady said in a rude manner, angry at her husband because of the smell in the elevator.

It seemed like the longest elevator ride in the history of elevator rides. It was only one floor, but it seemed like a lifetime. The elevator doors opened up, and everyone hurriedly exited the elevator. The small talk ensued again, revolving around business writings and percentage to targets. As everyone exited the elevator, a huge sigh of relief was heard from someone.

At that moment, a teenager ran past them at full speed to catch the elevator before the doors closed. The kid was probably around fourteen years old and looked like a smart-ass. He ran past Michael and almost hit him while running by, and Michael exclaimed, "Kids these days!" Michael thought, *Well, good for him; he gets to enjoy my fart in the elevator, the little bastard. It couldn't happen to a nicer little fuck.*

The kid forced the doors open and punched the button. The group headed toward the breakfast area, still discussing business, still within earshot of the elevator. The little bastard got a whiff of the fart and yelled out as loudly as he could, "Smokin'!" He followed up with a loud "Wow!"

Michael could no longer hold in his laughter, and neither could Nicole; they laughed sparingly but out loud. They excused themselves to a quieter area and started laughing uncontrollably. Michael said in between laughs, "That little bastard! I know it was bad, but he didn't have to scream it out so loud, because that made it so much worse." They both continued to laugh near the breakfast area entrance. Michael said, "We have to gain some composure to walk into this breakfast, and if we don't hurry, we are going to be late."

They gained their composure and walked into the breakfast area, where they found T. J. and his wife already seated. "Hey, Michael," T. J. said, "did you get some rest last night?"

"Yeah, we did, but I've got to tell you a story when we get a few minutes alone," Michael said with a laugh.

The ladies were in line, filling up their plates for breakfast. Michael and T. J. joined them in line. "What's on the agenda for today?" Michael asked.

a great week, because she had never been treated like a queen before and never had had so many orgasms in a single week.

Michael raised his left eyebrow and said stoically, "You're welcome." They laughed but did it quietly so they would not interrupt the CEO's speech.

Michael thought about how nice a week it had been, and he felt the Alicia debacle was finally behind him. He was a realist and didn't know what the future held with Nicole, but he was optimistic. This was his first affair with a dancer, and he didn't know how things would go when they got back to Houston or even if they would talk. *Well, just live for today*, he thought, *and not the future, because no one knows how long they have together, so just make the best of things while things are going well.*

Michael finished his thoughts and looked over at T. J., who, naturally, was staring at Nicole's boobs. T. J. looked up at Michael, licked his lips, and turned away with a big grin on his face. T. J. and Joyce had had a great time in Kauai but were ready to go home, much like everyone else.

Ed finished his speech and introduced the band; there would be music and dancing after dinner. The men took off their ties, and the women took off their heels to get down to some music and cut a rug. Most folks pretty much assembled near their counterparts—executives with executives and sales reps with sales reps. Everyone surrounded Nicole, and the women talked to her about things women talked about, such as marriages and divorces. In between dancing with Michael and refilling their drinks, Nicole talked with a gaggle of women, and it was obvious everyone was having a great time, laughing and chatting about whatever.

The band began to play a slow song, and Nicole came over to Michael for a dance. He was talking with T. J. about some dumb joke, when she came up behind him and grabbed his hand for a dance. Kauai was a great place to fall in love, and while they danced and looked into each other's eyes, Michael snuck in a quick kiss. Nicole said, "This was the best week of my life, and it is a shame it has to end tomorrow," and she thanked him again. Michael agreed wholeheartedly.

The great thing about dating and being crazy about each other was that neither one had to ask the other if they were going to have sex. It was an accepted fact that it was going to happen as soon as they got back to their room or maybe even in the elevator. That depended on whether there was anyone else in the elevator.

Nicole asked Michael, "Do you know what the ladies were curious about and why we were laughing and cutting up?"

"They were asking if I'm gay, correct?"

She laughed and said, "No! We both already know the answer to that question, you silly boy." They both laughed. "They wanted to know how long we have been dating and why you haven't popped the question. They saw us having so much fun the whole time we were here and how we got along so well, holding hands and stuff, so it made prying eyes curious."

"What did you tell them?"

"That we had been dating only a few months, but I'm very impressed with your looks and a few other things unmentionable. Those damn women sounded so classless, talking about their husbands' lack of bedroom skills and the small dicks they had. It felt like conversations back at work in Houston." They both laughed. "Everyone had a story, and it was not pretty in the least bit, but it was hilarious to hear all this talk from soccer moms."

Reality had a way of rearing its ugly head, and Michael began to think about the future with Nicole and how he could explain her employment to his folks, but he put that thought out of his head and continued the conversation with Nicole. "Okay, keep going," Michael said.

Nicole said she'd told the ladies she wasn't ready to get married yet, but if she was going to get married, she had a good idea of what she wanted in a husband after that week.

Michael looked at her and said, "Okay, understood, Nicole. So you have had a great time here in Hawaii?"

She looked at him and said, "The best time ever," and they kissed. It truly was a great week in Kauai, Hawaii, but the trip was almost over.

The next day, a long plane flight ensued, and they got home safely back to Houston. They shared a kiss and a hug goodbye. Michael went to work the next day with great memories and was on the wagon to dry out from all the booze and food.

That Monday was especially disappointing after the past week in Hawaii. T. J.'s first question was "Have you heard from Nicole?"

Michael was a bit incensed. "She just went home yesterday after we got back from Hawaii, and after seven days of sex, it makes one week—and makes one weak too." They both laughed loudly. Michael said, "It's early, so we'd better hold it down. Art is never in a good mood on Mondays, and I'm sure Davis and Art both want to hear about all the happenings in Hawaii. They don't know who was with me on the trip, unless you told them."

T. J. said, "No, I did not say anything."

Michael continued. "My plan is to tell them now, but it appears they are on a conference call in Davis's office, which doesn't bode well for you or me but mostly for me. I'm hoping the secret did not get out about Nicole, but if it did, who gives a fuck? It's not a firing offense."

T. J. agreed, and just then, Art walked out of Davis's office and said, "Welcome back! Let's talk in my office," pointing toward T. J. and Michael.

Art shut the door, which was never a good thing, but the first thing he said was "Tell me about the trip."

T. J. started, and Michael finished up with all the news about how well everything had gone, how good the food had been, and all the free booze. They explained the activities, such as riding four-wheelers into the mountains, and how much fun they'd had in Kauai. Art asked T. J. how his wife had liked the trip, and T. J. said, "She loved it and didn't want to leave."

"And how did you and your date like the trip?" Art asked Michael.

"It was great. Nicole loved every minute of it and didn't want to leave, just like Joyce." Michael was waiting on a nasty comment from Art or a complaint from the home office, but just then, Art's damn phone rang.

Art answered. It was an agent with a quick question, so he answered it, hung up, and continued. "It seems everyone liked your date, Michael," he said in a serious tone.

"Oh really?" Michael said.

"Yeah, the home office called, and more so, Ed Daniel called Davis first thing this morning and indicated how much he enjoyed meeting you and T. J. both again in Hawaii and your wife, T. J., and your date, Michael."

Michael asked, "Does he want her phone number or what?" Art's office erupted with laughter loud enough to hear in the underwriting department.

"Nothing like that; everyone from the home office indicated she was the hit of the trip."

"Oh wow, that's good news," Michael said, relieved. "We met at a club, and we've only been dating for a few months. This part slipped my mind, but she is a dancer at Rick's."

"Oh shit, are you serious?" Art asked with a laugh.

"I'm very serious," Michael replied, "and I'm in shock that no one figured it out in Hawaii."

Art laughed loudly. Michael and T. J. never had heard Art laugh that loud and long before. Art thought, *Oh my gosh, what balls this kid has to pull off such a thing and even make the home office complimentary about the situation.* "Oh geez, I'm in shock you pulled that off." Coming from Art, who wrote his mortgage and boat note off on his expense account monthly, it was a huge compliment. Art said, "Wait right here," and he left his office and jogged down to Davis's corner office.

Davis looked up from his desk and said, "What?"

"You're not going to believe this. Come down to my office!"

Davis, with a big grin on his face, said, "I'm right behind you, Art." He knew something was up because of Art's hurried speech. He knew it was some good shit or good gossip. Davis was bored and, surprisingly enough, in the office on a Monday.

The two returned to find T. J. and Michael laughing about what the hell the next conversation would entail and how crazy the day was turning, and it wasn't even ten o'clock yet.

Art said, "Tell Davis what you just told me about the trip to Hawaii!"

Michael said quickly, "The trip was great, the food was great, and the activities were a lot of fun."

Art looked in the air and said, "Damn it, not that part! The part about your date!"

Michael always enjoyed fucking around with people, including Art, Davis, and especially T. J. He played dumb and said, "Yeah, she had a good time too." T. J. laughed because he knew what Michael was doing.

"No!" Art shouted. "The other part!"

"Well, Nicole's blonde, with big tits, a nice ass, and a great personality, much like my regular dates."

Art crossed his arms and said, "No, motherfucker, the other part."

"Oh, okay! We met at a club a few months ago, and it turned out she is the self-professed best-looking dancer at Rick's."

Davis laughed loudly and said, "Seriously? She is a dancer at Rick's?"

Michael said, "Yeah, she is, and everyone in Hawaii thought she was the best thing since sliced bread." Everyone laughed.

Davis said, "Only this sales department in Houston could get away with that shit, and we have all hit a new low." Everyone laughed again. "When do we meet her anyway? We need to meet this gal," Davis said sternly.

"We haven't talked today. It's only Monday, so let's give it a few days; my energy reserves are on low at this point. Let me rejuvenate, please."

"That's fine, but we have the large-accounts meeting in about fifteen minutes, so get ready for that meeting, okay?" Everyone agreed, and as Davis left Art's office, he laughed and said, "Unbelievable."

Art said, "I'm in shock. You not only pulled that off, but no one questioned it, and I'm assuming she is gorgeous and smart."

"Yep," Michael said, "all of the above!"

"This meeting should make for an interesting evening. We have met your girlfriends in the past, but none seemed smart or impressive, except they were good looking."

"Thanks, Art," Michael replied in a smart-ass manner.

"It's true," Art said.

Michael said, "I'm young and like them gorgeous, young, stupid, and sex-starved, and I'm not concerned with their IQ, okay? Nicole is smart, gorgeous, and young and knows how to talk to folks. Dancers are really like sales reps, like T. J. and myself; they know how to talk to people and are usually good looking. Nicole fit right in with all the other sales folks in Hawaii. Is there a future between her and me? Who knows? We had a great time in Hawaii, but there are no dating guarantees, especially since she is a dancer. She might meet some rich motherfucker who sweeps her off her feet and takes her all over the world, which isn't in the cards for me, so I'm just enjoying it for what it is currently." Everyone was satisfied with Michael's answers, and it was time for the meeting, so the sales department went to the conference room to do what they did best: write business.

The large-line meeting went well; they wrote another couple of large accounts, which totaled more than $1.5 million of new business. Davis and Art were pleased and in shock over the explosive growth.

A few days later, the weekend was fast approaching, so Davis stopped by Michael's desk and said, "When are we going to meet this gal anyway?"

Michael said, "Her name is Nicole, and I'm surprised you didn't go by Rick's to meet her already."

"How do you know I didn't?"

"Because she would have told me," Michael said, and they both laughed. "It's Thursday, and we are meeting for a drink tonight. I'll talk to Art about his plans tonight. I'm sure you can change whatever plans you have tonight to meet us out, okay?"

"Oh, hell yeah, just tell me where and what time," Davis said. "By the way, what is the parking garage record up to now?"

"Well, it stands at nine, but after tonight, it should stand at ten."

Davis said, "Seriously? Are you going to bang her in the garage tonight?"

"Hell yes, I'm trying to pad my lead against all the new young fuckers human resources keeps hiring. As you well know, I'm in it to win it."

"Yeah, no shit, fucker, so where are we meeting tonight?"

"I'm going to suggest Yucatan Liquor Stand to Nicole because it is a new club that just opened up off Richmond Avenue, and it will be loaded with women. Just so you know, I'm always looking out for my fellow single brethren." They both laughed.

About fifteen minutes later, Michael walked down to Davis's corner office and said, "It's on for tonight, so see you there. Do you know where it is located?"

Davis said, "Yes, but give me the address."

Michael told Art the same thing and told them both to try to keep their dicks in their pants after they met Nicole. Art and Davis were curious about the gal who'd impressed the company's CEO.

Michael arrived first before Art and Davis. He walked into the club and saw Nicole standing there with a guy talking to her. He walked up and gave her a big French kiss, and when the guy talking to her saw that, he walked away in shame.

"Hey, Nicole," Michael said.

She said, "Hey, good looking!"

He gave her another kiss and then said his sales manager and branch manager would soon join them. They were the real guys to impress, he added, because he reported to them, and they conducted his reviews every year. "On the other end of things, these guys are fun to be with, so no need to put on any airs. Just be yourself, because these guys are down to earth and fun to be around."

Nicole said okay and then looked into Michael's eyes and said she had missed him that week. Michael agreed and said the same thing. He felt something inside that he hadn't felt in a good while, much like the feeling he'd had when dating Alicia.

"How was your week?" Michael asked.

"It was okay. Just tired of the same old shit," Nicole replied. "My plan is to finish college, get away from this lifestyle of dancing, and be the person I posed as in Hawaii. The money is good, but there's so much bullshit."

Michael agreed and ordered a few drinks for them, and as he was paying the waitress, Art and Davis walked into the Yucatan. Michael waved them over and introduced them to Nicole. They were almost speechless over her looks but said it was nice to meet her. Davis asked, "How was Hawaii?"

Nicole said, "The place truly is paradise, especially if a person has great company to share it with, and the people were amicable too."

Art and Davis were taken aback and having trouble finding words because she was just that gorgeous. They were both caught staring at her chest, and she was not shy about pointing it out. Davis asked where she was from, and she said, "Davis, my eyes are up here," pointing to her eyes. Art and Davis laughed loudly.

Art asked about her future aspirations and what she wanted to do with her life, and she indicated she was trying to finish college and would decide from there, but she felt her future was bright. The conversation was cordial and respectful, but even Nicole could see her beauty overwhelmed the two.

The shots began soon afterward, and Nicole was a shot expert, so after about four rounds of shots, Art and Davis excused themselves for a bit to find the bathroom. Nicole asked Michael, "Did you notice they had semiwood in their pants?"

Michael laughed and said, "No, looking at men's crotches doesn't interest me."

She laughed and said, "These guys are a lot of fun but not in your league, Michael."

Michael thanked her but said, "These are my bosses, so be nice to them, and they are also my friends."

She understood that but said, "Davis is way overweight and kind of gross to look at for an extended period. Art is like a father figure to you, isn't he?"

"Yeah, he is, but it wasn't always the way it is now. There were many things to accomplish to prove my worth to the company first. Things kind of came into the way they are now after the sales department was audited and a few other positive things happened afterward. Finally, I've become the fair-haired boy. Now, if I shit in the middle of the office and blame it on a loose dog that got into the branch office, everyone would believe me." They both laughed.

Davis and Art returned and indicated they were leaving because it was late, or at least late for them, even though it was only eight o'clock. They told Nicole how nice it was to meet her, and Davis indicated how magnificent it was that she'd impressed the company's CEO and said he hoped they would all get together again. She agreed and bid them goodbye.

Michael said, "Let's go by the office, and I'll show you the office."

She said, "You can get into the office still?"

"Hell yes, I'm the fair-haired boy, damn it!"

They had one more drink and went to his company car, and Michael drove them to the office. He used his security card to get into the office and showed her his desk, which was to the right of the receptionist's desk, the second desk to the right in front.

"Ah, you have front row?" she asked.

"Yep, I'm the first person everyone sees after the receptionist's desk, but it's not by choice." He pointed out Art's and Davis's offices and the power they wielded in the office and the industry. She was impressed.

Michael had conveniently parked in the parking garage to pad his record. After they left the office, he opened her door, as any gentleman would have, and then got into the driver's side. He looked at her and immediately began to kiss her, exactly as it had happened nine times before. The parking garage was fairly dark at night, and he suggested they move into the back of the company car, which they did to finish the night off. He lifted her skirt and began to enjoy the fruits of the night and also a new record in the parking garage. After the deed was done, they went back to the club to pick up Nicole's car. They kissed and drove into the night.

The next day, Art and Davis wanted to have lunch to rehash the trip to Hawaii and talk about Nicole. They had a few items of interest to go over with Michael too. They went to the Hofbrau Steak House, the usual place, where the most important sales meetings took place. It was also a noisy place to have lunch, so no one could overhear what they were talking about, which was good since most of the time, it was sensitive corporate information.

The conversation continued about Nicole, and the first comment came from Davis. "My balls are big to pull off some of the shit I've pulled off in the past, but taking a dancer on a company trip trumps anything I've ever thought of doing."

"Thanks, Davis. Maybe you could nominate me for an honorary master's degree from the Wharton School," Michael joked. They all laughed, and the waitress came by and took their drink orders, which were the usual: a beer for Art and Michael and two for Davis. The waitress knew them all because they were regular customers.

After the waitress walked away, Davis indicated he was going out with her next weekend. Art and Michael gave their congratulations to him because she was a hottie.

Art then said, "Since things have been going so well in recent history, I've got some good news for you and your career, Michael."

Michael said, "Oh shit, not another job offer from the regional home office."

"No, a promotion!" Art had never gone over the different positions of a sales rep, so Michael had thought that senior sales rep would always be his title. Art said, "There are three levels of sales reps at the company. To start is a senior sales rep, the next level is sales specialist, and the top level is a sales consultant."

Immediately, Michael asked, "I'm going to be a consultant?"

Davis and Art both laughed. Art said, "Not so fast, tiger; you've only been with the company for three years, so just slow down. T. J. has been with the company for over ten years and just got the consultant title."

"Taking a dancer on the company trip got me this promotion, so to get to the next level, I have to invite a movie star of sorts on the next trip?" Michael asked.

They both laughed, and Art said, "The reason you got the promotion is your sales results, not your dating habits, even though they make us all jealous."

The beers arrived, so Michael offered a toast to Art and Davis. He was thankful for his promotion and asked if there was a raise in pay for the promotion.

Art said, "Of course! You get about a nine percent bump in pay."

Michael was ecstatic and thanked them both again for the raise in pay and promotion. Art said, "Just keep doing what you're doing, and things will fall into place. The future is bright for you at the company, but I'm not sure you should be taking any more dancers on company trips in the future."

Michael indicated it had been a fluke because he had just broken up with his last girlfriend a month or so before the trip, and no one else was on the horizon except for Nicole. "But you've got to admit," Michael said, "she is drop-dead gorgeous."

They both chimed in and said, "No question about that fact."

Art continued the conversation, talking about the future again. "The company is talking about going to the team concept in the future. No one knows about this, so keep it under your hat because it will take a while for the company to implement this big of a change for this size of company." The company was growing by leaps and bounds nationally, and going to a team concept would take a few years and hundreds of headaches to implement.

"By the way, what the hell is a team concept anyway?" Michael asked.

"The team makes all the decisions, not supervisors and managers, and the real power is within the team. The team concept is some Japanese invention to have the team make the decisions and eliminate levels of management," Art said.

"That will take a while to implement," Davis said, "but let's not get off track. The home office is known to change their minds and do so regularly. They will try to talk more about this and figure out it would take too much time and interfere with business. They'll probably shelve the whole plan or just say, 'Fuck it.'" Everyone laughed.

Everyone ordered his usual steak and drank a few more beers. Michael said, "There is a new parking garage record after last night, and the record stands at ten."

Davis said, "You talked her into it, huh?"

"Sure did, but do you ever get one of those feelings in the back of your mind that something isn't right?"

Davis said, "Yeah, every Monday when I'm on a conference call with the regional home office."

They all laughed, but Michael continued. "She was fun last night, but my sixth sense told me her thoughts were elsewhere. Kind of like when you're talking to an agent about a problem, and you can tell he would rather be on a golf course or just somewhere else than talking about that problem shit?"

"Oh yeah, I'm sure Marco gets that no matter whom he talks with, because he is such as asshole," Art added. Everyone laughed again.

"I'm not sure what message Nicole sent, but I'll find out this weekend because we are going out on Sunday. After all, she works on Friday and Saturday," Michael said. "I'll probably hang out with my friends and see what kind of trouble we can stir up over the weekend, as they have been missing my company with the trip and all."

Art picked up the check, and they walked out of the Hofbrau. Michael felt as if he had the world by the balls at that point. He thought on his drive back to the branch about all the golf he was playing, all the women, and how much business was growing. *How could things get better?* Alicia crossed his mind, but he deleted that thought because he felt that lady was ancient history. His thoughts were of the present and all the good things currently happening in his life.

The weekend was crazy because all his friends had missed his wild personality, and Michael always attracted the best-looking gals. Friday was okay, but Saturday at Midnight Rodeo was fantastic, with shots flowing and lots of dancing with all the gorgeous ladies. Michael's good friend Chuck was present at the festivities and asked how it was going with the topless dancer.

"Chuck, her name is Nicole, and she is hotter than ever; plus, the sex is out of this world. Do you want to see pictures?" Michael asked.

Chuck said, "Sure don't, but you know that is a temporary deal, right?"

"True, but it sure is a lot of fun. Let's find some other gals to dance with," Michael said. "I'm going to dinner with Nicole tomorrow, so I'll find out if there is a future with her, but let's have some fun tonight. This place is crawling with gorgeous women."

After he danced with a few gals, Chuck indicated he was interested in the gal he was dancing with, but Michael put a thumbs down on her. Chuck asked, "Why? What's wrong with her?"

"I know her, and she is crazier than a peach-orchard boar." They both laughed loudly. "She is pretty, but it ends there. I went out with another friend she works with, and she is crazy and a stalker, much like Deborah, always hiding out and waiting in the shadows."

"Oh fuck, sure don't need that type of situation," Chuck said. "I'm feeling pretty crazy tonight, so maybe when we get done here, we should check out our old high school, St. Thomas, and retake the hill for old times' sake." Chuck was always melancholy over his history with Michael because they had done so many crazy things in high school and gotten away with it all. Even though there had been several totaled vehicles in the process, Chuck was always fun, and his New Year's Eve parties were legendary. Chuck had a New Year's Eve party every year, and they got bigger and better every year because more people showed up. No one knew how they heard about the party. They just showed up, and most of the ladies who showed up were beautiful, so no one gave a shit.

Chuck got a phone number from a gal at the bar, and they decided to go for a ride after they dropped Michael's car off at his house. It was a company car and couldn't be totaled without serious repercussions, much like what had happened years ago with Hal. Chuck was driving a Porsche 911, but it was about eight years old, and he wanted a newer one. He drove the shit out of it, hoping he would total it and get another with the insurance money.

They drove by the school and looked at how it had changed over the years, and they decided to look at the infamous hill next to St Thomas. "Can you believe we took that doing seventy?" Chuck asked Michael.

"No, I can't believe it, but I sure as hell don't want to do it again."

Chuck looked at Michael with a grin. "Why not?"

"We were bulletproof in high school, and now my mortality is closer. My life is going well these days, and the scariest thing I've accomplished these days is going out with topless dancers." They both laughed.

Chuck continued. "Maybe we should just take the hill for old times' sake and hope we don't get killed."

"Hope we don't get killed?" Michael asked. "I just got a promotion at work, and my girlfriend is gorgeous, so what makes you think I'd agree to this insanity?"

"Probably because you like doing crazy shit just like me," Chuck said, laughing.

"Agreed, but my résumé does not include blowing up a water bed in someone's house, as yours does, so I'll pass on that action."

They both laughed, and Chuck immediately floored the gas on the Porsche. Chuck got close to the hill, let up on the gas, and took the hill at fifty-five, which was nothing like the previous attempt, but the car from years ago had been an older Chevy and not the elegant Porsche. The Porsche left the asphalt for a split second with no damage on the landing. They both laughed at this attempt and the attempt from years ago and how much fun it had been to do crazy shit in high school. It wasn't the same thrill as it had been years ago, but it was fun nonetheless.

Michael said, "That was fun with no casualties, so let's stop at a stop-and-rob convenience store to get a couple of beers for the drive home. I've got a date tomorrow."

The drive home was uneventful, but Michael received a joyous call from Chuck the next morning, indicating he'd fallen asleep on the way home and totaled his Porsche on the Southwest Freeway.

"Congrats, Chuck," Michael said in a droll way. "Were you hurt?"

"No, I'm fine," Chuck said.

"Did you really fall asleep, or was that bullshit?"

"Who the fuck cares? I'm ready for a new car anyway, and I've got to report this to the insurance company tomorrow and find a rental car."

"Congrats, Chuck. I've got to go because I'm expecting company in a bit, so let me know what you end up buying."

As they hung up, the doorbell rang. It was Nicole. Michael answered the door, Nicole walked in, and he said, "Hey, gorgeous!" Michael invited her into his condo.

She had a different look on her face, and Michael felt a twinge of a look from the past he could not place while they talked about work. She went to the bathroom, and after thinking about it more, he recognized the look she had given him a few minutes earlier. It was the same look Alicia had given him months ago, but at least this time, he was better prepared for any bad news, because even though she was gorgeous, Michael was not going to fall in love again. Michael thought, *Oh shit, not again*, but he was better prepared this time.

Nicole came out of the bathroom and announced she was taking him to dinner at his favorite Italian restaurant, Paisano's, off Hillcroft.

"Great," he said. "Let's get going."

Michael filled her in on Chuck's latest escapade from the night before and the infamous St. Thomas hill. "Not as much fun as in the past but still a good way to end the night," Michael said with a laugh. They were seated quickly because Michael was a regular customer, and the waiters knew he tipped well. Of course, the fact that Nicole was with him helped out too. Everyone had a big smile because she was gorgeous and had on a beautiful low-cut dress to show off all her attributes.

Michael ordered a bottle of wine—Italian, of course, from the Banfi vineyards in Italy—and they began to talk about work. After they ordered an entrée of tortellini, Michael's favorite, he told her he'd received a promotion. She ordered the same thing, as she knew Michael knew the best-tasting food in Houston, and congratulated him on his recent promotion. She said his future was looking good at CIC, even though he was so young. They clinked their glasses together and said cheers to each other.

The food arrived quickly, and Michael asked Nicole if anything was wrong, because he felt her demeanor was off.

Nicole said, "I've never met someone as intuitive as you," as she finished her dinner. She was waiting for them to finish the wine to talk about a few things.

Michael said, "You're not pregnant, right?"

She laughed. "No, but we need to talk something out. Our Hawaiian vacation was incredible, and the memories are enough to last a lifetime. The last few months have been what every girl would want in a relationship."

"I'm listening intently, so what is the problem?"

"There is no problem, Michael, but I've recently met a very wealthy man, and he wants to start going out with me and only me. Based on the time we have gone out, how you treat a woman is outlandishly great and fun, but I don't want to be a dancer for the rest of my life. The man I've met owns his own oil company, and of course, he is older than me, but everything he has promised would make my life a wonderful life. He's offered to let me drive one of his Ferraris if I move in with him. You have a bright future, Michael, but this guy has already made it, and it's what I've always dreamed about for my future."

Michael said, "Nicole, you're a great catch, and I can't blame you for trying this on for size. We have had a great time together, but we weren't exclusive, so I'm not angry, just a bit disappointed because I was starting to feel some confidence in the relationship." Michael knew how to soft-soak a conversation, or make it sound as if her announcement desensitized him. It was the salesman in his blood.

As they left Paisano's, Michael questioned her one more time as he opened her car door. "So this is what you want, Nicole?"

"Yes, it is, Michael, but just don't hate me, please."

He got into the driver's side and said, "No, Nicole, I'm not the hating type, but it will be tough to replace you. It will be difficult, to say the least, but not impossible."

They arrived back at Michael's condo, and he walked her to her car. He gave her a hug and a kiss goodbye and wished her all the best in the future. He watched her drive away into the Houston night and sat outside his front door, as Deborah used to do, because it was dark, and no one could see him. His head was in his hands, and his thoughts ran across the movie *Casablanca* again, but he was not giving in to being upset. His thoughts were of the last few months and what he was doing with his life, which was a lot of fun but felt empty in his soul.

Tomorrow is Monday. I'd better get some sleep because the office will be lit up after Nicole's announcement, Michael thought. *Maybe it's time to step up my game in the future because it seems like not only nice guys but also assholes finish last.* Michael walked into his condo, and it was morgue quiet, but he was thankful for the quiet because of the conversation earlier, and he was tired and ready for bed.

Monday arrived again with its usual array of meetings and people interested in hearing about Michael's escapades over the weekend, mostly T. J., Art, and Davis. Everyone was disappointed about the news because everyone had been crazy about Nicole. Michael said, "This was anticipated, so it was no big surprise."

The large-account meeting was about to start, and T. J. indicated his disdain for dancers anyway. Michael said quickly, "Coming from the guy who took me to a topless bar the first week my employment began here, that's a pretty surprising comment." Art, Davis, and T. J. all laughed loudly.

T. J. said, "The welcome mat was out, and the best way to get to know you was to take you out for a bit."

"Yeah, well, underwriting is about to come in, so let's change the subject," Michael said. Before the room filled up with underwriting types, Michael added, "It's no big deal because the gal from a new appointment, the Dargon agency, is ready to go out, or at least that is what she indicated in the voice mail she left me this morning."

Davis asked, "What is her name?"

"Ginger, and she is a hottie. Not as hot as Nicole but pretty hot and not a dancer." Michael looked at T. J. and laughed. The rest of the guys in the room smiled too as the other attendees walked into the conference room.

The meeting started and ended within thirty minutes because Davis just wanted to know what new accounts had been written to report the information to home office. As everyone filed out of the conference room, Art indicated he had an appointment and left the office. Davis asked Michael to follow him to his office.

Michael asked, "What's up?"

"I've got a favor to ask."

"Okay, shoot."

"I have a national conference call with the home-office idiots in ten minutes, and it's all bullshit, but I also have a golf game lined up. Can't do both, so I'm sure you know who will win this foot race, right?"

"Oh yeah," Michael said. "The golf game always wins." They both laughed.

"I'll start the call off and indicate I'm here in Houston. At the end of the call, they will ask if there are any questions, so just say no, using a loud voice. We should be good. Afterward, call me to tell me everything went fine and to enjoy my day of golf, okay?"

"No problem. I'll be back in five minutes," Michael said because he had to use the bathroom.

While he was in the bathroom, one of the young underwriters was in the bathroom too; his name was Bill Harris. He looked at Michael as if he were some sort of movie star and said, "Wow, the stories that go around the office about you are amazing. Is it all true?"

"For the most part, yes, but I'm never too sure about what stories go around about me or how well some folks imbibe a story, so my answer would be probably yes. Since you're new with the company," Michael said, "you will have my respect if you break my parking garage record."

Bill said, "I've heard about the record and heard it was around seven. Is that true?"

Michael laughed. "That is an old total. Now it is up to ten and counting."

Bill was stunned and didn't know what to say; he just stood there as Michael took a piss in the urinal.

Michael said, "I've got a conference call with Davis, so write some business, okay, fucker?"

They both laughed, and Bill indicated he would try his best to break or get close to the record. Michael figured it was time to break the kid in, so as he left Bill in the bathroom, he turned the light off with a big laugh.

Michael got to Davis's office in time to hear him say, "Davis in Houston is here for the roll call." Davis looked up with a grin on his face, stood up, and left his office. His only comment was "Don't get too comfortable in my chair, okay?"

Michael grinned and nodded. He sat in the chair and could almost feel the power of the branch manager's chair. It was a comfortable chair with a high back, so Michael took off his shoes and put his feet up on the desk. The conference call was mostly about the direction for the year, and every branch manager was on the call. The conference call was similar to ones Michael had listened to with the regional home office, and mostly, it was boring. While the call was going on, Michael dreamed about being the branch manager of a branch office and the power and prestige of the position.

As the conference call was coming to an end, the home-office idiots went down the list to ask each branch manager if there were any questions. It got to Texas and then to Houston. "Any questions, Houston?"

Michael said in a loud, booming voice like Davis's, "No questions." The voice kept going down the list after Houston. *So no big deal*, Michael thought.

Since Art and Davis were gone, Michael lingered in Davis's office because he thought, *When will this ever happen again?*

Davis's secretary walked in and said, "There is a call for you on line one."

She didn't say who it was, so Michael started to shit his pants as he picked the phone up and said, "Hello?" It was Davis.

"Hey, how did it go?" Davis asked.

Michael breathed a sigh of relief. "It went fine. No problems."

Davis said, "I knew you would still be in my office," and he let out a big laugh.

Michael answered, "Yeah, it's a very comfortable chair too!" They both laughed.

Davis said, "I'm about to tee off, so we will talk soon, and by the way, that was the CEO on the conference call—Ed Daniel. I'm glad you didn't fuck up."

Michael about shit his pants again and said, "Wow!"

They hung up as T. J. walked into Davis's office and said, "Hey, Michael, you got a promotion!" They laughed and walked out of Davis's office to go to their Monday luncheon at the typical Mexican restaurant so T. J. could hear the real story about the demise of his relationship with Nicole.

As they rode in T. J.'s car to their usual Monday lunch, Michael said, "It was pretty much like the discussion was in the meeting earlier. She met some rich fuck at work, and that was the end of things."

T. J. asked, "Are you messed up like you were when the Alicia situation went south?"

"No," Michael answered quickly, "Nicole was a dancer, so I expected this to happen, but in retrospect, it sure was a lot of fun with everyone watching our every move when we were out on the town. But I've already got a new one, Ginger, to take out next, so it's no big deal. This will be a no-brainer Hammer Protocol situation." They both laughed. "Nicole was a big spender, and I'll save a lot of money by going out with someone not as gorgeous as Nicole. Now it's someone else's wallet that gets to suffer." They both laughed again, but deep down, Michael missed Nicole. He had known this would happen, and it wasn't a huge deal, just another in his long list of ex-girlfriends.

Ginger was next on the list, and he made an appointment to call on the agency midweek to explore the possibilities with a new target-market gal. She was gorgeous, though not Nicole beautiful, and was fun to hang out with, especially when they'd had lunch a few months back.

The day of the appointment arrived. Ginger was over her ex-boyfriend and ready to move on with someone new, as Michael and Ginger discussed at lunch at a Chinese restaurant off Buffalo Speedway and Richmond Avenue after Michael went over business stuff.

Both Ginger and Michael loved Chinese food, so it made sense to have lunch at one of the best restaurants in the area, especially since CIC was paying for it, as the lunches always went on Michael's expense account. It seemed expense accounts were just to use and abuse until someone bitched about it in the regional home office. Then he'd slow it down a bit for a few months and then go right back to it with a vengeance. The budget for any sales department was always cut back every year, usually by 10 percent, so the idea was to blow it out every year, mostly if there was a lot of growth during any given year. That was always Davis's advice—to blow expenses out every year—and since he had been a sales manager at one time, he knew the ropes.

As Ginger and Michael finished eating, Michael moved in for the kill. "Hey, what are you up to this weekend?"

"No plans," she said.

"Hey, let's go dancing. Do you know how to two-step?"

"Of course. Who doesn't?"

Michael laughed and said, "Let's shoot for Saturday."

They agreed, but Ginger did not exit the vehicle quickly, as she had done before; she lingered for a bit. Ginger was not shy in the least bit and thanked him for lunch with a big kiss. Michael said afterward, "Thank you too," and they both laughed. They exchanged home phone numbers, and Michael thought, *The game is on.*

The week blew by, and Michael and Chuck were at Confetti's in Houston for a special black-tie event, a charity of sorts. They knew there would be gorgeous women everywhere, and after walking in the club's front door, they saw they were right. It was the place to be that Friday night, with many gorgeous upper-crust gals nicely dressed in gowns.

"What vehicle did you get to replace the Porsche?" Michael asked.

"I ordered a new one," Chuck boasted.

"You fucker. Good job, but since this is a new one, you will take better care of this one, right?"

"Of course. Plus, I'm sure it will attract any gal in Houston whenever it gets here, damn it."

"Don't put a water bed in it." They both laughed about Chuck's recent water bed debacle, and Michael continued. "There sure are a lot of gorgeous ladies here tonight, so let's get to work, even though I've got a date tomorrow night."

Chuck was surprised. "You just got dumped by the dancer and already have another date?"

"Sure do."

"Is it another dancer?"

"No, I'm working on a contract with a customer service rep. She's hot too—another blonde-haired, blue-eyed gal."

"I'll bet she is. Do you introduce yourself as 'Michael the male slut' now?" Chuck asked, pronouncing the word as *shlut*.

They both laughed loudly. Michael and Chuck always employed that action because it attracted the best-looking gals' attention, as they could always sense a good time and wanted to find the fun people. When Michael and Chuck were together, it was always a great time, and they stocked up on phone numbers from the gorgeous gals just to keep the pipeline full of new prospects.

They had a few shots and figured it was time to call it a night. They went by Chuck's condo in Sugar Land for a nightcap with a few nameless stragglers from Confetti's. It was another triumphant night.

Michael and Chuck met in the kitchen after the gals left to talk about the night. Before Michael left, he had to use the bathroom. Michael looked in the shower and was shocked at what he saw. After he exited the bathroom, he told Chuck, "I've never seen a bathtub completely black with dirt; maybe you should hire a house cleaner, you pig." They both laughed, and Michael drove to his condo.

Michael called Ginger the next day to see if things were still on for that night. Ginger said, "Of course! Here is my address. Be here around seven."

Michael said, "The reservation is at eight at the Hyatt downtown, at the Spindletop." It was his sure-thing restaurant.

They arrived with no big fanfare, and the usual maître d' greeted Michael by his last name and indicated his usual table was ready. The food and wine were great, and Michael pointed out Houston's landmarks as the restaurant slowly spun around. Ginger was impressed; she hadn't even known the restaurant existed, like most of his dates.

As he paid the check, Michael used his selling skills and offered to show her the office with the hope of getting the parking garage record up to eleven. He was, however, met with some resistance, though it was positive resistance. Ginger was a bit more refined and suggested they go to Michael's house. Michael reluctantly agreed, but he figured it was best to do what she wanted to do with the parking garage record increase in jeopardy.

They got to his condo in record time, and their clothes were off in no time. Michael knew the walls were thin in the bedroom, so he settled for his sofa and love seat in the living room. It was just as comfortable as the bedroom and had more area to move around in.

After about thirty minutes of loud wailing from Ginger, Michael heard a knock on his door. He ignored it because Ginger was truly enjoying herself, and he was enjoying listening to her enjoy herself. Then the doorbell rang, and Michael yelled out, "Fuck! Hang on for a second, Ginger; it might be the police." They both laughed.

Michael went to the door and said, "If this is not the police, go away!"

Outside Michael's condo door, Chuck was with a few friends who wanted to party because it was Saturday night. After knocking and then ringing the doorbell, Chuck had put his ear to the door because he saw Michael's car outside and said, "I'm hearing screaming. I've known Michael for ages and don't think he is a serial killer, so I think he is in there fucking."

Michael heard the talking outside, and since he was naked, he peeked his head out the door. "Damn it, Chuck, you know I'm on a date tonight, and I'm sure you heard all the wailing, hollering, and loud, pleasurable noises from my condo, so why the hell are you here?"

"Oh, sorry, buddy. My friends wanted to party tonight," Chuck said with a laugh.

"I only need about twenty more minutes, you fucker, so do you want to meet somewhere, or are you guys coming back here?"

"It's late, so I figured we could just party here," Chuck said in a formal voice. He stuck his head in the door and inhaled through his nose. "Smells kind of funny in there. What is that aroma?"

"It's called Chanel with a hint of puss, okay? Why am I talking to you idiots anyway? I'm in here getting what the cats fight over, so come back in thirty minutes, okay? And damn it, be quiet, and don't wake the neighbors, please. I'm surprised they haven't called the police already with all the noise she is making."

"Okay, buddy," Chuck said with a sheepish grin.

Ginger was still on the sofa and asked, "Who the fuck was that?"

"Oh, just some friends who want to party," Michael said as he got back into position to finish.

The deed was done within fifteen minutes, and Michael indicated they should get dressed since his friends were coming over soon. Ginger ran off to the bathroom to fix her hair, and the doorbell rang again. Michael opened the door to Chuck and his friends. Michael asked, "Did you bring some booze too? I'm a bit low since no company was expected tonight." He gave Chuck a dark glare.

"Hell yes," Chuck said, "plenty of bourbon for everyone. Wow, that is a pretty powerful Chanel smell here."

Ginger walked out of the bathroom. It was an awkward moment since Michael and Ginger had just finished having sex, and the group of guys had heard a lot of it through the condo door. Michael introduced everyone, and Ginger indicated she had heard a lot about Chuck and the history of many shenanigans.

Chuck said, "Don't believe all that shit Michael comes up with. It's mostly true, but some of it is bullshit." He started to pour everyone a drink at Michael's bar near the kitchen. Chuck looked at Michael and Ginger and, with a smile, jokingly asked what perfume she was wearing. "It smells wonderful."

Ginger had not heard the conversation at the condo door earlier, and Michael turned away, trying not to laugh. That was Chuck's style; he always joked around when another person could not laugh out loud, and he was an expert at that type of comedy. It took a lot for Michael not to start laughing, because the condo still smelled like sex and Chanel.

Ginger said, "Oh, thanks. It's Chanel."

Chuck and Michael couldn't stand it anymore and started laughing loudly along with the other guests in the condo.

Ginger asked, "Why is Chanel so funny?"

Michael thought quickly because he didn't want to be honest about the answer. He said, "Chuck's last girlfriend wore Chanel, so he is familiar with the scent. She also was into other women, so the joke was we all just called her Chanel on Chanel."

"Okay," Ginger said with a smile.

Michael gave Chuck a glare that said, "You're an asshole for putting me on the spot to think quickly."

Chuck looked back at Michael, chugged his bourbon, and grinned from ear to ear with a chuckle.

The party raged through the night until Michael ran everyone off around two thirty because he wanted round two with Ginger. He also had his Sunday golf game with Dave the next day. He wasn't sure if he would make it or not, but he knew Dave would understand.

Ginger and Michael woke up Sunday afternoon. Ginger needed to get home and asked Michael for a ride. Michael said after making a vat of coffee, "No problem." He filled them both up large coffee cups, and they got into his car and left his condo.

They kissed goodbye, and Michael was back at his condo quickly. He sat on his sofa, where most of the action had happened the night before, and that odd old feeling of being empty hit him again. Michael thought, *This is a pretty good spot to be in life, but there has to be more than this type of living. I'll find Dave on the golf course and enjoy the rest of the day.*

After thinking a bit more about it, he grabbed his clubs and proceeded to the clubhouse, which was a short walk away. He found Dave on the ninth hole, and Dave shook his hand as if he hadn't seen him in a while and asked, "How was last night?"

"Oh, same old stuff: sex, booze, and the like. I have a new blonde with a gorgeous body named Ginger."

"Ah, so just a typical weekend, eh?"

"Yeah, but I'm ready for some golf because my back needs loosening from all the action last night. It's kind of sore." They both laughed.

They played eighteen holes together, and at the nineteenth hole, they had a beer and discussed a subject Michael had been thinking about recently. "Dave, this lifestyle is a lot of fun, and every guy out there would love to trade places with me, but I'm having this weird feeling that there has to be more in life. Maybe a steady girlfriend, but every time the situation presents itself and I let my guard down, they screw me around."

"I'm engaged to be married, as you know from the Jacuzzi incident recently," Dave said as he laughed, "and I'm glad to be in this position, but you're right: anyone would gladly change places with you in a New York minute. You're successful, the gals think you're good looking, and you fuck every weekend, so enjoy it, brother! Enjoy the notoriety while you can because you're not going to look like you do for the rest of your life."

Michael laughed and said, "Very accurate, you fucker, but how about some better advice other than 'I'm ugly as shit,' please?"

"Okay, fine. Then stop going out with dancers and gals you know there is no future with. It's almost like you date these gals because you know there is no future with them, and then, when the relationship goes south, the blame goes on the gal."

"Yeah, I see your point, Dave, so should I find some gal at church or something?"

Dave laughed and said, "Probably not, because you would be way too nervous in church." They both laughed loudly.

"Like a whore?" Michael asked.

"Exactly," Dave said with a laugh, "and try to find a higher-class gal. They are out there! One just has to find them." Dave finished his beer.

They walked back to their respective condos, and Michael thought, *He goes back to his fiancée waiting on him, and I get to*

go back to my empty condo. Well, fuck it. I'll work on finding a
classy gal in the future.

〰〰〰

Monday was in full swing with the usual meetings. The office folks wondered about Michael's weekend exploits, which he told about in detail. Davis called a meeting with Art, T. J., Susan, and Michael that afternoon to discuss the future. Davis opened up about how successful the branch had become over the last five years and said, "With all the growth we are experiencing, the branch could be a two-hundred-fifty-million-dollar-in-premium branch within five years if things stay the same." He thanked everyone in the room for his or her hard work and the large increases in premium growth. Davis added, "Maybe we will even get the Branch of the Year award or some accolades from the maniacs in the home office. Who knows?" He singled out Michael and T. J. for their hard work and efforts over the recent years. He said he was having a golf day at his private club for everyone in the next few days as a token of his appreciation and added, "We will make a party out of it too!"

A few days later, the party commenced on Davis's club with fully stocked beer coolers, free high-end golf balls, and golf shirts for everyone. It was a beautiful, sunny day in Sugar Land, a suburb of Houston. Davis and Art rode in one golf cart, and Michael and T. J. rode in another, with Susan riding alone. T. J. was not a golfer but always had wanted to be on a golf course to see what all the fuss was about playing golf. It was mostly about drinking, camaraderie, being outdoors, and being out of the office for an afternoon of fun.

The golf game was fun, and Michael was competitive on the golf course, but his mantra was "Never beat your boss in any game, especially golf. Keep it competitive, but blow it on the last hole."

The golf that day was fun, with jokes thrown out as if they'd just been invented yesterday. After the spectacular round of golf, Susan bid everyone goodbye, so everyone else went to the nineteenth hole to enjoy more drinks and play some poker, which was the norm after a game of golf. Instead of the bar, they retired to the men's locker room, where deals were made between members and guests. Just about everything under the sun happened in the men's locker room. There was a huge bar located in the men's locker room as well, so one could stumble to the bar for another drink if applicable. The usual games of poker with bonuses, such as Low Chicago or High Chicago, were added for fun.

Poker continued into the night until everyone had had his fill, and the foursome broke up to drive home, if they could make it. Everyone shook hands and thanked Davis for a fun day.

Davis and Art hung around for a bit and discussed Michael and T. J. and their futures with the company. Davis indicated T. J. was the old guard and had been with the company for more than ten years, while Michael was the new guard and had been with the company for four years and had a bright future with the company if things stayed the same. They both agreed things would probably remain the same.

Davis said, "The gals Michael goes out with are incredibly gorgeous. Where does he meet these gals anyway?"

Art said, "Every weekend, he goes out, so he probably meets them at nightclubs, but they are all gorgeous, with great figures. Michael is not the shy type, especially around women, so he does fine. The last parking garage total was ten, but that was a few weeks ago." They both laughed.

Davis and Art went to their respective vehicles and disappeared into the night. Tomorrow was another day at the Cleveland Insurance Companies. No one knew what the day or the next week would hold, but one thing was for sure: it would be fun and eventful for everyone involved.

Takeaways

*T*he Houston branch of the Cleveland Insurance Companies was by far the best sales job any sales rep could ever have wanted. It was the 1980s, with a growing economy under Reaganomics, so market conditions were excellent and the perfect storm for business growth. Every person in the Houston branch loved his or her job because it was all about growing the business and having fun. Most, if not all, employees couldn't wait to get to their desks to figure out ways to write more business. The positive atmosphere was due to the management style of Davis and Art.

Unfortunately, the future was not as kind. Davis made many enemies in the home office because they all knew his mistrust for the home office employees and regional home office employees. He didn't like any of them in the least. Davis was around CIC for so long because the CEO of the company loved his management style and the fact that under his direction, he always blew out the branch's targets every year he was at the helm.

However, within five years, the CEO, Ed Daniel, was forced into retirement because the company had a strict policy for every home office executive to retire at age sixty-five. Ed reached that age in 1994, and a new CEO was installed. Ed didn't want to retire, and it was like an emperor's assassination. Everyone moved up in class and rank. The new CEO did not know or give two shits about Davis, but his underlings hated Davis and made it a point to provide the new CEO with plenty of ammunition to get Davis fired or transferred into a job they all knew he would hate.

Soon after CIC bought a competitor company, Davis had to interview for his job again. He was given a choice to take over as a jumbo account manager in another state or lose his job, because he would not be the branch manager of Houston any longer. The underlings had done their job to perfection in ruining Davis's reputation in the home office, and since Ed was no longer CEO, Davis was out as branch manager in Houston. Davis loved running a branch office, and his management style was to make a small branch into a significantly larger branch office. Politics usually spelled the end for those types of people, as with Julius Caesar.

Davis was not happy about the turn of events and did not want to leave Houston, and during a beer-drinking discussion with Michael after work, he said he didn't know if he could succeed at the new job, but that was another story. There was speculation that Marco, the underwriting manager, had had a hand in Davis's demise, but it was never confirmed. Marco left the company soon afterward because he received a better financial offer from a competitor and resigned from CIC, much to everyone's delight because no one liked Marco.

During that time frame, CIC changed their operating procedure to employ the team concept, which gave the teams more power to make decisions and write more business. The real reason was to lay off supervisors and managers to accommodate the team concept. Art was no longer the sales manager, because T. J. and Michael were absorbed into the teams created for the team concept. Art's new job was invented to control and manage distribution, but the job was eliminated within about five years of its inception. The job was not his cup of tea and was a waste of talent for CIC. Art did not care much for Davis's replacement either and started to look for another job. Most of the Houston branch office didn't like Davis's replacement either, so just about everyone in the office was looking to get out.

It was a stark contrast to previous years at CIC and a disappointing development because many people had put a lot of blood, sweat, and tears into the company. Davis, Art, Michael, and T. J. had been responsible for the business coming in the door. With the help of other departments, the business had grown substantially. The branch office had grown to around $240 million in premiums—not an easy task to accomplish. The growth and ascendancy of a company was a great thing to be part of, and most employees had learned a tremendous amount of strategies from Davis and Art. Having an enormous amount of fun had been the icing on the cake.

However, every party came to an end. Art had had enough of all the bullshit and left the company in 1995 because the new branch manager worked more than a hundred hours a week and wanted everyone else to be there too. She was single and in her midforties and had no intention of ever getting married. She was married to the company. Most people could not handle that type of work schedule because they had family commitments and a life. Many employees left the company within a few years. Art's wife was a vice president at one of CIC's largest agencies, so Art ended up working there after a quick stop at a competing company.

Michael knew Art's absence would affect him in many different ways because there was no longer a buffer between himself and the home office. Art and Davis had been buffers and mentors, and Michael felt there was no one in the company to help manage his future. The new branch manager was neither a buffer nor a mentor and was an acidic individual. The mass exodus started with Art but continued for years afterward because the job was no longer fun or appealing. The branch decreased its writings and became a shadow of its former self. It was no longer the first insurance market to go with and would never again be thought of as the Cadillac of companies.

T. J. stayed with the company until he retired in 2002 and lived with his lovely wife between Houston and San Antonio. A charismatic individual who took it upon himself to help out new employees and teach them how to have fun in the process, T. J. always had a great joke and was the life of the party, but deep down, he was just a good ole country boy—a country boy who'd gone to the big city and become a legend in the insurance business. T. J. always joked he was "a legend in his own mind," a play on "a legend in his own time."

Michael's life did not exactly turn into a beautiful experience of marital bliss and happiness in which he rode off into the sunset with his lovely wife and kids. Extreme highs and extreme lows characterized his life, but that was the way Michael's life had always been.

When the new branch manager took over from Davis, everyone knew her from the regional home office. The fact that she was a workaholic and didn't have a life concerned everyone at CIC. As the months and years dragged on, no one liked to work for her, because it was all about meetings and projects. As the years went on, business writings went down so far under her reign as branch manager that layoffs soon happened. The new branch manager and her workaholic tendencies meant no more golf with agents, no more screwing off, and certainly no more parking garage records to obtain. During that time frame, CIC bought a competing company, which created many tasks to accomplish in conjunction with the normal days' work and made for an incredibly difficult working atmosphere.

The company had already instituted the team concept program by then, and Michael became a team leader, much to his chagrin. As months went on, Michael was promoted to a team leader of two teams and seldom called on agents or conducted business the way he used to, which made for a completely different job and atmosphere. The past sales jobs were phased out, but Michael wasn't aware of that fact until later in his career.

The promotion to team leader did not come with a pay increase, so he was doing four to five different jobs without any compensation. The promotion didn't give him warm fuzzies; it just made for a poor working environment. The new management didn't create good morale in the office either; it was a slave-labor-type environment with constant meetings about nothing and projects that never amounted to anything.

After a year and a half of that work atmosphere, Michael had had enough and started to look for another job. CIC had been his dream job at one time but had become an albatross around his neck. Michael left CIC in July 1996 for greener pastures. The decision was not an easy one, but it was apparent CIC wanted fewer employees, and the best way to eliminate them was to treat them like shit.

There was a bright spot in 1991 before Davis was unceremoniously shipped off to uncharted waters: Michael met his future wife.

In early 1991, Michael was set up on a blind date by one of his agents. Michael hated blind dates because a recent one had been disastrous. They agreed to meet at a Houston club, but Michael decided to bring a friend in case things went south. Once they got a closer look at her and Michael figured out he was not interested in the least, he had his friend distract her while he ran out the club's front door.

Another blind date, which Michael also was reluctant to agree to, occurred a few months later. This time, they met for lunch at a restaurant called Lavaca Bay, off Highway 6, near Interstate 10. The woman was beautiful, smart, and blonde, so Michael was interested in getting to know her. They began to date and hit it off, which was unusual. Things went so well they were married a few months later, in August 1991.

Over the years, they had three gorgeous kids—two girls and a boy—who were the apples of Michael's eye. Marital bliss agreed with Michael; there were no more empty feelings on Sundays. Michael and his wife raised their three kids in a suburb of Houston, and he felt his crazy days were in the rearview mirror because his kids and wife were so significant to him. His family made him happy. When his children were born, he felt a euphoria that surpassed everything in his life, and the love he felt was a love like no other. Children were a blessing.

Michael worked for another insurance company for nearly sixteen years. Amid corporate America's layoffs, especially with the older folks, he was laid off for no good reason. Even though he was an overachiever and finished strong every year, ageism was alive and well in corporate America.

Michael kept playing golf but not as much as in the 1980s and '90s, and his golf days weren't as insane as in the past. The past brought back many memories of people and places and all the crazy times he'd lived through. Most of Michael's old golfing buddies and friends moved on to different areas and jobs, and he lost touch with the bulk of them. Michael lost contact with them but didn't lose the memories.

Most people thought of the insurance business as boring. Michael had made it fun and enjoyable, and he reveled in the great memories of it all. Davis, Art, T. J., and Michael's years at CIC could be summed up with the statement "I can't believe we got away with all of that shit back then." Those times were the good old days. It was a shame not to realize they were the good old days before the good old days ended.

When Davis was unceremoniously shipped off to his next assignment out of state, the good old days ended. The branch maxed out premium growth that year at $240 million. The total shrank every year after 1994 because new management was not interested in development; they were interested mostly in useless meetings and projects. No one was out obtaining new business for the company or calling on the agent force any longer to uncover new business opportunities. There was too much grunt work to accomplish in the branch office under the new management.

The acidic atmosphere affected everything from growth to employee morale, but that was the new way of conducting business at CIC. The company as a whole, including the Houston branch office, was a shadow of its former self, and gone were its days as a market leader, because there were no more Davis and Art types around to foster growth. The glory days of CIC were the 1980s and '90s.

Printed in the United States
by Baker & Taylor Publisher Services